Fear of Crime

As a concept, the 'fear of crime' has produced considerable academic debate since the 1960s. Attention to the 'fear of crime', 'anxiety about crime' and 'insecurity' in general has found its way into governmental thinking, policy interventions in crime prevention, and popular discourse. Many national, regional and local governments now conduct their own studies into the fear of crime, as do media companies and polling organisations.

Bringing together a collection of new and cutting edge articles from key scholars in criminology, geography, sociology, psychology and related fields *Fear of Crime: Critical Voices in an Age of Anxiety* sets out to challenge many assumptions which remain submerged in attempts to measure, and attribute cause to, crime fears. Questioning the orthodoxy through which models of fear of crime are conceptualised, and critically engaging with inquiries that have supposed that fear is objectively quantifiable, measurable and frequent, the essays collected here offer new paradigms and methods of inquiry for approaching the fear of crime. They will be essential reading for academics, practitioners, policy makers and students interested in this field.

Murray Lee is a Senior Lecturer in Criminology and is currently co-director of the Institute of Criminology at the University of Sydney Law School.

Stephen Farrall is Reader in Criminology at Sheffield University.

Fear of Crime

Critical voices in an age of anxiety

Edited by
Murray Lee and Stephen Farrall

Routledge·Cavendish
Taylor & Francis Group
a GlassHouse book

First published 2009
by Routledge-Cavendish
2 Park Square, Milton Park, Abingdon, Oxon OX14 4RN

Simultaneously published in the USA and Canada
by Routledge-Cavendish
270 Madison Ave, New York, NY 10016

A GlassHouse Book

*Routledge-Cavendish is an imprint of the Taylor & Francis Group,
an informa business*

Reprinted in 2009.
Typeset in Sabon by
HWA Text and Data Management, London
Printed and bound in Great Britain by the
MPG Books Group.

British Library Cataloguing in Publication Data
A catalogue record for this book is available from the British
Library

Library of Congress Cataloging-in-Publication Data
Fear of crime : critical voices in an age of anxiety / edited by
Stephen Farrall & Murray Lee.
      p.   cm.
    1. Fear of crime. 2. Victims of crimes. 3. Criminology –
Political aspects. I. Farrall, Stephen. II. Lee, Murray, 1965–
HV6250.25.F435 2008
362.88–dc22   2008000863

ISBN 13: 978–0–415–43691–5 (hbk)
ISBN 10: 0–415–43691–5 (hbk)

ISBN 13: 978–0–415–43692–2 (pbk)
ISBN 10: 0–415–43692–3 (pbk)

ISBN 13: 978–0–203–89440–8 (ebk)
ISBN 10: 0–203–89440–5 (ebk)

Contents

Illustrations

Contributors

Derek A Chadee is Senior Lecturer in the Department of Behavioural Sciences and Director, ANSA McAL Psychological Research Centre, The University of the West Indies, St. Augustine. One of his major research tracks is in the area of fear of crime, currently undertaking a three-year longitudinal fear of crime study. In 2004, he was a Fulbright Scholar undertaking research on fear of crime at two American universities. His other research interests include fear and HIV/AIDS stigmatisation, media depiction of crimes and antecedents of emotions. He has maintained a cross-cultural research agenda.

Kristen Day is Professor of Planning, Policy, and Design, at the University of California, Irvine. Her research addresses issues of social justice tied to race and gender, in the use and perception of public spaces. Her current research examines the impacts of local anti-immigrant policies in Latino communities.

Jason Ditton was Professor of Criminology in the School of Law, Sheffield University until 2006. He is currently Senior Research Fellow in the Scottish Centre for Crime and Justice Research at Glasgow University, and is currently researching knife carrying and drug use by young offenders.

Mike Enders is the Senior Consultant/Lecturer in the Continuing Education Directorate, NSW Police College – Westmead Campus. Currently, his main duties involve facilitating and lecturing on the Crime Managers Development Course. Mike has over 20 years policing experience and was a Senior Investigator with the Independent Commission Against Corruption from 2000 to 2002. He was a Lecturer in Policing Studies at Charles Sturt University from 1995 until taking up his present position. He is co-editor with Benoit Dupont of *Policing the Lucky Country* (Hawkins Press).

Stephen Farrall is Reader in Criminology, School of Law, Sheffield University. His research has explored the reasons why people stop offending; petty forms of criminality amongst the middle classes; patterns of offending in the late eighteenth and early–mid nineteenth centuries, and the fear of crime. He is currently embarking upon research into the long-term impact of neo-conservative social policies on crime, and designing new survey measures of confidence in the criminal justice system for the European Commission.

David Gadd is Senior Lecturer in Criminology at Keele University. His research focuses on the biographies of offenders, the psychosocial dimensions of crime, masculinities, racism and violence. His first book *Psychosocial Criminology* was written with Tony Jefferson and published by Sage in 2007. David is currently writing a research monograph about the perpetration of hate crime with Bill Dixon and editing the *Handbook of Criminological Research* with Susanne Karstedt and Steven F. Messner.

Jonathan Jackson is Lecturer in Research Methods and Member of the Mannheim Centre for Criminology at the LSE. His research – which centres on public attitudes towards crime, cohesion and criminal justice – has been published in *Risk Analysis, British Journal of Criminology, Journal of Social Policy, European Journal of Criminology, Policing and Society, Journal of Applied Social Psychology, Science, Nature Materials,* and *Public Understanding of Science*. With Stephen Farrall and Emily Gray, he is currently writing a book based on an ESRC-funded project into the fear of crime. He is also embarking on two new studies. The first (funded by the European Commission) seeks to provide European Union institutions and member states with new social indicators for the assessment of public confidence in criminal justice. The second (funded by the Suntory and Toyota International Centres for Economics and Related Disciplines at the LSE) tracks the trajectories and correlates of public sentiment towards crime and criminal justice over the past 25 years.

Tony Jefferson is a Visiting Presidential Scholar at John Jay College of Criminal Justice, City University of New York. He has researched and published widely on questions to do with youth subcultures, the media, policing, race and crime, masculinity, fear of crime and, most recently, racial violence. His more recent published works include: *Psychosocial Criminology*, 2007 (with Dave Gadd); *Resistance through Rituals*, 2nd edn, 2006 (edited with Stuart Hall); and *Doing Qualitative Research Differently*, 2000 (with Wendy Hollway). Formerly the British editor for *Theoretical Criminology*, he is currently working on a book on racism.

Christine Jennett is a political sociologist and a Senior Lecturer in Justice Studies in the School of Social Sciences and Liberal Studies at Charles Sturt University. She has taught in various policing programmes for CSU and is currently Course Coordinator of the Bachelor of Justice Studies (Policing) and the Bachelor of Social Science (Criminal Justice). Her publications are in the areas of race and gender relations, public policy, social movements, fear of crime and intra-community violence.

Murray Lee is senior lecturer in criminology and co-director of the Institute of Criminology in the Faculty of Law at the University of Sydney. His research interests include fear of crime, law and order politics, and criminalisation through social isolation and exclusion. His current research includes exploring the geographies of criminalisation and the spatial distribution of recorded offending. He is author of *Inventing Fear of Crime: Criminology and the Politics of Anxiety* (Willan 2007)

Dennis Loo is Associate Professor of Sociology at California State Polytechnic University, Pomona. His research revolves around the use (and misuse) of polls, the making of public policy, and the rise of the neoliberal state. His publications include articles on the social construction of crime and policy-makers' use of the fear of crime. Loo is a recipient of the Alfred R. Lindesmith Award and Project Censored's Award. His book, *Impeach the President: The Case Against Bush and Cheney*, co-edited with Peter Phillips, was published by Seven Stories Press in 2006.

Rachel Pain is a social geographer at Durham University, UK, whose research interests have centred on fear of crime for over 15 years. Her current participatory action research project with young people is examining everyday fears, migration and the war on terror. Her books include *Fear: Critical Geopolitics and Everyday Life* (Ashgate 2008), *Connecting People, Participation and Place: Participatory Action Research Approaches and Methods* (Routledge, 2007) and the *Handbook of Social Geographies* (Sage, 2008).

Susan J Smith is Professor of Geography at Durham University, UK. Her research has focused on racism, the health divide, the threat of crime, social justice and the management of a wide range of social, financial and environmental risks. She was one of the first British social scientists to take fear and its effects seriously. Her books include *Crime, Space and Society* (Cambridge University Press, 1986), *The Politics of Race and Residence* (Polity Press, 1989), *Children at Risk?* (Open University Press, 1995), *Fear: Critical Geopolitics and Everyday Life* (Ashgate 2008), and the *Handbook of Social Geographies* (Sage, 2008).

Robbie M Sutton is Senior Lecturer at the Department of Psychology, University of Kent. His research on strategic aspects of communication and on perceptions of crime and justice has been published in the leading social psychological journals, such as the *Journal of Personality and Social Psychology* and *Personality and Social Psychology Bulletin*, as well as the *British Journal of Criminology*. He is currently working on a model of how the justice of social situations and systems is socially constructed

Marian Tulloch is a psychologist and is the Director of Charles Sturt University's Centre for Enhancement of Learning and Teaching. In her previous position as Head of the School of Social Sciences and Liberal Studies, she was the statistical consultant on the project with Mike Enders and Christine Jennett.

Nikiesha J Virgil is Assistant Lecturer in Psychology. She was a Fulbright Scholar and teaches at The University of the West Indies in the areas of Industrial Psychology, Statistics and Research Design and Community and Environmental Psychology.

Leanne Weber is Senior Lecturer in the School of Social Sciences and International Studies at The University of New South Wales. She has studied the detention of asylum seekers in the UK and is currently researching migration policing networks in Australia. She is the editor, with Sharon Pickering, of *Borders, Mobility and Technologies of Control* which was published in 2006 by Springer.

Acknowledgements

Our first debt of thanks is to Colin Perrin and his hard working team at GlassHouse, who had to endure several months of missed deadlines, changes in author teams and general tardiness on the part of the editors. The collection grew out of a conversation between the editors whilst Farrall was a Visiting Fellow at RegNet, ANU, and we would like to extend our thanks not only to John Braithwaite for making Farrall's stay possible in the first place, but also to the universities we have worked at whilst editing this book (Keele and Sheffield in Farrall's case) and (Western Sydney and Sydney in Lee's), and also to our colleagues who have supported this (and other) endeavours. Lee also benefitted as a Visiting Fellow in the Department of Criminology at Keele, during which the original ideas were 'firmed up' and we extend our thanks to UWS and Keele for making this possible. We would also like to thank our contributors for making the task of editing the book a fairly easy one through their timeliness and the quality of their submitted chapters. Finally, we thank our partners and families for putting up with us for the duration of the editorial and writing process – and, indeed, just for putting up with us.

Chapter 1

Critical voices in an age of anxiety

A reintroduction to the fear of crime

Stephen Farrall and Murray Lee

When faced with writing an Introduction, or indeed any sort of overview of the fear of crime, one is immediately struck with two questions. The first is 'where to begin?' and the second is 'is there anything left to say?'. We think that there is still plenty left to say about the creature which has become known as the fear of crime (and since we do not intend to attempt an overview of the field, we give the first question a bit of a body-swerve). Those hoping to find between the covers of this book a review of the relationship between the fear of crime and various socio-demographic variables, or looking for a 'quick fix' to issues of how to reduce the fear of crime for some or other government target will find themselves sorely disappointed. We make no apologies for this. Such is the generally repetitive nature of most research on the fear of crime that Hale's review (drafted in the early 1990s and published in 1996) is still an excellent summary of the field. However, this collection, we hope, drives on the debates which surround the fear of crime. All of the chapters are written by people who have some considerable experience of researching and thinking about the topics at hand. Our 'critical voices' come from around the industrialised world and from a variety of perspectives and backgrounds (urban geographers, sociologists, psychologists, psycho-analytically-inspired criminologists, political studies, and so on). Yet each, in some way, challenges some of the basic premises of the field. We shall return to these voices and what they have to say presently, but before we do we want to locate the fear of crime both in terms of the shifting nature of the debates and in terms of its place in wider social and political processes.

Locating the fear of crime I: An example from the UK

Interest in the fear of crime has ebbed and flowed since it was first discovered in the 1960s (some, see Loo, Chapter 2, in this book and Lee 2007, may prefer the word 'invented'). Initially, the fear of crime was viewed as legitimate topic of research, expressing as it appeared to a range of concerns about urban disorder in the US and rises in crime rates in the UK. Debates at this point focused on the seemingly strangely high levels of fear given the objectively low levels of risk. 'Why were fear levels so out of kilter with risk levels?', we asked ourselves. However, the tone of the debates changed', at least in the UK, from the 1980s onwards, as left realists and feminists waded into the field, questioning what crime surveys 'did' and what the fear of crime 'meant' and was 'used for'. Some answered the 'rationality question' with a further question (along the lines of 'what would a rational level of fear be, anyway?', Sparks 1992) whilst others suggested that if one viewed levels of fear through the lenses of patriarchy and low level but enduring intimidation then the higher rates of fear for, amongst others, women, ethnic minorities and the urban working class, started to make sense. Following these debates, the UK's Economic & Social Research Council (ESRC) commissioned a programme of research entitled Crime and Social Order. A number of the projects touched on the fear of crime (or as it was sometimes called 'anxieties about crime' or 'public sensibilities towards crime' – and some of those most centrally involved in that programme and its work as it pertained to the fear of crime are amongst our contributors).

The Crime and Social Order programme ended towards the end of the 1990s. Various of the projects which had explored the fear of crime ended on notes which suggested that the fear of crime was a confused and congested topic (which indeed, it was and still is). For example, Wendy Holway and Tony Jefferson (2000) pointed to the importance of making sense of individual biographies when exploring the fear of crime. Others, such as Evi Girling, Ian Loader and Richard Sparks (Girling et al. 2000: 66) suggested that public sensibilities and 'crime talk' constitute 'a means of registering and making intelligible what might otherwise remain some unsettling, yet difficult to grasp, mutations in the social and moral order'. This involves, they suggested, the use of metaphor and narrative about social change and the folding of stories, anecdotes, gossip, career, and personal biography together with perceptions of national change and decline. Yet others, for example the team lead by Jason Ditton, reported that they had pretty much lost faith in the then current survey measures used to explore the fear of crime (see Farrall et al. 1997 most notably). So, just as the Labour Party (or New Labour as they preferred to be called) came into office, academic criminologists in the UK dropped the fear of crime as a research topic and went off in pursuit of new toys. However, as Lee (2007) notes, despite the critical nature of this later qualitative turn, fear of crime had already become an object of intense governmental interest.

As academic research on the fear of crime in the UK pretty much dried up completely, so the fear of crime 'industry' switched homes; leaving academe and taking up residence first in central government departments before, like many approaching their forties, moving out to the provinces as part of a key plank in the Crime and Safety Audits inspired by the Crime and Disorder Act 1998 (see also Lee, Chapter 3, in this book, for a review of the situation in Australia). If academics had appeared reluctant to engage with the fear of crime for methodological or conceptual reasons prior to this, there was now no way that many of them were going to get their hands dirty with the messiness of 'delivery'. This is not to suggest, by any stretch of the imagination, that there are no UK academics prepared to 'roll up their sleeves' and put the concept to good (and critical) use, for some notable exceptions do exist. Betsy Stanko, now of the Metropolitan Police, but formerly well and truly of academe, is amongst the best known of UK-based researchers who has taken on this task, and of course, her work will be familiar to more than just British readers. Still, by and large, academic criminology in the UK has fallen out of love with the fear of crime.

We hope that, perhaps, this book can go someway towards reinvigorating academic interest in the topic – certainly if this collection of voices cannot inspire further research, it is hard to see what can. For while many contributors to this book might lament the invention of fear of crime as an organising principle for this body of research and literature, most would also be wary of it becoming the exclusive domain of an 'administrative criminology' conducted only in the service of government and government-inspired targets. To disengage with the debates now runs the risk of a poor organising principle, and a range of mediocre if not counter-productive methodologies, becoming even more ingrained. As we have seen with the development of this body of knowledge, time-series data can often become normalised in a way that reinforces its own truth value (Farrall 2004; Lee 2007).

Locating the fear of crime II: Where 'is' the fear of crime, what does it 'do'?

By posing these questions, we do not mean to embark upon a series of (frankly, quite tedious) paragraphs devoted to discussions of 'hot spots' of crime, 'sink estates' or to go through the houses on poorly-lit underpasses. Nor do we see ourselves initiating a review of the fear of crime as enforcer of after-dark curfews or of reducing levels of social cohesion (although, undoubtedly for some, it does have this effect). Rather, we see these (and similar questions) as a way into our own efforts to think through what it is that the fear of crime does to debates in contemporary societies and how it influences debates about 'law and order' (for want of a better term). We sketch these ideas out as Figure 1.1.

This figure attempts to describe the relationship(s) between the fear of crime (at the centre of the figure) and key political, social and economic organisations and institutions (in bold in the square boxes). The relationships are represented by the arrowed lines, and their operational characteristics described in italics in smaller square boxes.

Let us start not with the fear of crime, but with government. Governments initiate crime surveys in order to assess crime in their jurisdictions. This is partly because of a widening disillusionment with official crime statistics

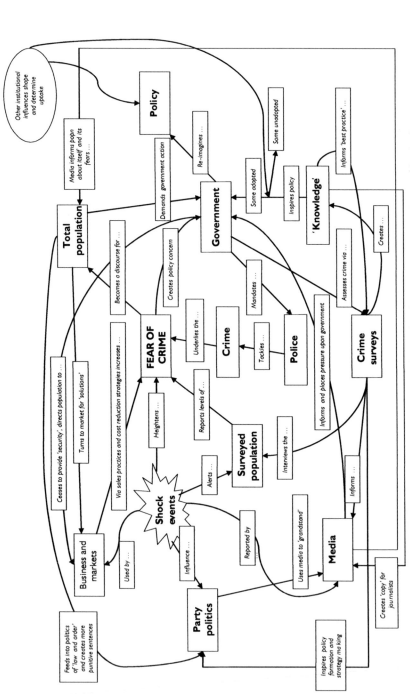

Figure 1.1 Relationship(s) between the fear of crime and key political, social and economic organisations and institutions

(which comes in part from 'knowledge, that is academic and officially-approved versions of truth which point to the failings of such official crime statistics) and the media (which report such views). Having commissioned crime surveys, samples of the population are surveyed, and over time, the information gained from such surveys fed back to the media and the wider population itself (the 'double hermeneutic' as Giddens (1984) would have it, or the fear of crime feedback loop in Lee's work, for example 2001). The surveyed population reports varying levels of crime fears (amongst other things, of course). Such fears become a discourse amongst the wider population for making sense of events (Girling *et al.* 2000) or for expressing other anxieties (Taylor and Jamieson 1998; Farrall *et al.* 2006), and also creates a pressure for the government of the day to 'do something' about crime. As well as placing pressure upon the government, the views of the populous (along with the data from crime surveys) are used by political parties to attune policies and encourage some to appeal to the electorate by making crime (and/or the fear of crime) an election issue. Survey data also, of course, assist in the formulation and reformulation of 'knowledge' and hence policy suggestions.

Meanwhile, back at the ranch, the government is slowly moving away from its role as 'provider of safety', instead pointing citizens towards the market for solutions to crime and their fears (which the population, with its understanding of budget restrictions and their own responsibility, has little choice but to embrace). Businesses operating in this market, which is – like all markets – competitive, need to exploit such fears and anxieties in order to sell their goods and services (new credit cards which are 'fraud-proofed', new windows which are burglar-proof and such like, see Hardy 2006 on the motor cycle insurance industry). Such practices remind the population that it is 'at risk' and serve to heighten crime fears. Shock events (murders of 'decent passers-by', abductions of children, serious crimes against members of the public, unexpected rises in crime rates, etc.) are used by those operating in the market to 'ram home' their message, and in so doing such events both directly and indirectly increase fears by their usage by businesses, media reporting and political grandstanding.

'Knowledge' suggests to government various policies which could be pursued to tackle the fear of crime. Some of these are adopted, others are not. The reasons for the adoption or non-adoption of such policies is influenced by a range of institutional pressures. Some of these relate to cultural norms which are unique to each nation, its history, political colour and popular ideas (which influence both government officials and academics, of course) about the causes of crime. All of these will vary over time and are not in anyway static.

This fluidity of crime fear discourse, its diffuse and yet often intensely localised nature, is often lost in its attempted quantification – or at least in the way it has traditionally been quantified. If there is one theme that, perhaps, defines this book, it is this inclination to move away from a static enumerated reading of fear of crime and to see it in its socio-political, psycho-social and geo-spatial contexts. That is not to suggest that the contributors here have disengaged with quantitative methodologies; rather they engage with these in new and reflexive ways with intense critical reflection which takes account of the researchers' own role in the production of knowledge. Reading this book will, no doubt, confirm that fear of crime is irreducible to specific 'causes', inherently political, discursive and yet intensely personal.

The collected essays

Our first essay is that by Dennis Loo. Loo takes us back to the 1960s, and to the US. Loo identifies the Republican Party's desire to challenge the bedrock of values which had produced and been consolidated by President Franklin Delano Roosevelt and his New Deal programme and the notion of a Great Society under Democratic President Lyndon Johnson. Loo argues that 'elites fabricated a fictive consensus around "law 'n' order" in the 1960s and employed it as a device to introduce momentous public policy changes', directly challenging the notion that these changes in social values occurred naturally. In a telling passage, Loo argues that:

> By combining several different items into a category created after the fact, Gallup created the impression that crime concerns were much higher than they actually were. Other polls publicised in the remainder of 1968 also either conflated categories, perpetuating the impression of more robust crime concerns than were actually justified by the data or particular polls were selectively presented in a manner that generated the same impression. The polls *not publicised* in 1968 actually revealed crime concerns were *dropping*.

The ultimate message of Loo's essay, however, is that the Republican Party shifted the terms of the debates from social injustices to a focus on law and order, pollsters manipulated or selectively reported their results to reflect this shift, leaving the Democratic Party little choice but to follow the agenda as it moved. A similar, although, of course, not identical process was witnessed during the UK's 1979 General Election campaign, when Mrs Thatcher (who won the campaign for the Conservative Party) spoke of citizens having the right to feel 'safe in the streets' (the central referent of a key measure of the fear of crime in many a crime survey) and needing 'less tax and more law and order' (see Farrall 2006).

Following from Loo's essay, we turn to that by Lee. Lee's aim is to 'identify a range of obscured dimensions of knowledge and power in relation to the representation of data concerning public anxieties about crime'. Lee argues that the intensely political dimensions of the fear of crime (and the resulting data, of course) and the socio-cultural implications of this, are often overlooked by government or 'administrative' criminologists who, on the assumptions that this thing 'exists' and is 'out there' to be measured, tend to reduce debates about 'fear of crime' to technical arguments. This, Lee argues, ignores all of that work (see Lee 2001, 2007; Stanko 2000; Loo and Grimes 2004; Loo, Chapter 2, in this book) which suggests that the fear of crime is contingent – something of a category of convenience. To paraphrase Lee, we created the concept (of crime fears) and only *then* reflected on whether or not it might be the most appropriate organising principal for a body of social scientific knowledge. This, naturally, is not to suggest that there was no anxiety about crime prior to the 1960s, for certainly there was (Pearson 1983). Rather, it is that the term 'fear of crime' was not an *organising principle*. As Lee elsewhere has noted (Lee 2007), the term was rarely if ever used before 1965. That the enumeration of such fear which resulted from surveys indicated significantly high levels of fear – or whatever was measured – meant that it became a governmental problematisation. Of course, once the fear of crime was enumerated and had become an organising principal for a range of criminal justice and social policy targeting, it also became a staple object of criminological inquiry attracting research funding and becoming the topic for thousands of academic publications (Hale 1996; Lee 1999; Lee 2007; Ditton and Farrall 2000). Consequently, not insignificant resources were invested in the 'new problem' of the fear of crime. As such, and this is also connected to the previous point, fear of crime became political from the moment it was enumerated.

Recent evidence (as if further evidence were needed) of the politicisation of the fear of crime and the associated concept of 'insecurity' has stemmed from the attacks on the US in 2001. Our next two essays consider this topic in some depth. First of all we have Smith and Pain's essay, in which they develop from two models of analysing fear – the everyday and the geopolitical – a third model of understanding the fear of crime. This is an approach which does not ignore global processes and events or attempts at political manipulation, and which accepts that outcomes at the rather more mundane or 'everyday' level, are not predictable, requiring that they 'make space for resistance to fear and fear discourses in everyday life too'. Ultimately, they argue that we need to shift the emphasis from 'authoritative, remote, top-down models of fear' towards more nuanced and grounded approaches based on everyday realities and perceptions. In so doing, Smith and Pain highlight the entwined nature of globalised fears and the processes which underlie them. Their ideas on the immediate local everyday fears and anxieties that are already present in some people's lives and the relationship of these to the wider world stimulates further thoughts about their connections.

Weber and Lee seek to 'critically assess the use of fear as a governmental tactic which has been employed as part of a national security discourse'. They go on to argue that the strategies for dealing with the threat of terrorism adopted by 'liberal' governments 'represent the ushering in of a new era of pre-emptive, and as-yet largely unconstrained, forms of governance'. In a tenor which is reminiscent of the opening essay by Dennis Loo, and building on Bauman's insights (2004), Weber and Lee argue that 'official fear' about terrorist attacks has been 'contrived' in such a way as to create a demand (or at least to create the image of a demand) for the ever-tightening of anti-terrorist legislation and the extension of state powers. Weber and Lee are careful not to suggest that governments have *created* the 'fear of terrorism' (nor do they deny the possibility of terror attacks nor the legitimacy of targeted and lawful action to prevent them), rather arguing that 'a politics of fear has tapped into generalised anxieties which have deep seated roots in wider structural change and that these anxieties often suit contemporary political agendas'. In so doing, they offer a critical assessment of the use of fear as a governmental tactic – one which has been employed as part of an ongoing national security discourse.

Our next two essays deal with the thorny issue of gender and the fear of crime. Most research undertaken has sought to assess if males or females were more or less fearful than one another (often finding that females 'win' the competition to be more fearful, Hale 1996). Both of the essays in this book come to the topic from a different perspective. Relying on qualitative interviews with men, Day explores the experiences of men of being feared in public, finding this to be heavily racialised. Such feelings of being feared, especially when experienced amongst certain ethnic minority men, become bound up in processes of physical exclusion from some arenas of public space (such as shopping arcades, city streets and bars). Such experiences, as Day notes, have the potential to scar the individual and collective psyches of the groups feared, leaving them left with an unconscious sense of their and their ethnic groups' position in society. Sutton and Farrall approach the topic of gender and the fear of crime from an altogether different position to Day (although we would invite readers to reflect on both essays simultaneously). Using quantitative data, they suggest that when answering survey questions aimed at measuring their fear levels, men suppress the extent of their fears, hence the oft found lower levels of fear amongst men when compared to women. As the authors are at pains to point out, they are not suggesting that men deliberately distort their fear levels. Sutton and Farrall go on to suggest that 'men and women share a consensus that females are much more fearful than males'. This result provides evidence of the gender stereotypes which have been assumed to underlie the tendency for men to minimise their fears (see also Sutton and Farrall 2005).

Since the publication of Hollway and Jefferson's book (2000) stemming from the UK ESRC's Crime and Social Order programme, there has been a resurgence in interest in psycho-social explanations within criminology. Gadd and Jefferson start from the assumption that 'subjects are not rational unitary beings with full self-knowledge, but psychosocial subjects with a split consciousness, constantly unconsciously defending themselves against anxiety'. With this in mind, they go on to argue that unconscious defensive activity affects what and how anything is remembered. Painful, fear-inducing or threatening events are either suppressed (that is forgotten) or recast in a modified fashion which renders the threatening aspects of the memory less challenging. Using the case study of one man, Gadd and Jefferson argue that the positions which any individual adopts are negotiated in relation to their biography and (any) attendant anxieties. Added to this are the discursive fields available to the individual (which are often influenced by their class, ethnicity, age and gender). As such, whether someone invests in the position of being fearful and preoccupied with the threat of victimisation depends, in part, as to how available that position is to him or her.

Jon Jackson's essay is an attempt 'bridge the social and the psychological in the fear of crime'. In this essay Jackson develops some of his earlier work in this area (see Jackson and Sunshine 2007; Jackson *et al.* 2006, 2007), and attempts to outline an approach to the fear of crime which draws upon cultural analyses of risk perception, the psychology of the individual, explanations inspired by sociological thinking, and geographical readings of the environment (see also Bannister 1993). Along the way he touches on survey methodologies, the circulation of narratives of fear and anxiety in society, and notions of morality. Jackson suggests that psychological analyses of risk perception need to account for the culturally embedded meaning of risk. However, he argues, psychologists have tended to ignore why people select one risk and not another. By arguing that a contextualised formulation of risk which bridges both levels of analysis (the psychological and the sociological) offers a promising way forward, Jackson points to new avenues for the quantitative investigation of the fear of crime.

Mike Enders and Christine Jennett revisit two large research projects conducted in Sydney Australia with the aim of further exploring the ideas of community cohesion and 'sense of community' and their relationship to fear of crime. They draw heavily on Sandra Walklate's (1997) research and are interested in how and in what circumstances community networks and relationships can mitigate against levels of crime fear. Their research identifies considerable problems with the ways in which New South Wales (NSW) policing policy and practice, including strategies such as high visibility policing, might not reduce but, in fact, increase problems associated with fear of crime in some circumstances. Enders and Jennett suggest the NSW police need to take seriously their stated objective to reduce both crime and fear of crime. Their research also has implications for the functions of local government suggesting that local strategies of community building can have positive effects in reducing crime fear and that local government needs to be funded accordingly to successfully conduct this work. While their work accepts that fear of crime is a problematic and contingent object of research, they believe that the concept still has the potential to operate as an organising principle for policy intervention.

The essay by Derek Chadee and his colleagues attempts to explore the relationship between anxiety and fear of crimes as articulated in the psychology literature. The literature on fear of crime has mostly dealt with this concept from a sociological or criminological perspective with no attempt to deconstruct the concept from an informed psychological perspective. Chadee and his colleagues find that the fear of crime (as measured in surveys) owes more to feelings of individual trait anxiety than it does to state anxiety, or even victimisation. As such, the fear of crime may simply be an articulation of altogether different anxieties, which are unrelated to crime.

Many of the essays in this book can be read as attempts to expand and challenge the existing narrow definitions of fear of crime. Others attempt to challenge the established methodologies and propose new, less reductive programs of research and methodologies in their place. Still others turn the concept on its head and attempt to situate the fear of crime and debates around it terms of a set of power relations which are played out at societal or interpersonal levels. It is perhaps pertinent to view this diverse range of essays through the lenses of power relations and the variety of ways they address questions of power. The power to define fear of crime in particular ways to particular political ends, the power of fear of crime to operate as a form of social exclusion, the power of fear of crime discourses to help construct our everyday geographies and subjectivities. As such, we are left with both a set of individual and collective research agendas and a collective challenge to current and future researchers in the field.

References

Bannister, J (1993) 'Locating fear: Environmental and ontological security', in Jones, H (ed), *Crime and the urban environment*, Aldershot: Avebury

Bauman, Z (2004) *Wasted Lives: Modernity and its Outcasts*. London: Polity.

Ditton, J and Farrall, S (2000) *The Fear of Crime*, Ashgate: Aldershot.

Farrall, S (2004) 'Revisiting Crime Surveys: Emotional Responses Without Emotions', *International Journal of Social Research Methodology*, 7(2): 157–71.

Farrall, S (2006) '"Rolling Back the State': Mrs Thatcher's Criminological Legacy", *International Journal of the Sociology of Law*, 34(4): 256–77.

Farrall, S, Bannister, J, Ditton, J and Gilchrist, E (1997) 'Questioning the Measurement of the Fear of Crime', *British Journal of Criminology*, 37(4): 657–78.

Farrall, S, Jackson, J and Gray, E (2006) *Everyday Emotion and the Fear of Crime: Preliminary Findings from Experience & Expression*, Working Paper No. 1, ESRC Grant RES 000 23 1108.

Giddens, A. (1984) *The Constitution of Society*, Polity Press: Cambridge.

Girling, E, Loader, I and Sparks, R (2000) *Crime and Social Control in Middle England: Questions of Order in an English Town*, London: Routledge.

Hale, C (1996) 'Fear of Crime: A Review of the Literature', *International Review of Victimology*, 4: 79–150.

Hardy, E. (2006) *The Fear Industry: Fear of Crime, Governance and Regulations – A Case Study of Motorcyclists*, PhD, Department of Sociology, Warwick University, available at: www.fearofcrime.co.uk/.

Hollway, W and Jefferson, T (2000) *Doing Qualitative Research Differently: Free association, narrative, and the interview method*, London: Sage.

Jackson, J and Sunshine, J (2007) 'Public Confidence in Policing: A Neo-Durkheimian Perspective', *British Journal of Criminology*, 47(2), 214–33.

Jackson, J, Allum, N and Gaskell, G (2006) 'Bridging Levels of Analysis in Risk Perception Research: The Case of the Fear of Crime', *Forum Qualitative Sozialforschung/Forum: Qualitative Social Research*, 7(1), available at www.qualitative-research.net/fqs-texte/1-06/06-1-20-e.htm.

Jackson, J, Farrall, S and Gray, E (2007) *Experience and Expression in the Fear of Crime*, Working Paper No. 7, ESRC Grant RES 000 23 1108.

Lee, M (1999) 'The Fear of Crime and Self-Governance: Towards a Genealogy', *The Australian and New Zealand Journal of Criminology* 32(3): 227–46.

Lee, M (2001) 'The Genesis of "Fear of Crime"', *Theoretical Criminology*, 5(4): 467-85.

Lee, M (2007), *Inventing Fear of Crime: Criminology and the Politics of Anxiety*, Cullompton: Willan.

Loo, D and Grimes, R-E (2004) 'Polls, Politics and Crime: The "Law and Order" Issue of the 1960s', *Western Criminology Review*, 5(1): 50–67.

Pearson, G (1983) *Hooligan: A History of Respectable Fears*, London: Macmillan Press.

Sparks, R (1992) 'Reason and unreason in left realism: some problems in the constitution of the fear of crime', in Matthews, R and Young, J (eds), *Issues in Realist Criminology*, London: Sage.

Stanko, E (2000) 'Victims R' Us', in Hope, T and Sparks, R (eds) *Crime, Risk and Insecurity*, London: Routledge.

Sutton, R and Farrall, S (2005) 'Gender, socially desirable responding and the fear of crime: Are women really more anxious about crime?', *British Journal of Criminology*, 45(2): 212–24.

Taylor, I and Jamieson, R (1998) 'Fear of Crime and Fear of Falling: English Anxieties Approaching the Millennium', *Archives Européennes de Sociologie*, 19(1): 149–75.

Walklate, S (1997) 'Crime and Community: Exploring the Interplay', paper presented at the First Australian Institute of Criminology Regional Crime Conference, Wagga Wagga, Charles Sturt University.

Chapter 2

The 'moral panic' that wasn't

The sixties crime issue in the US

Dennis Loo

'The sixties' (referring herein to that period stretching from the early years of the 1960s to 1973) was a time of great social and political turmoil worldwide. Within the US, the civil rights, anti-war, black power, and women's liberation movements rocked the country. Hundreds of riots (some described as 'insurrectionary') occurred along with the assassination of a string of political leaders: Malcolm X, John F Kennedy, Martin Luther King, Jr, Fred Hampton, and Robert F Kennedy. Powerful divisions opened up in US society and, as a result of this, President Lyndon Johnson, who had crushed Republican Party nominee Barry Goldwater in the 1964 presidential election, was so besieged a few years later that he renounced running for re-election in 1968. The sixties, put simply, represent a watershed: a touchstone for both the political Left and the Right. Reverberations from it are being felt to this day, including on the topic of most concern in this chapter: the matter of street crime.

According to collective memory and scholarly opinion, the sixties' 'law 'n order' issue,[1] reached unprecedented levels of public concern in the US. Further, the era's social insurgencies allegedly provoked heightened crime fears within the public, especially among white Americans, and led to a number of important outcomes, including:

- the 1968 election of conservative Republican Party nominees Richard Nixon and Spiro Agnew to the presidency, marking the end of the liberal policies of the Great Society under Democratic President Lyndon Johnson;
- the subsequent (and still ongoing) criminal justice system's expansion, unhinged in its growth from actual changes in index offending rates;[2]
- a shift in the public's mood towards greater intolerance, punitiveness, self-centeredness and stinginess; and
- the supplanting of the New Deal/FDR[3] class alliance by a social/religious/race issues-driven Republican Party alliance.

In short, according to the prevailing view, the 'law 'n order' issue *originated* within the public and precipitated a major shift in US public policy (Cronin *et al.* 1981; Smith 1985; Niemi *et al.* 1989; Skogan 1995; Flamm 2002).

The collective memory and scholarly consensus is, however, fundamentally wrong (see Loo and Grimes 2004).[4] Poll-measured crime concerns did not show a highly aroused public preoccupied with street crime. To paraphrase Mark Twain's famous retort to reports of his death: accounts of the birth of punitive and social Darwinist public policies as a result of a public obsessed with crime have been greatly exaggerated. Instead, elites fabricated a fictive consensus around 'law 'n order' in the sixties and employed it as a device to introduce momentous public policy changes. This consensus lacked a genuine popular component. It was, rather, the *representation* of a popular consensus.

Moral panics

Moral panics are instances in which the public, the media, and the state are disproportionately aroused about a putative problem. The term 'moral panic' comes from Cohen (1980) whose classic study on the English Mods and Rockers drew upon the groundwork of Durkheim and Marx.[5] Durkheim and Marx make uneasy bedfellows because they locate the initiating agency in very different places. Durkheim sees crime concerns as emanating from the public (offenses to the conscience collective), whereas Marx locates the origins in elites (the ruling ideas of any epoch are the ideas of the dominant classes). As a result of this uneasy co-existence between Durkheim and Marx, the moral panic and the social problems literature (moral panics are a subset of social problems) has contained divergent models ever since: the interest group model, the grassroots model, and the elite-engineered model (Hunt 1997; Goode and Ben-Yehuda 1994).

The interest group model holds that social problems start from the advocacy work of mid-range interest groups such as Mothers Against Drunk Driving. An issue rises to a social problem level when an interest group succeeds in getting the attention and approval of media and/or the state. The media and state are considered secondary claims-makers to the primary claims-makers: the mid-range interest group. The interest group model is the most popular one for scholars in the field, usually employed in combination with the grassroots (also known as structural strain) model (Goode and Ben-Yehuda 1994).

Structural strain attributes social problems to a generalised sentiment within the public that becomes attached to a specific issue – such as stranger kidnappings of children. This surrogate issue acts as a vehicle for these generalised public anxieties to express themselves. Structural strain thus posits a kind of mass psychological displacement phenomenon (Best 1990; Luttwak 1999). Because structural strain suffers from an inability to explain why a specific social problem arises at a specific point in time, it usually accompanies the interest group model in social problem studies to create a kind of hybrid explanation. The elite-engineered model locates the initiating agent in the media and/or the state. It is considered by many scholars to be inapt for most social problems/moral panics and is rarely employed (Goode and Ben-Yehuda 1994).

This preference among scholars for the interest group model and structural strain appears, however, to rest upon theoretical or ideological assumptions rather than upon empirical findings. That is, if one wanted to trace who or what the initiating agents were for a given social problem or panic, one would have to very carefully reconstruct the historical chronology. While chronologies make up an invariant aspect of social problems' accounts, a full examination of the critical initial stage and an inspection of a full and verifiable polling record are extremely rare. In the absence of this kind of detective work, the *assumption* is usually made that interest groups and/or public sentiment led the way. What must be proven is, therefore, instead assumed. The data, in other words, do not seem to have settled the issue; preferences of theory and ideology have.

This chapter seeks to make two interrelated contributions to the social problems literature in order to help resolve this overlooked problem. First, I employ and advocate a particular methodology for social problems' studies. The critical questions in social problems' analyses, after all, are 'who started it and what happened to it once it started?'. Since what is at stake in the social problems 'game' is public resources and their allocation, knowing who gets what and how this happened is a vital question for any putatively democratic polity. We cannot assume that 'the people' got what they wanted unless we can demonstrate empirically and with rigor that this is what actually occurred. In order to do this, minimally, we need to do the equivalent of the following:

- Inspect the entire polling record as available in 'raw' form at locales such as the Roper Center for Public Opinion that houses the full record of major polling organisations' polls. Without a full record of polls we can only use a partial polling record and what may be a *response* by the public to initiating activities by the state or media might otherwise appear to have *originated* within the public.
- Track media coverage of an issue across various major media outlets (newspapers, TV, news magazines, the internet) to see when coverage began. Since media are highly self-referential in nature (they look first and foremost to each other to determine what is 'newsworthy'), inspecting all of the major media outlets is vital if you want to pin down when media first started paying attention to an issue. Commonly, by contrast, social problems accounts select exemplary media sources (for example, the *New York Times*) rather than looking at the whole media universe.
- Track public officials' actions and pronouncements to see when the state got involved.

Second, based on this approach, the usually overlooked elite-engineered model appears to do the best job of explaining the sixties crime issue. The lacunae that interest group models together with structural strain create – their inability to explain why one issue wins out over another – can only be addressed properly if elites (media and the state) are not seen as invariably reactive agents or as secondary claims-makers, as Spector, Kitsuse and Best labelled them (Spector and Kitsuse 1973). The winning issue is characteristically understood to have triumphed because its claim must have been more compelling (Lowney and Best 1995). How do we know that it was more compelling? The fact that it won proves that it was more compelling. This is, of course, a circular argument. It does not tell us what distinguished the winning issue from the also-rans. In an attempt to overcome this post hoc problem, Lowney and Best (1995) cite three variables as decisive: an issue's resonance with cultural themes, the mobilisation of greater resources by the winning claims-making group, and contingent events (such as the drug-induced death of basketball player Len Bias which contributed to the mid-1980s US Drug War).

Unfortunately, upon closer examination, Lowney and Best's answer to the post-hoc problem still does not resolve the problem. Briefly put, their resolution does not fully answer the following objections: (1) There are numerous possible issues that could resonate with cultural themes. Why did *this* issue and not another get selected? (2) Did the successful interest group actually mobilise more resources than other groups? Frequently, the state and/or media decide *on their own* to pay more attention to an issue. Interest group mobilisation does not necessarily enter into the picture at all. (3) While contingent events can play a role in the genesis of a social problem, whether those events are publicised heavily or not is a decision that rests ultimately with media and/or the state. If mainstream media elect not to call a great deal of attention to an event, then that event will almost invariably pass relatively unnoticed. The post-hoc problem in social problems accounts remains unresolved because a key element is being overlooked both by Lowney and Best, and more generally, by the predominant models in social problems theory, structural strain and interest group: the key role media play in selecting, initiating and framing social issues.

Best contends, for example, that media usually act as secondary claims-makers: 'While press coverage may be especially visible and influential, claims-making rarely begins with the media; the press usually covers other, primary claims-makers, and its coverage is a secondary-claim' Best (1990: 109). Best's remark is an assertion, unsupported by convincing empirical data. The media studies literature, in fact, contains a plethora of examples of media initiating attention to an issue, demonstrating that the media themselves should be seen as primary claims-makers.

Media and the state, briefly put, do not simply adopt the interpretive frame presented them by interest groups, contrary to many of the scholars operating in the social problems sub-discipline.[6] Media and the state generate their own interpretive frame the majority of the time. In so doing, not only is their very substantial power in the social problems game expressed, the fact that they frequently decide what will be called to the public's attention without the involvement of mid-range interest groups or the public at the start – at all – makes them claims-makers *of the first order*.

A moral panic?

The sixties' 'law 'n order' issue is the tale of *a moral panic that wasn't* in that the public did not actually panic. The fact that they did not is interesting in at least three respects.

First, if a moral panic did not occur, then what it produced in consequences can now be called into question since its principal rationale no longer holds and never did. The increasingly draconian and exceedingly expensive criminal justice policies that date from the early 1970s, for example, are subject to challenge.

Second, if the panic did not happen, given the dramatic and ongoing social upheaval of the period, the constantly rising index crime rate (index crime rose yearly from 1960 until 1977), and the centrality of the 'law 'n order' issue in the election campaigns of the period, *why* not?

Third, is it a moral panic if it is fundamentally confined to the actions of media and/or the state?[7] Is it a panic if the public is not involved in panicking? What, if any, modifications are in order for the moral panic literature? What does this tell us about how carefully we need to treat polling data? What theoretical conclusions might be drawn from this?

Methodological issues – mode of approach

In this chapter I review the polling evidence which shows that sixties era public crime concerns did not, in fact, rise to unprecedented levels. I then move on to answer the question (albeit briefly): if crime concerns were not high, then how was the false impression of high crime concerns accomplished? Finally, I address the question of what this case study can tell us about how public discourse and public policy are socially constructed. What matters, it turns out, is not what the majority sentiment is (a basic tenet of the functionalist model); what matters is what is *seen* as the majority sentiment.

Scholars take polling data, particularly from reputable polling organisations, as reliable and valid empirical data – as well we should. Polls provide valuable insight into public opinion when properly: (a) constructed; (b) administered; (c) analysed; and (d) reported. Listing (a) through (d) is not revelatory to anyone who works with polling data professionally. But what has not previously been explored are instances where highly respected polling organisations such as Gallup have been guilty of harnessing their polls to particular public policy objectives. This would be at variance, of course, with George Gallup's stated objective when he started his polling organisation in 1935, '[H]e would provide the public with a powerful tool to learn what the American people truly believed, not, he said, the lies they were being fed by vested interests'. Poll reports would permit people 'to make wise judgments [from] the mountain of polling data collected'.[8]

The polling data

The conventional view that polls showed high crime concerns rests upon a mixture of conflated poll results (disparate answers aggregated together), partial and misleading poll reports in mass media, leading questions that assumed the answers the pollsters were apparently seeking, and fabricated polls (that is poll 'results' that did not exist). 'Cleaned up' poll data – that is, the polls taken in their entirety and as originally administered – show that crime concerns in the polls rose surprisingly modestly during the period. The numbers were *especially* modest given the tremendous turmoil of the period. One would have thought that all of these factors would have and should have created a 'perfect storm' of public arousal about crime and disorder. The fact that it did not is a fascinating and telling story itself and something that I address in my concluding remarks.

Arguably, the most important purveyor of the conventional view on the sixties crime issue was James Wilson's 1975 book *Thinking About Crime* which single-handedly helped push debate about crime to the right. As Miller (1996: 138) points out, it 'came to shape the nation's policy on crime for most of the 1980s, culminating in the misinformed and destructive legislation of the 1990s'.[9] Wilson claimed in his book that on four occasions in the 1960s, crime topped the 'most important problem' in the nation (MIP) polls.[10] 'In May 1965 the Gallup Poll reported that for the first time "crime" (along with education) was viewed by Americans as the most important problem facing the nation' (Wilson 1975: 65). Contrary to what Wilson stated, the May 1965 Gallup poll actually found only 1 per cent of respondents citing crime and 2 per cent citing juvenile delinquency (see Table 2.3). Wilson goes on to state '[i]n the months leading up to the Democratic National Convention in 1968 – specifically in February, May, and August – Gallup continued to report crime as the most important issue' (Wilson 1975: 65–6).

Where Wilson got these figures is a puzzle as he is wrong on all counts. Gallup did not conduct a MIP poll in February 1968. The May 1968 poll was a conflated category (I discuss this later in this article, see Table 2.3 herein). Even as a conflated item, it was far below the leading items such as the Vietnam War and civil rights. The August 1968 poll Wilson refers to showed 8 per cent citing crime and 1 per cent citing 'hippies' (see Table 2.3). These percentages were well below the numbers cited in other categories on that date such as 47 per cent for 'Vietnam' and 20 per cent citing 'civil rights'.

1964: LBJ v Goldwater

The sixties' crime issue is commonly dated from Senator Barry Goldwater's acceptance speech at the Republican Party's presidential nomination's convention on July 16, 1964. In it he famously stated that:

> The growing menace in our country tonight, to personal safety, to life, to limb and property, in homes, in churches, on the playgrounds, and places of business, particularly in our great cities, is the mounting concern, or should be, of every thoughtful citizen in the United States ... History shows us ... that nothing ... prepares the way for tyranny more than the failure of public officials to keep the streets from bullies and marauders.

Goldwater was not, however, the first to make this claim. *US News and World Report* (the most conservative of the three major American news weeklies) was, and Goldwater was only one of several different elite voices, such as the Federal Bureau of Investigation (FBI), making this claim. In commenting on the presidential contest between Democrat Lyndon Johnson and Republican Barry Goldwater, *Newsweek* opined that the '"safety-in-the-streets" issue's real potency could be its close association with civil rights in the minds of many voters'.[11]

Similarly, Cronin *et al.* (1981: 13) cite a 'Gallup poll taken shortly before the election [that] showed that popular sentiment [on civil rights and crime's connection] more closely resembled Goldwater's campaign statements than Johnson's' (Cronin *et al.* 1981: 13).

'Crime' and 'juvenile delinquency,' as Table 2.1 shows, barely registered in the 1964 polls. By comparison, 'civil rights, integration, racial discrimination (no reference to demonstrations or riots)', an indicator of those who presumptively thought that civil rights was the central issue, drew numbers ranging from 24 to 58 per cent, the 58 per cent being registered in July 1964.

If social protest, riots and racial challenge were intimately intertwined in the public's mind, then we should expect that as riots increased in number and ferocity after 1964, crime concerns should have also risen. Between 1965 and 1969, however, polls indicated that few among the public were linking civil protest to crime.

At least 257 riots broke out in 1967 (Baskin *et al.* 1971) and preceding that, in 1965, the famous Los Angeles Watts Rebellion emblazoned itself in history and in headlines across the country. Despite this, poll-measured concerns for 'crime and juvenile delinquency' between 1965 and 1967 remained low, ranging from 1–4 per cent from 1965–7.

White antipathy *to the riots* grew overall as time went on throughout the sixties, but crime concerns and riots did not move together. Why did

Table 2.1 1964 polls: most important problem in nation (%)

Sampling dates	Crime	Juvenile delinquency	Civil rights, integration, racial discrim- ination (no reference to demos or riots)	Civil rights. demos, negro riots, violence, lawlessness connected with them
27 March–2 April 1964	0.0	1.0	34.0	0.0
24–29 April 1964	0.0	2.0	42.0	0.0
25–30 June 1964	0.0	1.0	47.0	0.0
23–28 July 1964	<0.5	<0.5	58.0	2.0
6–11 August 1964	1.0	<0.5	36.0	2.0
27 August–1 Sept. 1964	<0.5	1.0	46.0	2.0
18–23 September 1964	<0.5	1.0	34.0	<0.5
8–13 October 1964	1.0	1.0	24.0	1.0

Source: Gallup

the polls *not* register elevated crime concerns after riots? A complete and rigorous answer to this question is beyond the scope of this chapter, but a suggestive hypothesis can be drawn based on the white reaction to the Watts Rebellion of 1965.

Watts 1965

The dominant analysis of racial attitudes in the sixties holds in essence that white Americans recoiled from blacks Americans' demands for equality as these demands became more insistent and militant. Collective memory holds that this was particularly true of the Watts Rebellion of 1965.[12] This dominant view holds out little hope that racial equity can ever be achieved because it posits that the more that white Americans' privileges are curtailed, the more they will oppose this. Without minimising the hold that racism can exert, the historical record – the fact that white racism is neither as pervasive nor as strong as it was prior to the civil rights movement – indicates that racial attitudes can and do change.

There are two other problems with the dominant analysis. First, it overlooks the fact that white Americans are a variegated group in terms of their attitudes. There is no singular, dominant stance among all white Americans with respect to race. Certainly the history of white skin privilege has had and continues to have an effect on white Americans as a whole. There is a taken-for-granted dimension to white skin privilege among those it favours that makes it more difficult for whites than ethnic or racial minorities to see white racism. But to posit a more or less uniform perspective is injudicious analytically.

Second, the character of a racial or ethnic group's reaction to its situation relative to other racial or ethnic groups is criss-crossed by other statuses and roles such as class. Reactions by any group to other groups' actions and demands are more contingent than inevitable in the sense that political leadership – the stance that political leadership takes on a given question or set of questions – can be *and usually is* decisive. Put another way: what is *seen* as the majority position matters much more than what the *actual* majority position is. Majority views do not hold sway as much as the dominant *presentation* of what the majority view supposedly is – at least in a putative democracy where rule by the majority is the dominant shibboleth.

The evidence from polling data about the reaction to the Watts Rebellion indicates a highly divided reaction by whites, with the majority sentiment actually sympathetic to black demands. This is diametrically at odds with the dominant interpretation of the Watts Rebellion's impact on white attitudes (see Loo and Grimes 2004 for a full presentation of these data). Extrapolating from my analysis of the data concerning Watts, I would hypothesise here that the reason why riots in general did not per se stoke crime concerns in the polls was because, at least in part, whites were politically divided in their reaction to the riots. They were divided in their reaction, in part, because whites were not uniformly hostile to black demands for equality and also because there was a powerful countervailing political 'pole' present in the sixties to that exerted by conservative elites in the form of the social insurgencies and the civil rights movement in particular. I discuss this factor more in the last section of the chapter.

Table 2.2 displays white responses to a question asking their views about the specific causes for the riot. Fifty-four per cent of those interviewed expressed sympathy for the riot compared to 42 per cent who were antagonistic. As Noelle-Neumann (1993) points out in her study of a phenomenon she labelled the 'spiral of silence', people who think their opinions are in the minority will tend to silence themselves and vice-versa. If you want to have your opinion carry the day, creating the impression (even if it is false) that your opinion is the dominant one helps to *make* it the dominant one.[13] Or, at least, it creates a reasonable facsimile of the majority sentiment, albeit a fragile facsimile. The question before Los Angeles and the nation then was which reaction to the rebellion would come to be seen as the dominant one.

Horne (1995: 281) observes that the widely propagated notion of a white backlash 'helped to create a momentum of its own and a self-fulfilling prophecy. Though certain studies showed substantial sympathy across racial lines for the grievances of South LA, this was not the message being broadcast by acolytes of the right'. Right-wing radio shows, ubiquitous in the US today,

Table 2.2 Causes of the Watts Riot – white respondents (%)

Sympathetic		Situational		Unsympathetic	
Unfair treatment	15	Heat, Frye arrest, etc.	23	Agitators & outsiders	14
History of injustice	11			Bad elements in community (troublemakers, gangs, hoodlums, delinquents, etc.)	12
Police brutality	2				
Just cause	**28**	**Situational**	**23**	**Hostile to riot**	**26**

were building a listenership in southern California, and helped push whites to the political Right.

White reaction to the Watts Rebellion (and by extension, the rest of the sixties' rebellions) was contingent and divided. There was, in other words, no uniform white response. Summations and interpretations of the rebellions were contested. The presence of powerful and influential social movements from below affected the degree to which the dominant discourse – the discourse originating from elites – was adopted. The MIP polls record is consistent with this view. Opinion-makers, politicians and media outlets such as Right-wing radio talk shows, played key roles in shaping and creating the elite discourse.

The MIP polls following the famous 1967 Detroit riots (the riots led to tanks being dispatched down the city's streets) further illustrate respondents' ability to distinguish crime from riots. In a Gallup poll on 3–8 August 1967, taken in the immediate wake of the 21 July to 1 August 1967 Detroit riots, only 2 per cent cited crime and juvenile delinquency as their chief concern. By contrast, 35 per cent cited 'Racial strife – arson, looting, etc.' as their chief concern. While the 1967 summer riots thus produced a large negative response in the 3–8 August 1967 poll, those polled distinguished riots from crime per se.

Respondents are allowed to choose more than one item as their top concern in the MIP polls and the tiny number citing 'crime' contradicts the belief that 'Racial strife – arson, looting, riots, etc.' was chosen as a simple substitute for 'crime'. Had respondents wanted to cite 'crime' as a major concern, they were free to do so and we might expect a much larger number to have done so then the 2 per cent who did.

A bifurcated reaction was evident between the public and media/political elites after the 1967 summer riots. On the one hand, polls revealed little mass public interest in the crime issue. Gallup's 3–8 August 1967 poll showed only 2 per cent citing 'crime and juvenile delinquency', and 4 per cent in its 27 October to 1 November 1967 poll. These polls received no media attention. 'Law and order', on the other hand, was the frequent topic in newspapers, on conservative talk shows, and among politicians. In October 1967, *New*

York Times' columnist Tom Wicker, a liberal, predicted that 'law and order' would become one of the 1968 presidential campaign's major issues.

1968: Elections and the crime issue

The two most prominently publicised polls in major media that supposedly showed crime to be Americans' foremost domestic concern were Gallup's 2–7 May 1968 and 26 June to 1 July 1968 polls. These polls showed that 15 and 29 per cent respectively of the public considered 'lawlessness' the top US domestic problem (for example, *New York Times*, 4 August 1968, p 45, col 1). Gallup created a category for these polls that they dubbed 'Crime and Lawlessness (including riots, looting and juvenile delinquency)'. Gallup had never used this category previously, nor have they used it since (see Table 2.3).

By combining several different items into a category created after the fact, Gallup created the impression that crime concerns were much higher than they actually were. Other polls publicised in the remainder of 1968 also either conflated categories – perpetuating the impression of more robust crime concerns than were actually justified by the data – or particular polls were selectively presented in a manner that generated the same impression. The polls *not publicised* in 1968 actually revealed crime concerns were *dropping*.

Table 2.3 Crime as the nation's most important problem 1967–9

Date	% citing crime/ juvenile deliquency
26–31 January 1967	2
3–8 August 1967	2
27 October–1 November 1967	4
4–9 January 1968	6
2–7 May 1968	[15]
26 June–1 July 1968	[29]
18–23 July 1968	11
7–12 August 1968	9
1 September 1968	12
26 September–1 October 1968	11
17–22 October 1968	12
1–6 January 1969	6
22–27 May 1969	2

[ ] indicates a conflated category: 'crime and lawlessness (including riots, looting and juvenile delinquency)'.

For example, Gallup's next poll, between 18–23 July 1968, recorded 11 per cent citing 'Crime (general), no references to juvenile delinquency, lack of respect for law and order', plus 'Juvenile delinquency – hippies'. This poll, therefore, actually recorded a *fall* in crime concerns – at least as compared to the May and June 1968 conflated polls. The 18–23 July 1968 poll was not publicised by any media or even by Gallup itself.

In its next poll, taken between 7–12 August 1968, Gallup found 9 per cent cited 'Crime (looting and lawlessness)' as their first choice, *down further* from its July 1968 sampling. This was particularly low given the fact that the Republican Party convention had just nominated – on 1 August 1968 – Nixon and Agnew on an explicit 'law and order' platform. In addition, two major riots had just occurred – in Cleveland between 23–26 July 1968, and Miami on 7 August 1968 – the same day Gallup began its August 1968 sampling.

This fall in crime concerns was not reported in media either. Instead, Gallup reported erroneously that its August 1968 poll showed that 21 per cent of respondents named 'crime (including looting, riots)' as their top choice. This figure of 21 per cent was in reality 9 per cent. The *New York Times* reported Gallup's inflated 21 per cent figure in its 8 September 1968 issue, noting that 'crime and lawlessness' were among the top four major worries of the electorate (p 77, col 4). This was true but misleading since the Vietnam War (at 47 per cent) and civil rights (at 20 per cent) outpolled crime (at 8 per cent) and riots (at 12 per cent) by a wide margin.

When disaggregated from disparate items and reported as actually answered in the poll, the 'crime' figure in August 1968's polls is only 9 per cent vs the 21 per cent reported as 'crime (including looting, riots)'. Similarly, the figure for 'crime and juvenile delinquency' as answered was 6 per cent in the 1 January 1969 poll vs the 17 per cent that Gallup reported as 'crime and lawlessness (including looting, riots and juvenile delinquency)'.

Gallup also administered three polls in the heat of the presidential campaign on 1 September 1968; 26 September to 1 October 1968; and 17–22 October 1968. These polls were not publicised by major media or by Gallup itself. The polls recorded elevated crime and riot concerns: 12 per cent (crime) and 14 per cent (riots), 11 and 12 per cent, and 12 and 12 per cent respectively. While elevated, they were not comparable to the recorded concerns over the Vietnam War that were running between 40–47 per cent in the same polls. These data are surprising in light of the hundreds of explosive and destructive riots throughout the sixties era, and the central status given the law and order issue during the 1968 presidential campaign.

The *New York Times*, despite its liberal editorial policy, publicised the following polls and did not report the fact that Gallup's September and October 1968 polls showed unimpressive crime concerns levels:

- A Louis Harris poll that reportedly found 81 per cent of the voters believing that 'law and order has broken down' (*New York Times*, 10 September 1968, p 31, col 1);
- A Harris survey showing Nixon had a spread of 12 percentage points over Humphrey on the law and order issue (*New York Times*, 13 September 1968, p 52, col 5);
- A *New York Times* survey showing that the law and order issue was the largest single issue turning voters to Nixon (*New York Times*, 15 September 1968, p 78, col 3);
- A Gallup poll that found that people's fear of using the streets in their own communities at night strengthens the law and order issue (*New York Times*, 10 October 1968, p 51, col 3);
- A Harris survey showing 52 per cent of negroes saying that police brutality is the major cause of the breakdown of law and order (with 10 per cent of whites agreeing) (*New York Times*, 16 October 1968, p 26, col 1).

In sum, then, with the exception of this last item of 16 October 1968, the polls that *the New York Times* selected to feature all conveyed the impression that the 'law and order' issue was of paramount importance to the electorate and that the electorate was in a 'law and order' mood.

The September 1968 Harris poll

The Harris poll showing 81 per cent of respondents agreeing that 'law and order have broken down,' published in the 9 September 1968 issue of the *New York Post* and picked up by the *New York Times* the next day, is very revealing. It is probably the most outstanding example of pollster misbehaviour on the crime issue in the sixties.

The *New York Post*'s headline for the piece was entitled '"Law & Order" Top Issue Next to the War: Harris'. The story began: 'Next to ending the war in Vietnam, the most urgent demand of American voters in this election season is to bring back a sense of law and order. By 81 to 14 per cent, a heavy majority of the public believes law and order has broken down in this country' (p 5).

On 24 August 1968, 1,481 voters were asked a series of questions beginning with: 'I want to ask you about some things which some people think *have been causes of the breakdown of law and order* in this country. For each, *tell me if you feel it is a major cause of a breakdown of law and order, a minor cause, or hardly a cause at all*' (emphasis added).

They began by asking respondents a series of questions structured as 'Many people say X has happened. Which of the following reasons would you say are responsible for causing X to happen?'. Harris next asked respondents a series of questions, one of which was: 'Do you think that X has happened?'.

In other words, the first series of questions *assume* the answer to a question asked later. Given this structure and sequence of questions, it is not surprising that 81 per cent of respondents should then agree that 'X has happened'.

In summary: (1) pollsters manipulated the results of some of their surveys (either in the way in which they framed their questions, or in the way they reported the results); (2) conservative politicians, the FBI, and major media linked protest with crime; and (3) media reported selectively the polls in a manner that fostered the impression that crime was uppermost in the public's mind.

Crime concerns did not rise higher than 12 per cent in the sixties. This fact does not obviate the observed fact that many Americans associate blacks with crime (see, for example, Skogan 1995). But the data from the MIP polls indicate that most Americans distinguished crime per se from racial challenge. Respondents who expressed opposition to racial challenge did so, but they did not also name crime in significant numbers as their choice for the nation's top problem.

Neither riots nor the rising index crime rate directly influenced the poll results with respect to crime concerns per se. What interpretation came to be understood as the dominant one was both contingent and central to the course of public policy-making. Were these riots a product of the 'tangle of pathology' of disrupted black family structures?[14] Were the riots to be understood as a form of righteous rebellion? Certain state actors, major media outlets, and pollsters played critical roles in the process of generating the elite interpretation.

As Spitzer (1975) points out, from the perspective of at least some social elites, street crime generates victims who are mainly members of an expendable class. Social protest, on the other hand, represents 'social dynamite' and is therefore much more threatening than ordinary street crime; it could lead to the system's demise. The conflating of riots and social protest with crime was, in short, an elite-sponsored social construction. Michigan Senator Robert Griffin, for example, equated the two in full in the 30 June 1972 issue of *Life* magazine (LXXII, p 52), calling the then-current crime wave 'a riot in slow motion' (cited by Conklin 1975: 1).

It is, of course, much easier to counter racial challenge by presenting one's self as 'anti-crime' instead of as 'anti-civil rights' (see Edsall and Edsall 1991). The FBI, *US News and World Report*, Goldwater, and subsequently, Nixon/Agnew did exactly this, invoking the race card by playing the crime card. John Ehrlichmann, Nixon's Special Counsel, admitted to this when he wrote about Nixon's 1968 campaign strategy: 'We'll go after the racists. That subliminal appeal to the anti-African American voter was always present in Nixon's statements and speeches' (Ehrlichmann 1970: 233).

Polls in the sixties and the representation of those polls were part of the production of the elite discourse. Interestingly, at times poll *results* were at variance with the dominant discourse. The dominant discourse, in other words, did not fully replicate itself in the poll results (see, for example, Shupe and Stacey 1982). To resolve that disjuncture – that is, to make the poll results 'look like' the dominant discourse – polls have sometimes been selectively reported, and in certain instances, individually erroneously reported or (re) presented. This is as one might expect: polls, after all, make up the key part of the rationale given for public policy shifts in contemporary times.

Discussion

On one level, the Republican Party was obviously implementing its so-called Southern strategy to steal away the southern white voter from the Democrats in being boosters of the 'law 'n order' issue (Beckett and Sasson 2000). They have obviously been very successful in this effort. But the Southern strategy hypothesis does not go far enough. It does not explain why the Democratic Party ended up adopting the interpretive frame being pushed by the Republican Party. Why, given the polling data, did the Democrats bow to the Republican Party's misrepresentations about the level of public concern about crime?

A common misunderstanding about the dynamics at work between the Republican Party and the Democrats is that they may *best* be understood by their mutual desire to defeat the other party in elections. Winning and holding office is believed, according to this view, to be the *primary* motivation for both parties. While the Republican Party and the Democrats are certainly in partisan rivalry with each other, there are other factors at work. What the Republican Party and the Democrats share in common – and what they share in common trumps overall how they differ – is their shared position as political elites. Anything that jeopardises the Republican Party and the Democratic Party's mutual status organisationally and institutionally, anything that could lead to social insurgency upsetting and possibly even toppling their governing status, is to be avoided at all costs (see Loo 2006). And this is only what we might expect. Expecting them to act differently than this is, after all, unrealistic.

In the 1960s, liberal elites argued that concessions (for example, the War on Poverty) needed to be made to the insurgents lest a conflagration result. Conservatives argued that concessions would only fuel the fires of insurgency and a crackdown was what was needed. The sixties insurgency breached the public agenda ordinarily generated by elites (Paletz and Entman 1981; Zaller 1992). A society-wide debate raged over whether the key social problem was crime or social injustice. The crime issue as authored initially by conservative elites in the sixties was challenged largely successfully by social movement activists who argued forcefully that social injustice, not crime, was the central social problem of the day.

This is one of the key reasons – probably by far the most important reason – that the public did not adopt the elite discourse that crime and social protest were one and the same thing. The sixties' insurgency created significant splits – for a short time – in elite ranks. The insurgency's influence *prevented* crime from emerging at the top of the MIP polls during the sixties because the public was split in its views and its loyalties, with the majority faction favouring the insurgencies.

Implications and conclusions

The data adduced and referred to here underscore the crime issue's socially constructed nature, demonstrating that the collective memory about the public's focus on the sixties' crime issue is inaccurate. The origins of that collective memory can be attributed to the collective efforts of conservative public officials, mass media, pollsters, and conservative intellectuals, such as James Q Wilson. If we use the customary definition for a moral panic in which the public is drawn into the panic, a moral panic around crime did not occur in the sixties. Instead, the impression of a panic was created.

The sixties' insurgency prevented the crime issue from becoming the number one domestic problem. Something similar could occur if and when a new social movement of sufficient force and influence develops and challenges the elite consensus. In that eventuality, a very fluid situation, pregnant with possibilities, would ensue. Contrary to the conventional view that the 'fear of crime' exists as a kind of inevitable social fact, 'crime' would then take its place among other issues that could rise or fall in prominence, depending upon the relative strength and influence of different political forces or movements.

Notes

1 It was also sometimes referred to as the 'crime in the streets' issue.
2 The incarceration rate in the US began its upward and still rising trajectory in 1973, the sixties era's endpoint.
3 President Franklin Delano Roosevelt.
4 Most of the data for the chapter herein are either based on that article or are recapitulated here.
5 Moral panic as a concept began originally with Durkheim (Downes and Rock 1988; Sumner 1994).
6 Best (2001: 15), for example, describes media's role as that of *conduit* for interest groups' claims, not as a framer of issues themselves: 'The *mass media* – including both the popular and entertainment media ... relay activists' claims to the general public'(emboldening added). Similarly, Surette (1998: 10–11) describes the relationship between media and claims-makers this way:

> The media serve the role of world knowledge *conduit* and playing field for the competition between claims-makers. Claims-makers compete for media attention and *media favour claims that are dramatic, sponsored by powerful groups, and related to established cultural themes* (emphasis added).

7 Tester (1994: 85) critiques the idea that 'simply because there was a moral panic in the media there must also have been a moral panic among the viewers and readers'.

 8 Gallup (1940).
 9 For example, the Pennsylvania Republican Party purchased Wilson's book for the entire Republican Party state legislative membership to use in planning state criminal justice policies (Miller 1996: fn 7, p 272).
10 Gallup first began polling in 1935 and offered its first 'most important problem' in the nation poll that year.
11 'The Curious Campaign – Point by Point', *Newsweek*, 19 October 1964, pp 27–8.
12 It was dubbed a rebellion by many because it was so clearly more than an average riot.
13 See also Sutton and Farrall, Chapter 7, in this book.
14 *The Negro Family: The Case for National Action,* written by Daniel Patrick Moynihan, then Assistant Secretary of Labor, was released in August 1965. In it Moynihan, a liberal, famously advanced the view that one of slavery's legacies was the broken black family. Moynihan linked this to the persistence of female-headed black families and a consequent higher delinquency and crime rate among blacks. His argument about matriarchal-headed families being at the root of the problem and 'tangle of pathology' resulting from it lent itself to adoption by Right-wing and as well as mainstream voices open to explaining the riots as due to family structure failures.

References

Altschull, J Herbert (1995) *Agents of Power: The Media and Public Policy,* White Plains, NY: Longman Publishers.

Bagdikian, Ben H (1997) *The Media Monopoly,* 5th edn, Boston, MA: Beacon Press.

Barlow, Melissa Hickman, David Barlow and Theodore Chiricos (1995a) 'Economic Conditions and Ideologies of Crime in the Media: A Content Analysis of Crime News', *Crime and Delinquency,* 41(1): 3–19.

—— (1995b) 'Mobilizing Support for Social Control in a Declining Economy: Exploring Ideologies of Crime within Crime News', *Crime and Delinquency,* 41(2): 191–204.

Baskin, Jane A, Joyce Hartweg, Ralph Lewis and Lester McCullough, Jr (1971) *Race Related Civil Disorders: 1967–1969,* Waltham, MA: Lemberg Center for the Study of Violence, Brandeis University.

Baskin, Jane A, Ralph Lewis, Joyce Hartweg Mannis and Lester McCullough, Jr (1972) *The Long, Hot Summer? An Analysis of Summer Disorders: 1967–1971,* Waltham, MA: Lemberg Center for the Study of Violence, Brandeis University.

Beckett, Katherine (1994) *The Politics of Law and Order: the State and the Wars Against Crime and Drugs, 1964 to the Present,* unpublished PhD dissertation, University of California at Los Angeles, Sociology Department.

Beckett, Katherine and Theodore Sasson (2000) *The Politics of Injustice: Crime and Punishment in America,* Thousand Oaks, CA: Pine Forge Press.

Best, Joel (1990) *Threatened Children: Rhetoric and Concern about Child-Victims,* Chicago, IL: University of Chicago Press.

—— (2001) *Damned Lies and Statistics: Untangling Numbers from the Media, Politicians, and Activists,* Berkeley, CA: University of California Press.

Blake, Phil (1974) 'Race, Homicide and the News', *The Nation* (7 December): 592–3.

Chambliss, William J (1994) 'Policing the Ghetto Underclass: The Politics of Law and Law Enforcement'. *Social Problems*, 41(2): 177–94.

Chiricos, Ted, Kathy Padgett and Marc Gertz (2000) 'Fear, TV News, and the Reality of Crime', *Criminology*, 38: 755–86.

Chiricos, Ted, Sarah Eschholz and Marc Gertz (1997) 'Crime, News and Fear of Crime: Toward an Identification of Audience Effects', *Social Problems*, 44(3): 342–57.

Cohen, Stanley (1980) *Folk Devils and Moral Panics*, London: MacGibbon & Kee.

Conklin, John E (1975) *The Impact of Crime*, New York: MacMillan.

Cose, Ellis (1993) *The Rage of a Privileged Class*, 1st edn, New York: Harper Collins.

Cronin, Thomas E, Tania Z Cronin and Michael E Milakovich (1981) *US vs Crime in the Streets*, Bloomington, IN: Indiana University Press.

Crouteau, David and William Hoynes (2001) *The Business of Media: Corporate Media and the Public Interest*, Thousand Oaks, CA: Pine Forge Press.

Downes, David and Paul Rock (1988) *Understanding Deviance: A Guide to the Sociology of Crime and Rule-breaking*, 2nd edn, Oxford: Clarendon Press.

Edsall, Thomas and Mary Edsall (1991) *Chain Reaction: The Impact of Race, Rights and Taxes on American Politics*, New York: WW Norton.

Ehrlichmann, J (1970) *Witness to Power: The Nixon Years*, New York: Simon & Schuster.

Erskine, Hazel (1974) 'The Polls: Fear of Violence and Crime', *Public Opinion Quarterly*, 38(1): 131–45.

Fishman, Mark (1978) 'Crime Waves as Ideology', *Social Problems*, 25: 531–43.

Flamm, Michael (2002) '"Law and Order" at Large: The New York Civilian Review Board Referendum of 1966 and the Crisis of Liberalism', *The Historian*, 64: 643–65.

Fritz, Noah J and David L Altheide (1987) 'The Mass Media and the Social Construction of the Missing Children Problem', *Sociological Quarterly*, 28(4): 473–92.

Furstenberg, Frank F, Jr (1971) 'Public Reaction to Crime in the Streets', *American Scholar*, 40(4): 601–10.

Gallup, George (1940) *The Pulse of Democracy*, New York: Simon and Schuster.

Gans, Herbert J (1979) *Deciding What's News: A Study of CBS Evening News, NBC Nightly News, Newsweek and Time*, New York: Pantheon.

Ginsberg, Benjamin (1986) *The Captive Public: How Mass Opinion Promotes State Power*, New York: Basic Books.

Goode, Erich and Nachman Ben-Yehuda (1994) *Moral Panics: The Social Construction of Deviance*, Cambridge, MA: Blackwell.

Gorelick, Steven M (1989) '"Join Our War": The Construction of Ideology in a Newspaper Crimefighting Campaign', *Crime and Delinquency*, 35(3): 421–36.

Hacker, Andrew (1988) 'Black Crime, White Racism', *New York Review of Books*, 3 March: 36–41.

—— (1992) 'The New Civil War', *New York Review of Books*, 23 April: 30–4.

Hall, Stuart, Chas Critcher, Tony Jefferson, John Clarke and Brian Roberts (1978) *Policing the Crisis: Mugging, the State and Law and Order*, London: MacMillan.

Hartley, John (1992) *The Politics of Pictures*, Routledge: London.

Hartmann, Paul and Charles Husband (1974) *Racism and the Mass Media: A Study of the Role of the Mass Media in the Formation of White Beliefs and Attitudes in Britain*, London: Davis-Poynter.

—— (1981) 'The Mass Media and Racial Conflict', in Stanley Cohen and Jock Young (eds), *The Manufacturing of News*, revised edn, London: Constable.

Herman, Edward and Noam Chomsky (1988) *Manufacturing Consent: the Political Economy of the Mass Media*, New York: Pantheon Books.

Horne, Gerald (1995) *Fire This Time: The Watts Uprising and the 1960s*, Charlottesville, VI: University of Virginia Press.

Hunt, Arnold (1997) '"Moral Panic" and the Moral Language in the Media', *British Journal of Sociology*, 48(4): 629–48.

Jacob, Herbert, Robert L Lineberry, with Anner Heinz, Janice Beecher, Jack Moran and Duance Swank (1982) *Governmental Responses to Crime: Crime on Urban Agendas*, US Department of Justice, National Institute of Justice, GPO No: J28.2:G74.

Kahneman, Daniel and Amos Tversky (1982) 'The Psychology of Preferences', *Scientific American*, 246: 136–42.

Loo, Dennis D (2002) 'Creating a Crime Wave: the 1990s', *Free Inquiry in Creative Sociology*, 30: 40–55.

—— (2006) 'Never Elected, Not Once: the Immaculate Deception and the Road Ahead', in D Loo and P Phillips (eds) *Impeach the President: the Case Against Bush and Cheney*, New York: Seven Stories Press.

Loo, Dennis D and Ruth-Ellen Grimes (2004) 'Polls, Politics and Crime: The "Law and Order" Issue of the 1960s', *Western Criminology Review*, 5(1): 50–67.

Lowney, KS and J Best (1995) 'Stalking strangers and lovers: Changing media typifications of a new crime problem', in J Best (ed), Images of issues: Typifying contemporary social problems, 2nd edn, New York: Aldine de Gruyterpp.

Luttwak, Edward (1999) *Turbo-Capitalism: Winners and Losers in the Global Economy*, New York: HarperCollins.

McAdam, Doug (1982) *Political Process and the Development of Black Insurgency: 1930–1970*, Chicago, IL: University of Chicago Press.

Miller, Jerome (1996) *Search and Destroy: African-American Males in the Criminal Justice System*, New York: Cambridge University Press.

Niemi, Richard, John Mueller and Tom Smith (1989) *Trends in Public Opinion: A Compendium of Survey Data*, New York: Greenwood Press.

Noelle-Neumann, Elizabeth (1993) *The Spiral of Silence*, 2nd edn, Chicago, IL: University of Chicago Press.

Paletz, David L and Robert M Entman (1981) *Media, Power, Politics*, New York: The Free Press.

Parenti, Michael (1993) *Inventing Reality: The Politics of the Media*, 2nd edn, New York: St Martin's Press.

Scholarly Resources (2000) *The Gallup Poll: Public Opinion, 1935–1997*, Wilmington, DE: Scholarly Resources.

Schudson, Michael (1995) *The Power of the News*, Cambridge, MA: Harvard University Press.

Shupe, Anson and William A Stacey (1982) 'Born Again Politics and the Moral Majority: What Social Surveys Really Show', *Studies in American Religion*, vol 5, New York: Edwin Mellen Press.

Skogan, Wesley G (1995) 'Crime and the Racial Fears of White Americans', *Annals of the American Academy of Politics and Public Policy*, 539: 59–71.

Smith, Tom (1985) 'The Polls: America's Most Important Problem', *Public Opinion Quarterly*, 49(2): 264–74.

Spector, Malcolm and John Kitsuse (1973) 'Social Problems', *Social Problems*, 21(2): 145–59.

Spitzer, Steven (1975) 'Towards a Marxian Theory of Deviance', *Social Problems*, 22: 638–51.

Steffens, Lincoln (1931) *The Autobiography of Lincoln Steffens*, New York: Harcourt Brace & Co.

Sumner, Colin (1981) 'Race, Crime and Hegemony: a Review Essay', *Contemporary Crises*, 5: 277–91.

Sumner, Colin (1994) *The Sociology of Deviance: An Obituary*, Buckingham: Open University Press.

Surette, Ray (1998) *Media Crime and Criminal Justice: Images and Realities*, Belmont, CA: Wadsworth.

Szykowny, Rick (1994) 'No Justice, No Peace: an Interview with Jerome Miller', *Humanist*, 54: 9–20.

Teeple, Gary (1995) *Globalization and the Decline of Social Reform*, Atlantic Highlands, NJ: Humanities Press.

Tester, Keith (1994) *Media, Culture and Morality*, London: Routledge.

Tuchman, Gaye (1978) 'Professionalism as an Agent of Legitimation', *Journal of Communications*, Spring: 106–13.

Van Dijk, Teun A (1991) *Racism and the Press*, New York: Routledge.

Wilson, James Q (1975) *Thinking About Crime*, New York: Basic Books, Inc.

Zaller, John R (1992) *The Nature and Origins of Mass Opinion*, Cambridge: Cambridge University Press.

Zimring, Franklin E and Gordon Hawkins (1991) *The Scale of Imprisonment*, Chicago, IL: The University of Chicago Press.

Chapter 3

The enumeration of anxiety

Power, knowledge and fear of crime

Murray Lee

> The young, strong body, now helpless in sleep, awoke in him a pitying, protecting feeling. ... In the old days, he thought, a man looked at a girl's body and saw it as desirable, and that was the end of the story. But you could not have pure love or pure lust nowadays. No emotion was pure, because everything was mixed up with fear and hatred. Their embrace had been a battle, the climax a victory. It was a blow against the Party. It was a political act.
>
> (George Orwell, *Nineteen Eighty-Four*, 1949: 104).

Introduction

This chapter has a very specific aim. It seeks to identify a range of obscured dimensions of knowledge and power in relation to the representation of data concerning public anxieties about crime. It argues that the intensely political dimensions of fear of crime data, and the socio-cultural implications of this, is often ignored by government or 'administrative' criminologists who tend to reduce debates about 'fear of crime' to technical arguments. Three specific examples of the power effects of enumerating fear of crime are identified. The chapter concludes by stressing that in the context of a range of contemporary neo-liberal political rationalities, the way we conceptualise and measure fear of crime has implications at both the macro and micro level.

Debates concerning the nature of public anxiety about crime have now spanned four decades. Indeed, 2007 marked the fortieth anniversary of the 'discovery' of fear of crime. Given this it is perhaps not a time celebration or even recrimination but for historical reflection. Fear of crime was first problematised in 1967 as a result of *inter alia* three large-scale victim surveys conducted in the US (Biderman *et al.* 1967; Ennis 1967; Reiss 1967).[1] As well as asking about respondent's experiences of victimisation the surveys asked a range of questions about a respondent's anxiety about crime. In particular, the surveys asked respondents 'scenario' type questions such as 'would you feel safe being out alone in your neighbourhood after dark'[2] in order to take a 'global measure' of crime fear. Generally, respondents had the choice one to five on a Likert scale; a range which went from 'very safe' to 'very unsafe'. Survey results were quantified and the resulting data is said to be representative of the public fear of crime. While many researchers involved in these early surveys were circumspect about what their data set actually measured or represented, the methodology has remained strikingly similar in most subsequent large-scale crime and victim surveys. As a result, analysts have been able to state 'facts' such as 'the level of worry about violent crime has increased' (Povey *et al.* 2005: 8) and 'more than two-thirds (68%) of women (compared with a third of men) said they did not walk alone in their neighbourhood after dark ...' (Morris *et al.* 2003). With the production of figures such as these has come the notion that fear of crime can be reduced or governed through policy intervention.

What is fear of crime?

When we discuss fear of crime it is unlike discussing material phenomena such as buildings, roads and bridges. It is also different from discussing natural objects such as rocks and mountains or birds and animals. Nor is it much like discussions of offence rates, mortality rates, literacy and numeracy skills and most other social scientific objects of knowledge. As Skogan succinctly put it more than 30 years ago, it is '... a diffuse psychological construct affected by a number of aspects of urban life' (Skogan 1976: 14). It is perhaps a shame that Skogan's very fuzzy definition of crime fear has not endured for it captures the very amorphous nature of crime fear; something that is lost through the process of quantification.

That is fear of crime is by nature and *was* by definition – at least in Skogan's terms – *subjective*.[3] It is an experience, or set of experiences, that are intensely individual – that is if we accept a 'techno-scientific' account that such a coherent *thing* even exists (Lupton 1999). While most natural and materially occurring objects can be counted and described, even if the categories by which we order or taxonomise these are largely arbitrarily constructed (Foucault 1970), and many social scientific targets of knowledge clearly categorised and delineated – for example we can statistically count an assault offence through a detailed police or victim account of the offence even while the accuracy of these accounts and levels of reportage might vary – fear of crime is both a conceptually poor construct (Hale 1996; Ditton and Farrall 2000) and a subjectively diverse set of experiences (Jackson 2004).[4] It is not something that exists 'out there' in the social world as some kind of Durkheimian social fact like crime or suicide. As Jackson (2004: 962) has put it, fear of crime has come:

> ... to name and classify in a nebulous form a range of perceptions, responses and vulnerabilities. Expressing or associating concerns about broader social issues that crime connects with the public consciousness.

In this sense it exists as an organising principle in the minds of statisticians, social scientists, criminologists, policy makers and politicians – and even these cannot agree on what that *something* is.

Some facts

Many of the debates that have followed and been provoked by the enumeration of the fear of crime are largely technical and somewhat reflect the broader 'managerialist' or 'administrative' turn in criminology; criminologist as 'system engineer' as Stan Cohen (1988: 23) has put it. Even many of its critics confine their arguments to statistical method and accuracy. Proponents seem to suggest that the enumeration of crime fear is somehow apolitical; results are seen to inform policy and the public in practical ways. However, while debate about what fear of crime is and how this might best be measured continue there are some historical facts about the phenomenon over which there can be little doubt and these tend to highlight its political implications.

First, as a concept fear of crime was *invented* via new technologies of enumerating crime that developed in the 1960s; most notably the victim or crime survey (Stanko 2000; Lee 2007a, Loo, Chapter 2, in this book). Thus, most of the technical debates to which I refer *followed* its invention rather than the other way around. We created the concept then decided to argue about whether it might be a decent organising principal for a body of social scientific knowledge, or not. This is not to suggest that there was no anxiety about crime prior to the 1960s, certainly there was (see Pearson 1983). Rather, it is that the term fear of crime was not an organising principle – indeed, the term was rarely if ever used before 1965 (Lee 2007a). Second, the enumeration of fear of crime that resulted from the surveys indicated significantly high levels of fear – or whatever was measured – that it became a governmental problematisation. Third, once fear of crime was enumerated and became an organising principal for a range of criminal justice and social policy targeting its reduction, it also became a staple object of criminological inquiry attracting research funding and becoming the topic for thousands of academic publications (Hale 1996; Lee 1999; Lee 2007a; Ditton and Farrall 2000). Not insignificant resources were invested in the new problem. Fourth, and this is also connected to the previous point, fear of crime became political from the moment it was enumerated. The initial surveys themselves were the result of an 'expert commission' assembled by US president LB Johnson.[5] As Ditton and Farrall (2000) have made absolutely clear, the political potency of 'fear of crime' was there at the outset. Harris succinctly plotted this political potency way back in 1969 (see Harris 1969; Lee 2007a), a fact that seems to be conveniently glossed over by many subsequent researchers. Thus, one cannot speak of levels of fear of crime without engaging debates about how fear plays out at a political level – it was at this level it was *invented*. With this in mind I will now identify three overlapping domains in which the power/knowledge capacities of fear of crime can be identified; its reportage, its democratisation, and its reduction.

Levels of fear and the politics of reporting

In 2004 *The International Journal of Social Research Methodology* published a series of three articles that debated the relative merits of the way in which fear of crime was recorded in the British Crime Survey (BCS) – two by my co-editor, Stephen Farrall (2004a, 2004b), and one by British Home Office analyst, Mike Hough (2004). Farrall, a long time critic of the questions used to measure the fear of crime by surveys such as the BCS, argued that the BCS significantly overstated crime fear. Farrall proffered a number of arguments as to why this was the case. These ranged from the inability of the BCS to capture the relatively *infrequent* nature of fearful episodes, through to his contention that the emotional responses to the threat of victimisation range from fear, to anger, through a range of responses – something the current BCS cannot control for (Gilchrist *et al.* 1998). Rhetorically, Farrall asked 'do we as a community of scholars, believe the data we have been producing for the last 20 years' (2004a: 163)?

For Hough, Farrall's question was misguided. He responded by suggesting that the specifics of what the BCS 'global questions' are measuring are secondary. More important was the rich time series data we have over a 20-year period that 'starts to yield some perspective about crime and people's experience of it' (Hough 2004: 175). Hough argued that despite there still being shortcomings in the methodology, and indeed in extrapolations made from these data, the time series data now available made variations in levels of fear (or whatever it is that is measured) from sweep to sweep of the survey intelligible. He also rightly noted the delicacy with which BCS analysts had handled the results; indeed, most government researchers and analysts had been quite circumspect about how much they could say about fear of crime from the results gathered.

Farrall's rejoinder went on to note the inherent conservatism of surveys like the BCS and their inability to be self reflexive about problems of data collection and analysis. As Farrall (2004a: 169) notes:

> ... there is a terrible conservatism that haunts crime surveys. No one wants to break the mold and ask new questions or to propose new ways of asking old questions for fear of making the previous 25–35 years of data collection redundant for comparative purposes. ... this is nothing short of an admission that the question wording influences data, and that changes in question styles will result in changes in the data produced.

Conservatism aside, Hough's defence of this body of data is not sustainable if we extend our analysis beyond these technical debates. As scholars we should not delude ourselves that the knowledge we produce is exempt from being co-opted into political agendas (a point also made by Farrall 2004b: 178), or that criminological work can ever be simply apolitical or technical. Crime statistics of any kind are political numbers and criminology as a discipline is closely aligned with the apparatus of control. There is massive media interest in the results of the BCS (take, for example, Hough's own frequent media appearances following sweeps of the BCS). Here levels do matter in spite of the efforts of Home Office statisticians to explain figures down. The difference between one-third and two-thirds of women being fearful, for example, is politically significant. Levels of crime and fear become topics of political contestation in election campaigns (rising fear being used as a reason not to re-elect incumbent governments for example). These figures have powerful effects – even as they are themselves constructs of power and knowledge (Lee 2007a). As Foucault has noted, the most dangerous aspect of power is that it be viewed as 'neutral' or 'politically invisible' (cited in Walters 2003).

Democratising fear of crime

As is probably quite clear by now, I believe fear of crime is a very poor organising principal or concept for understating – and particularly quantifying – anxiety or concern about crime. The recent qualitative turn examining 'crime talk' has clearly emphasised these shortcomings (see Girling *et al.* 2000; Hollway and Jefferson 2000; Farrall *et al.* 2006; Lee 2007b). As Henry and Milovanovic (2000: 51) put it in relation to constitutive nature of crime generally – and I think this is even more pertinent to a concept like fear of crime:

> ... [I]t is the co-produced outcome, not only of humans and their environment, but of human agents and the wider society through its excessive investment, to the point of obsession, in crime, through crime shows, crime drama, crime documentaries, crime news, crime books, crime films, crime precautions, criminal justice agencies, criminal lawyers and criminologists. All are parasitic of the crime problem ... but they also contribute to its ongoing social and cultural production and ongoing reproduction.

It seems to me this embedded socio-cultural nature of crime fear is conveniently overlooked. This is more than suggesting that fear of crime is an artefact of the survey method – although certainly it is in part. Rather, it is an artefact of a range of socio-cultural practices and representations that themselves make the crime or victim survey a legitimate regime of truth through which to speak about offending, victimisation and fear of crime (see Pratt 1997). And it is here we can identify a second set of power effects or productive capacities of fear of crime – both as a concept and as a body of data. While initially the victim survey was the domain of government criminologists in criminal justice agencies, today it is democratised. The broader truth effects of the data and the concept now mean that the survey instrument is reproduced by news organisations, pollsters, women's magazines, websites, insurance agencies, local government, criminal justice evaluations and the like. This democratisation of the concept feeds it back into our cultural (and, indeed, social scientific) mix making fear of crime broadly intelligible as a thing, and object. Once it becomes a 'cultural theme' (Garland 2001) it helps to unify experiences. One can thus present as being fearful of crime, and report that such and such has happened to one, and in so doing can create an experience which is intelligible to others. Here I am following the work of Hacking (1995) who convincingly argued that the naming and identification of a range of psychiatric conditions and diagnostic indicators throughout the twentieth century resulted in a huge increase in the presentation of cases with the prescribed symptoms. This is not to argue that symptoms were faked, nor to suggest that the diagnostic categories were simply illusory. Rather, it is to suggest that human subjectivity and experience is malleable and subject to the productive effects of power at the micro level of experience and action; to what Foucault speaks of as the micro-physics of power that has the capacity to take hold of the body and inscribe it with meaning.

I have argued elsewhere that the term 'fear' is itself saturated with meaning that genders the concept; fear being the providence of women; risk being the providence of men.[6] This problematises women's fear while leaving men's lower levels of fear unproblematic (Lee 2007a; but see also Sutton and Farrall 2005 and Sutton and Farrall, Chapter 7, in this book); the result of this is risk/fear paradox[7]. Betsy Stanko (2000) succinctly noted that when fear of crime became a 'discourse' in the UK in the 1980s and 1990s it had the effect of feeding on modes of crime prevention. It, along with its inherent relationship with the victim survey, helped us imagine narratives of the 'blameworthy' and 'blameless' victims based on composite imaginings of 'lifestyle'. The closer one's characteristics were to being to an average offender, the more likely they were to also become a victim. And most importantly, all this fed into broader criminological and political strategies aimed at ensuring individual citizens engage in their own risk avoidance behaviours where avoidance of victimisation neatly translated into the individual management of risk – O'Malley's (1992) 'private prudentialsim' mixed with Garland's (2001) 'criminologies of the self'; individuals are implored to both insure and securitise themselves. The language of the Home Office makes this seem technical:

> The BCS helps to identify those most at risk of different types of crime, and this helps in the planning of crime prevention programs. ...

The BCS looks at people's attitudes to crime, such as how much they fear crime and what measures they take to avoid it.

(Home Office 2007b).

This is not simply technical, it is political and regulatory, and fits neatly into a specific element of contemporary neo-liberal governmental and political rationalities which aim to produce 'active citizens' who can be 'governed at a distance'. Of course it has policy relevance, but more than this is has bio-political effects. While on the one hand these effects shape our understandings of victimage (deserving, or undeserving, lifestyle based or random and unlucky) they also begin to drive policing practices – both of the self and of the Other. As Garland (1997: 180) has noted:

> Statistical knowledge fuels bio-political technologies – and is produced by them – in the same way as that knowledge of individuals spirals in and out of disciplinary practices. Budgetary calculations, economic forecasts, demographic projections, actuarial tables, scientific surveys, market research and epidemiological studies all function as technologies of government in the modern state. Statistical information forms the basis for political problematisations.

Numbers have bio-political effects. They not only produce and are produced by political and governmental problematisations, they actually 'make up people' (Hacking 1986). Individual subjectivities are adjusted via linkages from governmental programmes to individual subject and *vice versa*. This ability to 'govern at a distance' or 'govern through freedom' allows welfarist rationalities of collective wellbeing to be replaced with a notion of the active consumer who manages ones own risk and fear. That measures of fear of crime mesh with this bio-political web seems strikingly obvious.

Fear of crime and meeting key performance indicators

In many jurisdictions, reducing fear of crime has become, at one point or another, a *key performance indicator* (KPI) for high-ranking police officers (failure to reduce fear may have repercussions on policing careers) and, indeed, an object for policing more generally.[8] In New South Wales (Australia) the current police commissioner's responsibilities are to 'reduce crime and reduce the fear of crime'. On the face of it, this is surely a worthy set of goals. However, there are a couple of major caveats. First, there is the simple technical problem as discussed above regarding the levels of fear measurement. If fear of crime is elevated by our technologies of enumeration – in other words, if surveys overestimate crime fear – we are trying to reduce a phantom figure. This might also explain the intransigents of levels of fear of crime and the difficultly those responsible for its reduction might have in meeting their KPIs.[9] For example the British Home Office (2007a) has stated that although reported crime is well down:

> ... we aim to reduce this level even further. And to reduce fear of crime which has risen, despite the drop in crime. For instance, only 3.2% of households become victims of burglary, but 13% live in fear of it. This is something we need to – and will – address.

And here again is where the technical and benign become political. Politicians of varying hues are willing to politicise our fears. Incumbent governments generally want to see the fear of crime reduced – even as they remind us of how crime might increase under their opposing party who will make thing increasingly unsafe. In this political environment not only is there an imperative for policing organisations to meet their KPIs for fear reduction, there is also increasing pressure from the political masters to see that these indicators are met, placing great strain on both the policing organisation and the traditional separation of powers. As McLaughlin (2000: 119) notes, '[p]olice forces have also developed aggressive, high profile operational strategies to shift the burden of fear from potential victims to offenders'. Fear of crime becomes not only a rationale – amongst others – for particular policing styles, it also becomes an object that politicises policing practice.

The results are strategies of high visibility policing, reassurance policing, and an increasing web of CCTV and the like. While some of these strategies in some cases may well have desirable effects in terms of reducing antisocial behaviours and building trust, in other situations, this might be to the detriment of other intelligence-led forms of policing; surely the imperative to reduce a phantom figure should not be driving policing policy? This victory of policing style over policing substance is indicative of the kind of representational crime control being driven by crime fear; where an aesthetic victory is enough; often in contradistinction to forms of community policing that might be truly inclusive. Further, to illustrate this is the notion that the visibility of police and the CCTV camera is no longer enough. The public apparently need to be reminded that such strategies are in place through media campaigns, signage or information packages. It is not the policing strategies in and of themselves that might reduce fear but the public information dissemination suggesting that something is being done. The criminologist can then quantify and qualify this change in perceptions. When respondents suggest that increased CCTV increases their sense of security in an area, as they did in responses to an evaluation of Sydney's 'Safe City' project (Coumarelos 2001), more CCTV can be installed and the information campaign can intensify accordingly. The phantom drives the policy and the policy has productive power effects on citizens we are yet to fully understand – we are left with something of a security loop; security begets security.

There are a couple of points I can make, however. Fear reduction strategies are generally played out in public space; indeed, it is fear of victimisation by strangers, and generally in public spaces, that the surveys allude to; the global scenario question is of course targeted precisely at this. Space is, somewhat ironically, manipulated, dominated or governed in order to re-make it as safe and welcoming – although in reality many Crime Prevention Through Environmental Design (CPTED) programmes potentially make the space bland and unwelcoming so as to dissuade loitering; for example, the removal of street furniture, the need for 'sight-lines', the cutting or removal of trees and shrubs. In this sense, the knowledge/information about fear of crime creates strategies of representing and (re)presenting social space which, while it might reduce the risk of a criminogenic 'situation', might also dissuade public usage.

Theoretically, the work of Lefebvre (1991) gives us some insight into how this plays out spatially. The very spatial technologies of security and crime prevention, driven by *inter alia* the fear of crime phantom, produce a form of domination over social space. 'Spaces of representation' (that is, spaces that are representative of a range of spatial practices) are dominated by simple representations of space. That is, in this case, the model of space driven by the crime and fear reduction specialist.[10] Perhaps such effects find their zenith in the fear 'hotspot' map where computer imagers of public space are constructed to designate levels of recorded fear. Here spatial practices – for Lefebvre the basis of bodily orientation and the base materiality of the production of social space – are dominated by the cartographic representation and subsequently the external surveilling eye.

In this context I am not suggesting that fear of crime is the only discourse deployed. Rather, a broader set of neo-liberal crime prevention rationalities are at play here. However, the enumeration of fear of crime dovetails conveniently with many of these neo-liberal rationalities. If reducing fear of crime is a KPI – whether for police or other governing bodies – strategies of crime prevention that are also understood to reassure the public will gain favour. This is not necessarily to accept the 'negative hypothesis' as Foucault might put it. On the contrary, it is to highlight the productive effects of fear of crime as a form of knowledge/power. Not only is it part of a subjectifying set of rationalities that govern subjects at a distance and through freedom, it also plays a part in the reconstruction of environment in which these freedoms will (or will not) be exercised.

Conclusions

I have attempted to map three overlapping areas in which the power and knowledge effects of enumerating fear of crime can be identified. I could name and map a range of subsequent areas such as insurance, criminal justice areas of law-making and sentencing, environmental design, planning and the like. Certainly the boundaries between these domains are anything but clear cut. In this context it is incumbent upon researchers in this field to acknowledge the political salience of fear of crime's enumeration and to move the debate from questions of technical accuracy to questions of political rationality.

The enumeration of fear of crime has created a concept that has become embedded in truth games and strategies of power that concern crime, its definition, its prevention and the politics, bureaucracies and instrumentalities engaged in these practices. Moreover, fear of crime has become a cultural theme, not only providing the conditions under which discussions of levels of crime fear and the like become intelligible, but also democratising the discourse and allowing the very methods of enumeration to be reproduced as part of popular culture. While I suspect it is too late to dispense with fear of crime as an organising principal, and as such we may have to treat the concept with what Cohen (1988) has called 'repressive tolerance', strategies of resistance are possible if the hidden dimensions of its power effects are made intelligible.

Notes

1 I have outlined the pre-history of these surveys and other socio-political forces at work elsewhere (Lee 2007a) and will not revisit this here.
2 More specific data is produced via questions such as 'how worried are you about being [mugged/raped/robbed/assaulted/]'.
3 In stating this, I am not suggesting that other social scientific objects are not also subjective. Rather, I wish to emphasise here the huge disjuncture between diverse individual experiences and this single descriptor.
4 Farrall et al. (2006) note, drawing from a recent study of 'everyday emotions' (Scherer et al. 2004), that there were almost as many emotions expressed by research participants as there were 'appraisal combinations'. Indeed, respondents reported 775 different words or phrases to describe the emotions of a single day. Moreover, where fear was reported as an experience, it was very rare and infrequent.
5 The President's Commission on Law Enforcement and Administration of Justice (1967). This Commission reported its findings in 1967 largely based on the three surveys discussed above.
6 In this sense women are fearful subjects who would best manage their fear via the regulation of their bodies, while men are risk takers who can, however, accurately calculate their risk of victimisation.
7 Put simply, those groups less likely to be victimised express higher levels of fear.
8 For example, the NSW Police Commission Ken Morony's message is that 'NSW Police Force remains fully committed to driving down crime and reducing the fear of crime through the provision of a range of services designed to ensure a safe New South Wales' (Moroney 2007).

9 In recent years, reductions in categories of offending in many developed nation states have not been mirrored by reductions in indicators of 'fear of crime'.
10 See Lash 2002: 114–24 for a discussion of Lefebvre's spatial materialism.

References

Biderman, A, Johnson, L, McIntyre, J and Weir, A (1967) 'Report on a Pilot Study in the District of Columbia on Victimisation and Attitudes Toward Law Enforcement', *President's Commission on Law Enforcement and Administration of Justice, Field Surveys 1*, Washington DC: US Government Printing Office.

Cohen, S (1988) *Against Criminology*, New Brunswick: Transaction Books.

Coumarelos, C (2001) *An Evaluation of the Safe City Strategy in Central Sydney*, Sydney: NSW Bureau of Crime Statistics and Research.

Ditton, J and Farrall, S (2000) *The Fear Of Crime*, Aldershot: Ashgate.

Ennis, P (1967) 'Criminal Victimisation in the United States: A Report of a National Survey', *President's Commission on Law Enforcement and the Administration of Justice, Field Surveys 11*, Washington DC: Government Printing Office.

Farrall, S (2004a) 'Revisiting crime surveys: Emotional responses without emotions? OR Look back in anger', *International Journal of Social Research Methodology*, 7(2): 157–71.

—— (2004b) 'Can we believe our eyes? A response to Mike Hough', *International Journal of Social Research Methodology*, 7(2): 177–9.

Farrall, S, Jackson, J and Gray, E (2006) 'Experience and Expression in Fear of Crime, Working Paper No. 1', ESRC Grant RES 000 23 1108.

Foucault, M (1970) *The Order of Things: An Archaeology of the Human Sciences*, New York: Random House.

Garland, D (2001) *Culture of Control: Crime and Social Order in Contemporary Society*, Chicago, IL: Chicago University Press.

Gilchrist, E, Bannister, J, Ditton, J and Farrall, S (1998) 'Women and "fear of crime": Challenging the accepted stereotype', *British Journal of Criminology*, 38(2): 283–98.

Girling, E, Loader, I and Sparks, R (2000) *Crime and social Change in Middle England: Questions of Order in an English Town*, London: Routledge.

Hacking, I (1986) 'Making up people', in T Heller, M Sosna and D Wellbery (eds), *Reconstructing Individualism*, Stanford, CA: Stanford University Press.

—— (1995) *Rewriting the Soul: Multiple Personality and the Sciences of Memory*, Princeton, NJ: Princeton University Press.

Hale, C (1996) 'Fear of crime: A review of the literature', *International Review of Victimology*, 4(2): 79–150.

Harris, R (1969) *Fear of Crime*, New York: Frederick A Praeger.

Henry, S and Milovanovic, D (2000) 'Constitutive criminology', in Muncie, J and McLaughlin, E (eds), *The Sage Dictionary of Criminology*, London: Sage.

Hollway, W and Jefferson, T (2000) *Doing Qualitative Research Differently: Free Association, Narrative and the Interview Method*, Thousand Oaks, CA: Sage Publications.

Home Office (2007a) 'How We're Reducing Crime', available at www.homeoffice. gov.uk/crime-victims/reducing-crime/ (accessed 14 August 2007).

—— (2007b) 'What is the British Crime Survey?', available at www.homeoffice.gov.
uk/rds/bcs1.html (accessed 14 May 2007).

Hough, M (2004) 'Worry about crime: mental events or mental states?', *International
Journal of Social Research Methodology*, 7(2): 171–6.

Jackson, J (2004) 'Experience and expression: social and cultural significance in the
fear of crime', *British Journal of Criminology*, 44(6): 946–66.

Jackson, J, Allum, N and Gaskell, G (2006) 'Bridging levels of analysis in risk
perception research: the case of fear of crime', *Forum: Qualitative Research*, 7(1):
Art 20, available at www.qualitative-research.net/fqs-texte/1-06/06-1-20-e_p.html
(accessed 16 August 2007).

Lash, S. (2002) *Critique of Information*, London: Sage.

Lee, M (1999) 'The fear of crime and self-governance: towards a genealogy', *The
Australian and New Zealand Journal of Criminology*, 32(3): 227–46.

—— (2007a) *Inventing Fear of Crime*, Cullompton: Willan Publishing.

—— (2007b) 'Fear, law and order and politics: tales of two towns', *Crime in Rural
Australia*, Annandale: Federation Presse.

Lefebvre, H. (1991) *The Production of Space*, Oxford: Blackwell.

Lupton, D (1999) *Risk*, London: Routledge.

McLaughlin, E (2000) 'Fear of crime', in Muncie, J and McLaughlin, E (eds), *The
Sage Dictionary of Criminology*, London: Sage.

Moroney, K (2007) 'Commissioner's Message', available at www.police.nsw.gov.
au/about_us/commissioner_ken_moroney/commissioners_message (accessed 17
August 2007).

Morris, A, Reilly, J and in collaboration with S Berry and R Ransom (2003) *The
New Zealand National Survey of Crime Victims 2001*, New Zealand Ministry of
Justice.

O'Malley, P (1992) 'Risk, power, and crime prevention', *Economy and Society*,
21(3): 252–75.

Orwell, G (1949) *Nineteen Eighty-Four*, Harmondsworth: Penguin.

Pearson, G (1983) *Hooligan: A History of Respectable Fears*, London: Macmillan
Press Ltd.

Povey, D, Upson, A and Jansson, K (2005) 'Crime in England and Wales: Quarterly
update to June 2005', *Statistical Bulletin 18/05*, London: Home Office.

Pratt, J (1997) *Governing the Dangerous*, Annandale: Federation Press.

President's Commission on Law Enforcement and Administration of Justice, The
(1967) *The Challenge of Crime in a Free Society: A Report by the President's
Commission on Law Enforcement and Administration of Justice*, Washington DC:
United States Government Printing Office.

Reiss, A (1967) 'Studies in Crime and Law Enforcement in Major Metropolitan Areas,
Volume 1', *President's Commission on law Enforcement and the Administration of
Justice, Field Surveys 111*, Washington DC: US Government Printing Office.

Scherer, KR, Wranik, T, Sangsue, J, Tran, V and Scherer, U (2004) 'Emotions in
everyday life: probability of occurrence, risk factors, appraisal and reaction
patters', *Social Science Information*, 43(4): 499–570.

Skogan, W (1976) 'Public policy and fear of crime in large American Cities', paper
presented at the Midwest Political Science Association, Chicago.

Stanko, E (2000) 'Victims R' Us', in T Hope and R Sparks (eds), *Crime, Risk and
Insecurity*, London: Routledge.

Sutton, R and Farrall, S (2005) 'Gender, socially desirable responding, and the fear of crime: are women really more anxious about crime?', *British Journal of Criminology*, 45(2): 212–24.

Walters, R (2003) *Deviant Knowledge: Criminology, Politics and Policy*, Cullompton: Willan Publishing.

Chapter 4

Critical geopolitics and everyday fears

Susan J Smith and Rachel Pain

Introduction

During the late twentieth century, fear was closely related to crime in the public and academic imaginations. In fact, a project of critical, feminist geography was precisely to ground fear in the very real acts of violence and appropriation that inspire it. Pain (1995, 1997), for example, shows how women's and older people's fears, so often dismissed as being disproportionate to the risks manifest in official statistics, are partly related to hidden abuse encountered in the domestic sphere. However, the events shaping the twenty-first century have focused attention towards a different kind of fear: towards anxieties that are new, (ostensibly) 'global', and which express the uncertainty of life in a fragile world whose disparate parts and peoples are more connected than ever before. Attention now given to issues (which are not new, but which have the appearance, at least, of accelerating) such as immigration and asylum, infectious disease epidemics, terrorism and environmental catastrophe, is indicative of the growing portrayal and experience of risk and fear as globalised phenomena. Fear has become part of the geopolitical terrain; it is drawn explicitly into political discourse and action, and increasingly into the commentaries of political scientists. The fears that inspire this seem very real. But what is curious about current understandings of these fears is how readily assumptions are made about people's emotional responses to internationally mobile threats, without the need for the firm evidence base, rooted in an appreciation of actual risks, which has previously fixated criminologists. Fear really has taken on a life of its own, and in this short chapter it is this we seek to explain, and resist.

Geopolitics and the spatial dynamics of fear

For example, a wave of academic analysis followed the World Trade Centre attacks in New York on 11 September 2001, much of which has not dwelt in depth on people's emotional responses to, or mobilisation against terrorist events, but rather has drawn 'fear' into analysis of international relations. Fear is increasingly deployed as a political tool (see Loo, Chapter 2, in this book) on the back of the idea that it is new, that it is inspired by real and ever present risks, and that extreme measures are needed if it is to be managed. Our suggestion, however, is that while September 11 did present a turning point of sorts, it was not the dawn of a *new* era, either for the nexus of international relations and everyday life or for the spatial politics of fear. In fact, the historical continuities are clear. For 'the West', September 11 triggered a deepening of oppressive governance, an extension of regulation and curtailment of liberties, and an intensification and redirection of the racism and hate that certain groups already experienced in everyday life (Hopkins 2007; McCulloch 2003; Poynting *et al.* 2004). For other parts of the world too – places the US and Britain have since targeted with military interventions – the ramifications of 'terror' can also be seen as having continuity with previous times. So our first thought when approaching fear in this era, as in others, is to emphasise its historicity as well as its spatiality in order to get a sense of what has and has not changed, and where.

A further concern is that commentators on this new preoccupation rarely stop to look back at the body of critical theory on fear of crime. This earlier work developed a strong empirical tradition, using local events and experiences to formulate theoretical and policy solutions to multifaceted lived experiences of risk. In contrast, empirical and conceptual work at the interfaces of geopolitical practice, public discourse and everyday life are relatively sparse. It is, indeed, extraordinary how far the everyday – the feelings, experiences, practices and actions of people outside the realm of formal politics – has been 'invisibilised' in the recent flurry of interest in the globalised geopolitics of fear. Instead, there is an uneasy yet taken-for-granted assumption as to what fear-provoking incidents *are* and how often they do (or would, without massive interventions) *occur* (see Farrall and Gadd 2004), triggering a cycle of fear-inducing discourses which are circulated, at one (global) scale/space, and are presumed to be relevant to (indeed, protective of) the lives of people who become fearful at other (more local) sites. This received wisdom is at odds with the recent 'emotional turn' in social and economic research which recognises the complexity, situatedness, sociality, embodied and – critically – constitutive qualities of emotional life. Fear does not pop out of the heavens and hover in the ether before blanketing itself across huge segments of cities and societies; it has to be lived and – crucially – made (see Bauman 2004; Lee 2007). Yet, as we shall show, this making may only in very small ways be about the 'large acts' of terror that are played, replayed, revisited and reconstituted on an almost daily basis in the press (also see Weber and Lee, Chapter 5, in this book).

In this chapter, we – two social geographers who have written extensively about the local geographies of fear of crime (for example, Pain 1997, 2000; Smith 1986, 1989) – offer a critique of the 'new' focus on geopolitical fears. To develop this argument, we draw especially on critical accounts of fear of crime in everyday life, which we argue have significant, but as yet neglected, implications for understanding 'global' fears. Bringing an established body of sociological and criminological inquiry grounded in the fears of local lives to bear on recent geopolitical analyses of post-September 11 we draw attention to the stark duality between the geopolitical and the everyday. We show how the former is 'scaled' above the latter in a hierarchical model of cause and effect and how this locks the fears of politicians and those of local communities into a self-reproducing cycle of unease.

We also argue for the importance of splicing the two currently disjunct approaches to fear together, to develop a spatial politics of fear that not only includes 'global' and 'local', but finds ways to bring them together in one account (see Megoran 2005). This does, inevitably, build from the two strands to analysing fear that have been prominent in social science scholarship to date – the everyday and the geopolitical – but in the end it is an argument against their hitherto separated trajectories. We want to find a different way of understanding fear, which does not ignore global processes and events or attempts at political manipulation; which accepts that outcomes at everyday scales are not predictable, and makes space for resistance to fear and fear discourses in everyday life too. Our point is that there are not two scales which inspire and address fear by variously *relating* to one another; rather there are assemblages of fear built, trained, embedded, woven, wired, nurtured and natured into the way specific times, places and events work.

To develop this argument, we begin by setting out the problematic: we address the conflicts and disunities that arise between two strands of the analysis of fear, geopolitics and everyday life. Here we examine lessons from existing scholarship on the fear of crime. We then go on to set out a new way of envisioning fear, suggesting that the lens and practice of moral and material geographies are helpful to understanding these new and increasingly complex patterns of fear. So while the two strands in analysing fear we turn to now look somewhat different, in the end, we will argue, they are part of the same assemblage.

The geopolitics of fear is everyday life ...

The most developed strand of work on fear has its starting point in everyday life. In this vein, research across the social sciences over more than three decades has emphasised the social and spatial constitution of the micropolitics of fear. Feminist scholars in sociology, criminology and human geography have been especially prominent here, seeking to draw out the way social politics become entwined with the particularities of place to produce emotional landscapes for marginalised groups (for example, Day *et al.* 2003; Pain 2000; Smith 1989; Stanko 1990; Valentine 1989). The emphasis in this literature has been on giving voice and credence to the fearful experiences and practices of everyday life, often using in-depth, qualitative methodologies. Such research has often exposed the partiality or irrelevance of the fears which tend to be publicised by the media or in safety guidance issued by the state. Instead, this body of research highlights two things.

First, echoing left realism, there is strong relationship between marginality and fear, as the contours of anxiety within cities tend to follow topographies of inequality. Second, and more crucially still, this work points to an extensive catalogue of hidden harm in private and unpoliced spaces stemming from racist violence, domestic violence, child abuse, elder abuse, police brutality against the young, homeless and dispossessed, and latterly Islamophobia. Exposing the fears of people who are sometimes more often constructed as fear-provoking in popular discourses has become a defining task in such work (see Day, Chapter 6, and Sutton and Farrall, Chapter 7, in this book). The political bent, as well as the rootedness in experience, of many of these accounts resists presumption about the immutable passivity of fearful subjects, and highlights the many ways of nurturing resilience and resistance to fear.

The second key strand of research on fear concentrates on those political geographies of fear inspired by events which have global and national reach. In this literature fear is most often analysed as a tool of governance, legitimising national and international actions on terrorism, informing issues of national security, restricting immigration and so on. The focus of this literature is fear and the state, and so the emphasis is not so much upon the emotional or experiential aspects of fear for individuals or communities, but rather with the way fear inspires actions which regulate and manipulate everyday life (for example, Gregory and Pred 2007; Robin 2004; Sparke 2007). The active agents here may be terrorists or insurgent groups, competing national regimes, or layers of domestic governance; the fears they inspire are communicated and mediated through the mass media, popular culture, the routine control of space and policy-making.

What is key here is not necessarily the newness of these 'world class' risks, but a gradual realisation of the globalisation of risk – an acknowledgement that perceived threats and dangers are much closer to the West than they used to be. Places are more intimately connected, and so too follows fear: any illusion of security by distance has been shattered by the continuing compression of time-space. In this way, the attacks on the US of 11 September 2001 acted to crystallise the emotional landscapes of the west which had been developing for some time. These fears, while we might think of them in some way as global, are in fact inward-looking, as terror and crisis affecting non-Western countries does not provoke the same emotions in 'the West'. One effect of the 'war on terror' has been to raise the prominence of the geopolitical almost beyond question, and submerge the everyday – what is actually going on with people's emotions has, by and large, been forgotten.

While these global and local bodies of work have tended to ignore each other, their subjects are clearly linked. Just as the accounts of everyday fear bind wider social and political structures into their explanations (for example, see Stanko's insistence on 'what it means to be universally vulnerable, a subordinate, in a male-dominated society' in shaping women's fear of crime, 1987: 134), global fears are also inherently, already everyday in their manifestations (witness Corey Robin's (2004) account of the impacts on terror discourses on Muslim workers in the US). More broadly, the scaling of social and spatial phenomena – of which global/local and geopolitical/everyday are two examples – is now more widely recognised as an artificial, hierarchical and essentially political device. We suggest (see also Megoran 2005; Pain 2008) that it is anomalous that longstanding critical scholarship on the fear of violence has barely been mentioned in recent interest in critical geopolitics of fear, precisely *because* it is scholarship rooted in the practices of everyday life.

Before going on to set out a new way of envisioning fear, we want to elaborate on some of the disconnections that arise when viewing fear through these two alternate lenses. For us, it is not enough to identify the everyday and geopolitical components of fear as equal partners in producing or exchanging fear, like pieces of a jigsaw: there are problematics, discontinuities and disconnections that need to be addressed. Everyday accounts tend to suggest it is the same old longstanding local fears which are most prominent in people's lives, rather than fears about terrorism or new killer viruses. There is also a concern that analyses of fear as geopolitical sometimes inadvertently reproduce the very state meta-narratives about fear they oppose, in failing to question who feels what (see Pain 2007, 2008). Further, geopolitical analysis often ignores people and their power, or uses representations as a kind of proxy for people's feelings and actions. What of people's consciousness, criticality and resistance in the face of geopolitical discourses and events? Equally, there are limitations to approaches to fear that overemphasise the everyday and place the local merely as a blank canvas for empirical description of broader processes. An inward-looking focus on experiences and practices becomes insulated from its political, social and cultural contexts at a time when fear is rapidly globalising. A final, crucial disconnection is that there seem few means of *connecting* the geopolitical and the everyday in convincing ways. We are quite ignorant of the movement of fear; how it circulates from global to local, or how it moves from discourses/events to the bodies and feelings of individuals.

We go on to suggest two related conceptual mainstays for understanding fear as simultaneously everyday and geopolitical – remoralising and rematerialising fear. To develop these themes, we want to suggest a change of visual motif for the way global and local fears work. This shift is represented in Figure 4.1. The existing model for thinking about the geopolitics of fear can be visualised as in Figure 4.1(a): here the political and the everyday are represented as two distinct realms, fixed in a hierarchical relationship.

Figure 4.1(b) offers an alternative visual metaphor for the reconceptualisation of critical geopolitics and everyday life, removing the

a)

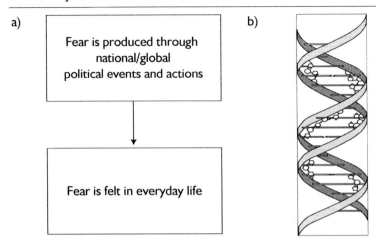

Fear is produced through
national/global
political events and actions

Fear is felt in everyday life

b)

Figure 4.1 A hierarchical view of fear: a) a visual motif for fear; b) the double helix – the parallel strands are geopolitics and everyday life, the connections the events, encounters, movements, dialogues, affects, actions and things that conjoin them.

spatial hierarchy linking large-scale risks with localised anxieties. The figure is in the form of a double helix, borrowed of course from the structure of DNA, which contains the genetic instructions for life. It has two equivalent strands (geopolitics and everyday life) that wind into a single structure and form the building blocks of every assemblage of fear. The 'two strands' carry the same information and are bound together by numerous connectors (in DNA, hydrogen bonds pairing complementary bases). We could see these connections as events, encounters, movements, dialogues, actions, affects and things: the materials that connect and conjoin geopolitics and everyday life. But these engagements are fragile – in DNA, the hydrogen bonds unzip and rejoin; that is why, as a safeguard, the genetic information is duplicated on each strand. The breaks and discontinuities that occur – both randomly and in patterned ways – might represent the awkward, unfinished, disunited, conflicting nature of relations between the geopolitical and the everyday; but ultimately they are inter-reliant and complementary. Our argument is that these connections and disconnections which are not just new and interesting, but also politically enabling – it is in these connecting and dynamic spaces and things where the opportunities lie to resist, have dialogue, influence and act. So while there is an inevitability about the fearful human condition, this model holds out also a prospect of designing in other ways of human being. Fear and hope are two sides of a single coin; they cannot be uncoupled but one is often more visible than the other. A new visual motif for the way fear works and is materialised is one route to a more rounded experience of this Janus-faced condition.

In the remainder of the chapter, we elaborate on how this newly envisioned relationship might be conceptualised. In particular, we suggest some ideas by which global fears might be grounded, and the scales of everyday and geopolitical at least partially dismantled.

What is 'fear', anyway?

A 'common sense' understanding of fear portrays it as an emotional response to a material threat. People are fearful of individuals, places, actions and events that have inflicted, or are very close to inflicting, physical or psychological harm on themselves or on the people and things they hold dear. Avoiding, evading, or removing real risks is, for this model of life, a logical way to deal with such grounded and immediate fears.

Another way of understanding fear is to regard it as an emotional geography that has somehow acquired a life of its own; a condition that is only loosely related to material risks. Then the challenge becomes one of working out what inspires levels of fear that are disproportionate to real risks, and addressing them in the interests of arriving at a less anxious world. One of the most debated mechanisms this model draws into the amplification of fear is that of 'moral panic' in which media representations, criminal justice scapegoating, and policing crackdowns whip up a frenzy of societal outrage against criminalised people and places. One result is toughened sentencing; another is heightened fear (Hall *et al.* 1978).

Reputations have been made, revised and subdued by a long-running debate around the 'old chestnut' of just what it is – reality, imagination or moral indignation – that inspires fear, and why. But it is a tired debate which does not take account of the way the world of fear has been changing, and in particular which sheds little light on the vexed question of how to apprehend simultaneously the global fears rewriting the landscape of international (and internal) relations, and the local lives whose fears have hitherto featured most prominently in conventional literatures. In an attempt to move understanding of fear forward through, within, and perhaps despite, the global/local paradox, we flesh out Figure 4.1(b) by suggesting two rather different ways into the geography of fearful lives. We offer first a moral, and then a material take on what fear is and how it works

Moral geographies

We view fear as a social or collective experience rather than just an individual state. But it is more than this – it is also a morality play and a product of the power relations that shape the moral codes of everyday conduct as well as those of international affairs. Fear does not just involve a relationship between the individual and a variety of societal structures; it is embedded in a network of moral and political geographies.

We can illustrate this by fleshing out the operation of two linked practices: naming and privileging. The naming and privileging of certain styles of fear implies that one kind of (authoritarian) politics has a grip on the moral geography of anxiety. But wound into the spiral of authoritarian morality is an everyday morality which contains a more radical politics – a politics that can reshape and recast the landscape of fear, a way of going on that could and *should* be interrogated for what it tells us about the way people experience, handle and recast fear.

Naming fear

How do we understand such a wide ranging term as 'fear', with its various nuances in meaning? The answer to this question is much more diverse than today's headlines might suggest. A glimpse into the debate over 'naming' is itself a stark reminder of the extent to which dominant discourses take for granted the privilege routinely afforded to some 'names' over others. So it is worth noting these three things.

First, some critics of 'the fear of crime' have argued that the concept has less meaning than is widely accepted; that it is a tautological discourse whose circularity is broken when people who are asked about other emotional reactions to crime choose these over 'fear' (Ditton and Farrall 2000). Fear from this perspective is 'misnamed'; it captures a range of experiences about which rather little is known.

Second, at the same time, some of the earliest accounts of fear of assault put forward by feminist scholars and activists (for example Stanko 1987; Wise and Stanley 1987), while countering the dominant individuated image of 'fear' as a physical response to an immediate threat where the heart races, palms sweat and body shakes, also recast gendered fear as an ongoing malaise engendered by people's structured position in a hierarchy of power. The wealth of detailed evidence on which these ideas were based told of the ways in which harassment, discrimination and other everyday 'normalised' encounters feed into a generalised sense of insecurity.

Third, and intriguingly, later work has also questioned the apparent universalism of feminist analysis. Whose label is fear? Do we call it fear before we know it is fear, and is this disempowering – for example identifying women as eternal victims and denying them the possibility of challenging that status (Segal 1990)? Following a predominantly Anglo-American debate, Koskela's (1997) work in Finland raised new questions about the cultural specificity of this malaise of fear, as well as the possibilities of boldness and resistance (see also Pain (1995) on old age and fear).

Far more remains to be said about resistance and hope, but for the moment, we raise these questions: Does naming certain groups as fearful do them a disservice? Does it become difficult to escape these categorisations, which have also been convenient vehicles for further constraining participation in social life (Lee 2007; Midwinter 1990; Stanko 1990; Valentine 1996)? For Muslims in North America and Europe during the 'war on terror', is there a danger that the allotment by critical researchers of 'fearful' in addition to 'feared' is not just a means of identifying oppression, but a way of further fixing marginality? And so on. In short, with naming fear comes a presumption about whose experience this is; a presumption about who could and should address fear and how. With the practice of naming come the politics of privileging.

Privileging fear

The question of who can and does name fear is answered partly by understanding whose voices, and whose labels, are privileged. Successive politicians have played to the 'fears' of middle class, white suburbanites, while validating and reinforcing them, and as explored elsewhere, some recent academic analyses do the same (Pain 2007). Terror fears, reflecting imaginary geographies of Western countries as newly risky (Gregory and Pred 2007; Katz 2007), are fears of the white, privileged and protected.

But it is often the quietest fears, holding apparently little political capital but having a more immediate materiality, which have the sharpest impacts (Shirlow and Pain 2003). While these impacts may not be headline seeking, they are moral practices which can have effects: which can jump from strand to strand in the assemblage of fear, potentially changing the way fearful lives are replicated for the future. A number of authors argue that there are, embedded in the conduct of everyday life – in ordinary people's hopes and fears, in the routines of human being, in the lay practices that make local geographies teem with life – normative themes that are too often overlooked by policy makers and academics alike (Sayer 2003; Smith 2005). In fact, lay practices can differ radically from political assumptions and predictions; they can – quietly, defiantly, routinely, inadvertently or in many other ways – help privilege different takes on fear, and shape different responses to it. If the world does work more in line with our connective model of fear assemblages (Figure 4.1(b)) rather than with the traditional hierarchical approach (Figure 4.1(a)), there is a moral prerogative to emphasise people's own accounts of the pattern of their emotional landscapes. Ordinary lives often hold the solution to some of the more intractable political problems.

Material panic

Hitherto, the power relations of naming and privileging fear have been understood through the lens of moral panic. Understanding the way fear works has been about being able to see how isolated events of criminality and victimisation are drawn into a frenzy of demonisation and vulnerabilities, and thereby into a politics of repression. Moral panic is an appealing explanation for the way in which fear becomes detached from material risk and takes on a life of its own. But it presumes too much about the way people come to know about, and react, to risks and threat; it assigns too much power to a press whose content is as likely to be taken with a pinch of salt as it is to be believed. The notion of moral panic might be in line with the understanding of fear represented in Figure 4.1(a), but our attempt to unsettle this model points to two other themes. Elaborating on the assemblage model depicted in Figure 4.1(b), we suggest the practices of knowing and placing fear give it a materiality of its own. Fear is not an abstract moral panic; it is an increasingly ingrained material practice. The uneven materialisation of some versions of fear and fearfulness is what drive the politics of control that have so much currency today.

Knowing fear

How do we know about fear? What frameworks of analysis apply, and what methods allow people to tell it? For a subject so complex, there has been heavy reliance on analysis of media representations and a reliance upon poorly worded survey questions. Material risk is hard to know, as few of those most at risk from crime, abuse and harassment ever report their experiences, but it is downplayed or ignored in many accounts of fear of crime. However, fear has a materiality of its own. Fears of all kinds are networked, hardwired and signposted into life in ways that variously alert, protect and control. Walk across any hotel lobby in a large US city today, and wait for the lift. There will be a sign warning you that there are carcinogens all around; you are there at your own risk. Walk through security in any UK airport: forget the metal objects that keep the electronic alarms beeping in the background, but remember to put toiletries into a clear plastic bag. That is a material reminder of one airport bomb scare; others will leave different traces. They, too, will be written onto the innocent bodies that move across borders, and will be carried with them as they travel through space and time (see Abu Zhara 2008). Fear has a creeping materiality that pervades, constitutes, and binds together the ostensibly separate spheres of geopolitical and everyday life (Figure 4.1). Even though 'real' risks are unknowable and may seem remote, the fear they inspire gains momentum at it is materialised at every turn and in everybody.

Placing fear

Imaginaries of fear have always been spatialised: located in certain places rather than others. The ways in which fear is materialised and embodied brings these spatialities to life. In mainstream accounts of fear, in the discipline of criminology and the public policies it services), imaginary geographies of fear have been encouraged by the focus on fear, crime and violence almost exclusively as problems of public space and strangers (Stanko 1987). Fear is viewed as a problem of city centres, urban streets and parks, rather than homes, semi-private spaces and people who are acquaintances or relatives. If it is possible to reduce fear by reducing risks, then the fact that most attempts at resolving fear are situational and limited to public space is problematic (Gilling 1997).

Yet tackling 'the wrong kind of fear' is still high on the agenda. And this is because these fears acquire a materiality, a facticity, of their own. What may begin as immaterial fears become materialised, for example through the safety industry which supplies technologies of surveillance and defence, supposedly to keep fears at bay, but they create more largely unnecessary concern. Katz (2007) suggests that terror fears have become a normalised part of the material urban environment in the US, as the presence of armed soldiers guarding bridges and streets no longer merits attention. Again, how much protection these materialisations of fear provide is dubious; but they can instil as well as reflect fear, allowing remote global fears to creep into our subconscious minds and routinised actions alongside those everyday fears we already know about and experience. Another example, the growth in popularity and marketing of sports utility vehicles as supposedly capable of keeping our (though not other) families safe (Lauer 2005), underlines that the materialisation of fear does not just lead to a changing landscape for all, but reflects a sharply unequal distribution of fear, privilege and risk.

Recognising the materiality of fear means that there are tracks and traces between the different lives of those who seek to control fear and those whose lives are pervaded by it. It is possible to follow the materialisation of certain fears into local landscapes; and it is important to show how everyday practices might be inspired by this, might tolerate it, could ignore it, will certainly pose alternatives, and may well have other, more pressing, 'things' to contend with – other materialities which could and perhaps should be privileged over the dominant manifestation of fear.

Conclusion

We began with the suggestion that to make sense of 'new' 'global' fears we need to attend to the historical and spatial contexts they enter. We argued that much is currently being assumed about how people's emotions are affected by political events and discourses, and for the general need to reconfigure the global and everyday. In drawing on research on the fear of crime in relation to these issues, we argued that it is time to shift the emphasis from authoritative, remote, top-down models of fear to more nuanced and grounded approaches. But more than this, we want to highlight the entwined nature of globalised fears and the processes underlying them; to work with the immediate local everyday fears that are already there; and to stimulate further thought about their connections and relationships with the wider world.

While it is increasingly acknowledged that political violences and fears are expressed in everyday and intimate spaces (Gregory and Pred 2007: 6), for us the task goes well beyond simply expanding the spaces and scales under consideration when charting the way politics has its effects. Indeed, we make the case for rupturing the very idea of these spaces and scales, because they tend to fix commanding notions about emotions, power, human agency and being. Instead, we have suggested a new motif to account for fear – a figure in which geopolitical and everyday processes, events and actions are interwined, building assemblages of fear that are trained, embedded, woven, wired, nurtured and natured into the way specific times, places, and events work. In particular, we want to underline the fact that the everyday always and already speaks back, resists, and changes seemingly immutable forces. Reimagining, indeed remaking, the nexus of geopolitical and everyday fears in this way opens up the possibilities for change: in that sense it is an empowering and enabling model of fear potentially resistant to political attempts to manipulate people's emotions. At the same time, it holds out the prospect of 'scaling up' the materialities of fear: small acts and practices can make a difference; the materialities of local geographies can find their way into the circuits of high politics. While materialising fear is substantially a bid to get a particular version of global politics ingrained into the everyday, there is no reason why it cannot also be about the way particular versions of everyday life travel into the geopolitics of fear. Potentially, at least, this opens up a space for hope to sit alongside fear in these changing geopolitical times.

Note

1   This chapter is an abridged and revised version of 'Fear: critical geopolitics and everyday life' in Rachel Pain and Susan J Smith (eds), *Fear: Critical Geopolitics and Everyday Life*, Aldershot: Ashgate (2008). It appears here by kind permission of Ashgate Publishing Limited.

References

Abu Zhara, N (2008) 'Identity cards and coercion in Palestine', in Pain, R and Smith, SJ (eds), *Fear: Critical Geopolitics and Everyday Life*, Ashgate: Aldershot.
Bauman, Z (2004) *Wasted Lives: Modernity and its Outcasts*, Polity: Cambridge.
Day, K, Stump, C and Carreon, D (2003) 'Confrontation and loss of control: Masculinity and men's fear in public space', *Journal of Environmental Psychology* 23: 311–22.
Ditton, J and Farrall, S (2000) *The Fear of Crime*, Aldershot: Ashgate.
Farrall, S and Gadd, D (2004) 'The frequency of the fear of crime', *British Journal of Criminology*, 44(1): 127–32.
Garland, D (2001) *The Culture of Control: Crime and Social Order in Contemporary Society*, Chicago, IL: University of Chicago Press.

Gilling, D (1997) *Crime Prevention*, London: UCL Press.

Gregory, D and Pred A (2007) *Violent Geographies: Fear, Terror, and Political Violence*, New York: Routledge.

Hall, S, Critcher, C, Jefferson, T, Clarke J and Roberts, B (1978) *Policing The Crisis: Mugging, the State, and Law and Order*, London: Macmillan.

Hopkins, PE (2007) 'Global events, national politics, local lives: young Muslim men in Scotland', *Environment and Planning A*, 39(5): 1119–33.

Katz, C (2007) 'Banal terrorism', in D Gregory and A Pred (eds), *Violent Geographies: Fear, Terror, and Political Violence*, New York: Routledge.

Koskela, H (1997) '"Bold walk and breakings": women's spatial confidence versus fear of violence', *Gender, Place and Culture*, 4(3): 301–19.

Lauer, J (2005) 'Driven to extremes: fear of crime and the rise of the sport utility vehicle in the United States', *Crime, Media, Culture*, 1(2): 149–68.

Lee, M (2007) *Inventing Fear of Crime*, Cullompton: Willan Publishing.

McCulloch, J (2003) 'Counter-terrorism, human security and globalisation – from welfare to warfare state?, *Current Issues in Criminal Justice*, 14(3): 283–98

Megoran, N (2005) 'The critical geopolitics of danger in Uzbekistan and Kyrgyzstan', *Environment and Planning D: Society and Space*, 23: 555–80.

Midwinter, E (1990) *The Old Order: Crime and Older People*, London: Centre for Policy on Ageing.

Pain, RH (1995) 'Elderly women and fear of violent crime: the least likely victims?', *British Journal of Criminology*, 35(4): 584–98.

—— (1997) 'Social geographies of women's fear of crime', *Transactions of the Institute of British Geographers*, 22(2): 231–44.

Pain, R (2000) 'Place, social relations and the fear of crime: a review' *Progress in Human Geography*, 24(3): 365–88.

—— (2007) 'Globalised fear: towards an emotional geopolitics', unpublished paper.

—— (2008) 'Whose fear is it anyway? Resisting terror fear and fear for children', in Pain, R and Smith, SJ (eds), *Fear: Critical Geopolitics and Everyday Life*, Aldershot: Ashgate.

Poynting, S, Noble, G, Tabar, P and Collins, J (2004) *Bin Laden in the Suburbs: Criminalising the Arab Other*, Sydney: Federation Press/Institute of Criminology.

Robin, C (2004) *Fear: The History of a Political Idea*, Oxford: Oxford University Press.

Sayer, A (2003) '(De)commodification, consumer culture and moral economy', *Environment and Planning D: Society and Space*, 21: 341–57.

Segal, L (1990) *Slow Motion: Changing Masculinities, Changing Men*, London: Virago.

Shirlow, P and Pain, R (2003) 'Introduction: the geographies and politics of fear', *Capital and Class*, 80: 1–12.

Smith, SJ (1986) *Crime, Space and Society*, Cambridge: Cambridge University Press.

—— (1989) 'Social relations, neighbourhood structure, and the fear of crime in Britain', in D Evans and D Herbert (eds), *The Geography of Crime*, London: Routledge.

—— (2005) 'States, markets and an ethic of care', *Political Geography*, 24: 1–20.

Sparke, M (2007) 'Geopolitical fears, geoeconomic hopes, and the responsibilities of geography', *Annals of the Association of American Geographers*, 97(2): 338–49.

Stanko, EA (1987) 'Typical violence, normal precaution: men, women and interpersonal violence in England, Wales, Scotland and the USA', in J Hanmer and M Maynard (eds), *Women, Violence and Social Control*, London: Macmillan.

Stanko, E (1990) *Everyday Violence: Women's and Men's Experience of Personal Danger*, London: Pandora.

Sutton, R and Farrall, S (2005) 'Gender, socially desirable responding, and the fear of crime: are women really more anxious about crime?', *British Journal of Criminology*, 45(2): 212–24.

Valentine, G (1989) 'The geography of women's fear', *Area*, 21(4): 385–90.

—— (1996) 'Angels and devils: moral landscapes of childhood', *Environment and Planning D: Society and Space*, 14: 581–99.

Wise, S and Stanley, L (1987) *Georgie Porgie: Sexual Harassment in Everyday Life*, London: Pandora Press.

Chapter 5

Preventing indeterminate threats

Fear, terror and the politics of preemption

Leanne Weber and Murray Lee

> Official fear can only be *contrived*. ... Earthly powers, much like the novelties of consumer markets, must create their own demand. For their grip to hold, their object must be *made*, and *kept*, vulnerable and insecure.
>
> (Zygmunt Bauman 2004: 49–50)

Introduction

The 'war on terror' and the associated spectre of terrorist attacks in the developed world – and on a global scale – has become perhaps the most potent international geo-political issue of the early twenty-first century. The political imperative to be seen to be doing everything possible to reduce the risk of terrorist attack has helped drive a new front in the politics of fear. Our apparent level of concern about the possibility of a terrorist strike has made us willing to trade off our hard earned rights and freedoms in the name of 'exceptional circumstances' and the need to increase national security. Fear of terror has helped, or been used to justify, the passage of a plethora of illiberal and potentially repressive legislation in democratic states such as Britain, the US and Australia. Yet we argue that this new politics borrows from an old model and a tried and tested blueprint (see also Smith and Pain, Chapter 4, in this book). Fear of terrorism did not need to be invented, it is assumed – even, as we shall see, in the absence of empirical evidence. Indeed, there is a continuum between fear of crime and fear of terrorism. The parallels between crime control and national security discourses are striking and both are characteristic of early twenty-first century modes of government where sovereign states reassert themselves in the face of a new globalised order (Garland 2001; O'Malley 2001).

This chapter critically assesses the use of fear as a governmental tactic which has been employed as part of a national security discourse. We also observe that this deployment of fear may give rise to bottom-up securitising strategies initiated by a responsibilised citizenry. This necessitates a discussion of the roles played by fear, risk and indeterminacy within wider strategies aimed at the control of terrorists, illegal immigrants, paedophiles and a range of dangerous Others. We suggest these strategies represent the ushering in of a new era of pre-emptive, and as-yet largely unconstrained, forms of governance. Following Bauman (2004), we argue that 'official fear' about terrorist attacks has been 'contrived', in certain respects, thereby creating demand (or at least a presumed demand) for the tightening of anti-terrorist legislation and an extension of state powers. In adopting this critical perspective, we neither deny the possibility of terror attacks nor the legitimacy of targeted and lawful action to prevent them. Nor do we suppose that governments have single-handedly *created* 'fear of terrorism'. Rather, we argue that a politics of fear has tapped into generalised anxieties which have deep seated roots in wider structural change and that these anxieties often suit contemporary political agendas.

Anxiety, risk and the precautionary principle

Theorists of reflexive (or late) modernity have long argued that we live in a period in which risks have multiplied, or at least have been seen to multiply (Giddens 1993; Beck 1992; Lupton 1999). Accounts of the role and nature of risk vary widely. The 'logic of risk' has been conceived to be driven by: a range of broad social and material changes beginning roughly in the 1950s which have resulted in a 'risk society' (Beck 1992,1996); a cultural milieu in which we have become increasingly risk averse as a result of media and political emphasis on exceptional (often horrific) events and the moral panics that follow (Furedi 2002; Glassner 1999); or, following the work of Michel Foucault (1991), neo-liberal rationalities and modes of government which both desocialise or individuate risk through responsibilisation and prudentialism (O'Malley 1992, 2001; Hudson 2003) and make risk the rational basis of predictive and preventative strategies (Freely and Simon 1992).

For Beck (1992, 1996) these changes include the erosion of unifying – if unstable – experiences of class, status and political organisation mediated by the market and an industrial society based on the distribution of 'goods'. Risk society is then characterised by a sense of uncertainty and is preoccupied not with the distribution of 'goods' but the distribution of 'bads' many of which are by-products of industrial and market expansion. While social inequalities become individualised and support networks provided by family or locality become increasingly frail (Giddens 1993), the 'ontological security' of the late-modern subject increasingly becomes dependent on positioning oneself amid a diverse range of disparate social identities (Rose 1990). Only constant reflection and vigilance and a 'colonising of the future' can offer security under such circumstances (Beck 2002). Risks must be constantly identified, managed and, wherever possible, preempted. Hudson suggests that risk society theory explains how expectations of safety and security are generated that can never be satisfied (2003: 44). Agamben (2005) observes that the new globalised order (or disorder) is an environment in which security/insecurity discourses can multiply. If there is one certainty about the new global order, it is its uncertainty. While our penchant for the identification and attempted management of an increasing number of risks appears unstoppable, and, indeed, the soft constructionism of risk society theory suggests that modernity itself helps to multiply risk perceptions, our tolerance for the mismanagement of risks – at least in developed societies – decreases. The pessimistic risk thesis has however been challenged by O'Malley (2001, 2004) who suggests that the logic of risk is not in and of itself decivilising or illiberal. Rather, the particular political rationalities through which risk logic has been deployed have proven to be moralising and never technically neutral.

Nonetheless, political rationalities do not generate in isolation. As Bauman (2004) has argued, much generalised insecurity is a creation of the processes of globalisation and the unfettered expansion of the global economy; forces that have broken down the historic protections of national sovereignty. The concomitant rise of an array of neo-liberalist political rationalities has further eroded the protections of the Keynesian welfare state. However, as its potency as a guarantor of material security recedes the coercive power of the state is not necessarily diminished but is redirected and concentrated, internally and externally, directly and indirectly, into projects of harsh punishments for convicted offenders (Garland 1996), securitisation (Loader 2002) and renationalisation (Sassen 1996). These strategies for the reassertion of sovereignty occur at multiple levels of governance. As Crawford (2002: 30) notes:

> The anxieties produced by the endemic insecurity and uncertainty of late modernity tend to be conflated and compressed into a distinct and overwhelming concern about personal safety. This localised concern finds its clearest expressions in the rise of discourses about 'community safety' across the Anglo-Saxon world. ... 'Community safety', in so far as it is concerned with 'quality of life' issues, is saturated with concerns about safety and 'ontological insecurity'. It evokes a 'solution' to crime, incivility and disorder, thus enabling the (local) state to reassert some form of sovereignty. Symbolically, it reaffirms control of a given territory, which is visible and tangible.

Or as McCulloch more brusquely asserts, the 'ascendancy of global corporations over nation-states marks the rise of the authoritarian state that rejects social support in favour of social control' (McCulloch 2004). However, O'Malley's (2001: 92) focus on the tensions between neo-liberal and conservative political agendas sheds further light on the current climate, noting that the state becomes 'a source of respect and power associated with potent nationalist symbols and moral agendas' even as it is given over to the internationalist and globalised travails of the market.

Despite all the uncertainty and anxiety of the late modern world, or more to the point because of it, populations have become more willing to allow governments to override long held individual rights and international conventions even as the possibilities and potentialities of sovereign states are being reconfigured. As it seeks to govern through crime (Simon 1997), security (Loader 2002; Valverde 2001) and terrorism (Mythen 2007b); mounting its various 'wars' on drugs (Bewley-Taylor 1999), immigration (Green and Grewcock 2002; Webber 2004) and terror (Welch 2003; McCulloch and Carlton 2006), populations are increasingly divided into those who stand within and without the 'orbit of protection' (Zedner 2006: 427). With the political abandonment of Keynesian notions of redistribution of risk, those who are considered risky become liable to exclusion and incarceration, while those considered at risk are deemed responsible for their own risk management:

> Demonisation has been replaced by the concept of 'dangerisation'. Political governance, therefore, has become partially dependent on the deviant other and the mobilisation of feelings of safety. Political power, and its establishment, as well as its preservation, are today dependent on carefully selected campaign issues, among which safety (and feelings of unsafety) is paramount.
>
> (Albrecht cited in Bauman 2004: 56)

In medieval times, before the great projects of geographical colonisation were commenced, it was the imagined dragons in the unknown lands beyond the visible horizon that fuelled the fears of European populations and governments. If the imperial project of late modernity is to 'colonise the future' (Beck 2002: 41) rather than conquer territory, it is the unpredictable actions of untrustworthy elements amongst us that come to embody the threat of the unknown. In the face of pervasive security narratives, a radical mantra of pre-emption has displaced the conservative doctrine of defence both locally and transnationally as part of a proactive policy of national 'security' (Agamben 2005). From a criminological perspective, this has been interpreted as the incorporation of international relations doctrines of 'anticipatory self-defence' into radically reconfigured law enforcement arenas, most notably in the field of counter terrorism (Zedner 2006).

Working from an international relations perspective, Aradau and Van Munster (2007: 89) contrast Beck's structural thesis of 'risk society', with its focus on uncontrollable, catastrophic events, with more reflexive Foucauldian notions of governing through risk. They conclude that the latter offers more purchase for analysing 'the heterogeneous practices that are defined as the "war on terror"'. They chart a development in risk management that goes beyond the calculable, individual risks associated with longstanding practices of *prudential* risk avoidance, towards the adoption of a *precautionary* stance (which they call 'drastic prevention') that promotes zero tolerance of essentially incalculable risks: 'What is new is not so much the advent of a risk society as the emergence of a "precautionary" element that has given birth to new configurations of risk that require that the catastrophic prospects of the future be avoided *at all costs*' (Aradau and Van Munster 2007: 91, emphasis added). While acknowledging the usefulness of Beck's conception of risk as *harm*, Gabe Mythen and Sandra Walklate concur that the characterisation of risk as *uncertainty* within a Foucauldian framework is crucial to understanding emergent preemptive strategies underlying the 'war on terror' (Mythen and Walklate 2006).

Similar developments in preemptive thinking are discernible in the preventive detention and surveillance of sex offenders (O'Malley 2001), the interception and military interdiction of asylum seekers (Weber 2007), and in the confiscation of financial assets and imposition of control orders on terror suspects (McCulloch and Carlton 2006; Zedner 2007b). Zedner (2007a: 262) argues we are witnessing a transition from a post- to a pre-crime society in which the 'post-crime logic of criminal justice is often overshadowed by the pre-crime logic of security'. Furthermore, modes of pre-punishment introduced in the terrorism context have been observed to migrate into more routine domains of criminal justice, such as the British proposal for Serious Crime Prevention Orders (Zedner 2007b). These practices represent a permanent adjustment of traditional forms of risk management (Aradau and Van Munster 2007) and a fundamental reordering of established legal rules amounting to what Zedner describes as a system of 'future law'.

Arguing along similar lines, Mythen (2007b) notes that, in the terrorist threat discourses of many modern states, a calculus of risk based on past events is being supplanted by 'future led risk judgments in which worst case scenarios are privileged'. Thus indeterminacy becomes tamed not through rational calculation but by imagining the worst that *might* happen. In effect, pre-crime society 'shifts the temporal perspective to anticipate and forestall that which has not yet occurred *and may never do so*' (Zedner 2007a: 262, emphasis added). More than that, the precautionary principle requires 'regulatory action on the basis of possible "unmanageable" risks, *even after tests have been conducted that find no evidence of harm*' (Aradau and Van Munster 2007: 102, emphasis added). As Malloch and Stanley (2005) have noted in relation to asylum seekers, it is their unknowability *per se*, rather than the specific risks that can be ascribed to them that defines them as dangerous.

The deployment of knowledge through profiling, surveillance and intelligence practices plays a key role in framing (although never quite knowing) these uncertain risks. In fact, according to Aradau and Van Munster (2007: 108), the war on terror incorporates both exceptional (precautionary) and routine (prudential) measures, and it is differences in the 'knowability' of risks that conditions the level of response: 'Governing terrorism through risk entails drastic prevention at the catastrophic horizon of the future as well as generalised and arbitrary surveillance at the limit of knowledge'. Returning to our medieval metaphor, it is the horizon of scientific and technical knowledge in the contemporary world, rather than the physical horizon visible to the human eye, which separates the known and predictable world from the fearful realm of dragons.

Supplementing this precautionary logic is a conception of the *incorrigibility or ungovernability* of certain individuals and suspect groups. Precautionary thinking leads to an image of a responsibilised citizenry threatened by an incorrigible minority who must be dealt with preemptively, and who therefore become the object of ongoing suspicion and surveillance. Under its influence sex offenders become 'serial' offenders and those who offend against children become 'paedophiles', regardless of whether their personal histories support these labels; asylum seekers and migrants are perceived as irrevocably different and unassimilable; and militant Islamists are recast as extremists operating beyond the reach of reason. The *dangerisation* of both the asylum seeker and the potential terrorist render them as 'categorically excluded' groups – 'they are not like us and cannot become like us' – subject to a very specific actuarial justice (O'Malley 2004: 328).

Mythen (2007a) notes that if citizens can be persuaded to imagine themselves as potential victims and consequently as a nation under threat, objections to legislative change can be reduced and devalued. Under such circumstances citizens can be controlled and order maintained. In this sense, discourses of insecurity have material effects, justifying the mobilisation of significant state resources: 'At an economic level, the British government has drastically increased the amount spent on national security, beefing up security measures, passing through anti-terrorist legislation and orchestrating a campaign to inform the public about emergency situations' (Mythen 2007a: 477) Moreover, the efficacy and legitimacy of these 'beefed up' measures, and the motivations of governments in introducing them, are open to question. Zedner (2007b) concludes her examination of British control orders by proposing that the state may have 'gone beyond this legitimate protective duty to develop measures motivated more by fear of incurring political liability for the next terrorist attack than by faith in the efficacy of prevention'.

It also possible to discern strategies of responsibilisation in efforts to harness a culture of fear; minimally associated with the criminally excluded Other, maximally with the new terrorist (Mythen and Walklate 2006). Here reductivist discourse in statements by politicians and public servants not only harnesses fears, but actively invites individuals to help manage the terrorist threat. The 'unintended' consequences of responsibilisation strategies may not be limited to the propagation of anxiety, but may also include direct action by citizens. Community participation in the co-production of local security has been broadly welcomed by many commentators (for example,

Johnston and Shearing 2003). However Johnston (2001: 967) notes the 'instability of responsible citizenship as a rationality of governance ... by mobilising the public to engage in acts of responsible citizenship, alternative modes of "autonomous" citizenship might also be encouraged, typically in the form of vigilantism'.

The implications of responsibilisation are particularly unpredictable in relation to national security, where the information available to citizen activists is likely to be limited and distorted, and where a high perception of risk combined with a low level of trust in the efficacy of authorities produces the preconditions for vigilantism. Governments can market fear, and thereby promote demand for fear-reduction, but do not necessarily control the means by which this demand is met. For example, Malloch and Stanley (2005) note that local communities in Britain have demonstrated their own form of risk management in relation to asylum seekers, mounting campaigns of local opposition to the establishment of detention centres on the basis of inflated concerns about the dangerousness of their intended occupants which have been fuelled by the government's own risk communications.

Fear, intolerance and the market for security

For Bauman (2004: 46–9) fear is an essential ingredient of governance. Fear enables the exercise of power to successfully discipline or subjugate populations and has historically taken differing forms. Religious power was derived by its promise of security. As Bauman puts it God freed us from the threat of 'cosmic fear' – the mortal being, the self in relation to the enormity of the universe. We then feared God and prayed for his benevolence, the 'soul court' was to decree away the random blow of fate. In contemporary times, we turn to more 'earthly powers' (see opening quote) to provide, and in turn create markets for our security. Police, military and intelligence officials are the present day 'professionals of threat management' who produce 'knowledge-power based on (in)security' (Bigo 2000: 94). This power is grounded not only in coercive force, but also 'in their capacity to define the sources of our insecurity and to produce techniques to manage them' (Bigo 2000: 94). The notion that governance requires fear and insecurity is anything but new. What changes is the context through which insecurity is identified and thus governed – or at least used as a tool of governance.

Rothe and Muzzatti (2004), writing about the US, suggest that terrorism constitutes the moral panic of our time through which 'the polity and the media' have elevated 'societal fear' (see also Welch 2003). But what is the empirical evidence regarding fear of terrorism? Does fear of terrorism simply suffer from the same conceptual ambiguities and problems of measurement that has plagued empirical research into fear of crime (see Hale 1996; Ditton and Farrall 2000; Lee 2007)? Indeed, it is clear that at present the data on fear of terrorism is difficult to separate conceptually from data on risk perception and opinions about official responses.

Drawing on 2004 Gallup poll figures in the US, Beirne and Messerschmidt (2006) argue that in the years following the attacks on the World Trade Centre the American public transferred their highest level of fear from *fear of violent crime*, to *fear of a terrorist attack*. However, 2007 Gallup poll figures provide for some refinement of the nature of these concerns:

> Terrorism is to a significant extent a latent concern for Americans. Along with the Iraq war, terrorism emerges as a top election or public policy concern when Americans are asked to rate the importance of a battery of specific issues. But the public is less likely to name terrorism in open-ended questions asking for the nation's most pressing problems or top issues for Congress to deal with – typically no more than 10% to 15%. Overall, Americans show fairly broad tolerance for strong anti-terrorism measures. Relatively few Americans think the Patriot Act 'goes too far' in compromising civil liberties to fight terrorism; a majority either thinks it is about right or would like it to go further.
>
> (Gallup 2007)

This analysis may suggest that preparedness to accept rights violations in the name of security could rest as much on a lack of human rights awareness or an absence of concern for those who may be affected, as on an overriding level of fear. The politics of fear might be more accurately described as the politics of fear *and intolerance*. (See Pyszczynski in Prewitt *et al.* 2004 for a psycho-social explanation of this response to anxiety.) Again, fear *per se* is revealed to be a most inadequate organising principle (see Lee, Chapter 3, in this book). A series of nationally representative surveys conducted in the US within a month of the September 11 attacks, suggested that fear increased individuals' risk estimates and was associated with support for both conciliatory policies and generalised precautions against further attacks; while anger responses, although associated with decreased risk perceptions, led to advocacy of more punitive and retributive measures (Lerner *et al.* 2003). This finding seems to be supported by the observation (based on rather tenuous research) that while only about half the respondents in a survey run by a Sydney newspaper in 2004 said they feared a terrorist attack in Australia, three quarters advocated the introduction of the death penalty for terrorist offences (Daily Telegraph 2004).

In a survey of 2083 Australians conducted in the wake of the Bali bombings in October 2002, the polling company ACNielsen (2002) reported that 71 per cent of respondents, when asked directly, were *worried* about a terrorist attack on Australian soil. This compared with 41 per cent in a comparable survey conducted prior to the anniversary of the September 11 attacks, suggesting the effect of political discourse and media coverage of these events in raising concern. It is significant that satisfaction with protective measures put in place by the government did not rise in parallel with fear levels, being measured at 51 per cent after the Bali bombings, compared with 47 per cent before the September 11 anniversary. This perhaps taps into the sentiment that despite increased levels of security, risk perceptions cannot be nullified.

It is not at all clear that terrorist attacks have had the impact on general feelings of wellbeing and security that are often supposed. An economist from Curtin University in Western Australia made use of an omnibus survey which was repeated before and after the September 11 attacks, to investigate the broad impact of these events on the general sense of wellbeing amongst Australians (Dockery 2006). The study found no evidence of a detrimental effect, including on a specific question about feelings of safety, and the author speculated that the attacks may, in fact, have served to increase feelings of wellbeing by highlighting the relatively secure environment in Australia. While the subsequent Bali bombings, closer to home and involving large numbers of Australians, may have had some impact, Dockery concluded that in both cases the effect on everyday lives was 'far less than the discourse of political leaders, the media and other social commentators might suggest' (2006: 2). Similar findings were reported in a Swiss study that investigated emotions and everyday life (Scherer *et al.* 2004). These researchers also surveyed before and after the September 11 attacks and suggested that these global events actually had little immediate effect on the everyday emotions of their sample group.

As already noted, even in the countries most directly affected by terrorist attacks, polls have stubbornly refused to demonstrate the *exceptionally* high levels of fear supposedly unleashed by the terror attacks. Moreover, a survey conducted by an American life insurance company found that 62 per cent of respondents were more concerned about financial security than their physical mortality (Yin reported in Dockery 2006). This apparent disparity between demonstrable fear of terrorism and the levels of risk reflected in political rhetoric seems to suggest a key role for politicians in the 'contrivance' of a climate of insecurity (to return to Bauman's terminology), or at least in the channelling of more demonstrable generic anxieties into concern about terrorist attack. As by Furedi observes (2004: 3): 'Today ... public fears are rarely expressed in response to any specific event. Rather, the politics of fear captures a sensibility towards life in general'.

In her book *Fear and Politics*, Carmen Lawrence[1] (cited in Allen 2006), assigned a leading responsibility to politicians in promulgating fear narratives, with the media playing a secondary role. Lawrence gives the graphic example of the collusion between media and government in the filming of pre-dawn raids on terror suspects. Of course, the fact that 'fear sells' suggests a receptive audience for terror narratives (Alterman in Prewitt *et al.* 2004), reminding us that the relationship between the media, politicians and public opinion is a dynamic one (also see Lee 2007). A Foucauldian appreciation of the dispersal of governmental authority suggests that an array of other agencies may also play an active role in promoting fear discourses for their own purposes. Politicians do not exercise a monopoly on the production of fear and a range of actors from politicians, business leaders and special interest groups, have manipulated public anxiety about terror to suit their own agendas (Furedi 2004). Similarly, Loader (2006) identifies 'politicians, police officers and pundits' as the promulgators of a securitised world view which is likely to exercise a 'deep affective allure' on insecure citizens.

It seems that the 'evidence' about fear of terrorism, as with fear of crime, is fraught with contradictions. While social and political commentators often observe that 'there is little question Australians are more fearful of their world, with every emerging issue assessed through the prism of a garrison under attack' (Parker 2006), it invariably proves difficult to pinpoint the precise focus for public fears. One commentator has characterised the public response to a generic politics of fear in terms of withdrawal and doubting acceptance of government action, rather than enthusiastic support (Parker 2006), and this would seem to be consistent with the limited empirical evidence that has been presented here. The literature on obedience to authority may have some explanatory value in this context, as it predicts that a significant proportion of citizens may concur, either actively or unreflectively, with potentially harmful measures, where they are presented by a legitimate authority as being essential (Kelman and Hamilton 1989; Bandura 1990). Furthermore, as the burdens of pre-punishment invariably fall on already marginalised groups, these protections appear to come at no particular cost to the majority community. This leads to the unpalatable conclusion that readiness to countenance mistreatment, or at least routine injustice, to suspect groups may be a more significant factor in promoting acceptance of pre-punishment regimes than intolerable levels of fear of terrorist attack.

As for the role of governments, even if we concur with Furedi (2004) that politicians 'cannot simply create fear from thin air', and that political parties of all persuasions have 'internalised the culture of fear' rather than created it, it is nevertheless clear that fear has proved to be a rich political resource which has been used to justify sweeping legislative changes for which governments can be held directly responsible. When combined with the politics of intolerance which arises from strategies of renationalisation, a particularly potent form of exclusionary governance emerges.

Politics and the governance of security

Lee has argued elsewhere (2007) that the discourse of fear of crime offered a blueprint on which could be imposed the public fear of terrorism. State elections in Australia now have a long history of being fought as 'law and order auctions' driven by the fear of street crime. Since September 11, and the Tampa affair,[2] this tactic has in part given way to federal elections fought on the issue of 'national security' – largely driven by the fear of a terrorist attack (McCulloch 2004). (In)security and (un)safety have become both new problematisations of government and new targets of political activity:

> The 9/11 attack on America only two weeks after the arrival of the Tampa provided the foundation for a shift towards a more purely security-based framework ... That there was no evidence or logic to back this representation did not detract from its political marketability. The 'war on terror' provided a seemingly durable new vehicle for the fear factor and rebranded security as the new federal law-and-order.
>
> (McCulloch 2004: 25)

National security, a term rarely used in Australia prior to 11 September 2001, is now used as the benchmark policy on which citizens are supposed to elect administrations. Politicians' national security credentials are held up as badges of honour and the other side of politics is ridiculed for being soft (a strategy all too familiar to those interested in law and order politics). In the US context, former key G. W. Bush advisor Carl Rove made this position clear when he noted '[Democrats] have a pre-9/11 worldview' of national security that is 'deeply and profoundly and consistently wrong' (cited in Robinson, *Washington Post*, 27 January 2006). Robinson (2006) noted in the *Washington Post* that 'once upon a time we had a great wartime president who told Americans they had nothing to fear but fear itself. Now we have George W. Bush, who uses fear as a tool of executive power and as a political weapon against his opponents'.

The former Prime Minister of Australia played a significant role in sustaining the fear factor by keeping the spectre of terrorist attack alive in the consciousness Australian voters. For example, in a motion to Parliament in March 2004 John Howard reinforced the exceptionalism of the terror threat (Parliament of Australia 2004: 27557):

> The threat of terrorism is unlike any other threat the world has seen. This is not the threat of invading armies poised on borders, ready to roll over those borders and to capture civilian populations and devastate towns, cities and villages; this is a different kind of threat, and it is a threat that requires a different kind of response ... The world did change forever on September 11, and this country had a terrible reminder of how the world changed on September 11 with the events of 12 October 2002 in Bali.
>
> (cited in Dockery 2006: 5)

The 'different kind of response' has included increased powers of surveillance and detention, and an array of preemptive measures targeted towards the *dangerous* rather than the *guilty* (see Lynch and Williams 2006 for a comprehensive review). The three planks of Australian anti-terror laws are wide ranging terrorism offences including sedition; banning of 'terrorist' organisations; and unprecedented powers for security organisations, including incommunicado detention for up to a week for intelligence gathering, and the issuing of control orders with no requirement to notify the recipient of the reasons (Otto and Tham 2006). The previous Australian government also stands accused of being complicit in secret renditions, denial of due process, torture and detention of Australian citizens (ABC Online 2007) and has openly supported US actions at Guantanamo Bay in the face of widespread criticism from human rights groups (for example Amnesty International 2007a).

In a statement relating to the control order imposed on acquitted terror suspect Jack Thomas, former Treasurer Peter Costello noted: 'All right, well, we observe the rule of law. That's fair enough. But the Government wouldn't want to be in a situation where our society was subject to *some* damage and we hadn't done *what we could* to protect the people of Australia' (ABC Online 2006a, emphasis added). Otto and Tham (2006) report that similar arguments proved persuasive to the magistrate who reviewed the police decision to impose the control order on Jack Thomas: 'The reasons given by the magistrate were based on speculations as to the risk that he may pose. In the words of the magistrate, Thomas is a "potential resource" and he "may be susceptible to the views" of others like Abu Bakar Bashir' (Otto and Tham 2006: 14). The likelihood of such events *actually* happening was apparently not considered germane to the granting of the order.

The initial response of the Australian Prime Minister after the foiled car bomb attacks in London and Glasgow in the summer of 2007 was notably more moderate, as he called for calm and warned against hasty judgements about the questioning of Indian doctor Mohamed Haneef in Brisbane over his family links with the bombers (Holyroyd 2007). With the expanded counter-terrorism powers firmly entrenched, the incident provided an opportunity instead to reinforce the value of the enhanced detention powers under which the suspect was being held, and to associate feelings of security with the government's new measures. News reports told daily of how police could extend his detention for further periods of questioning under the new terrorism laws, and statements by politicians and federal police fuelled public perceptions of guilt by association. Charges of 'reckless support for terrorism' were eventually dropped amid widespread criticism of the actions of police, prosecutors and government. However, going by discourse on talkback radio and in letters pages, although many seemed to see this as a political stunt a sizable proportion of the Australian population believed the recently introduced legislation did not go far enough if a suspect could be freed when the government still suspected his motives.

However, can a nation and its citizens ever be completely 'secure' against a terrorist attack? It cannot of course. As Zedner (2007a: 274) concludes, 'security is the indefinite pursuit of the unattainable'. Thus there will always be a level of risk and uncertainty, and we can never hope to have 'enough' security under conditions of extreme risk aversion. As Hardt and Negri (2005) argue, the so-called war on terror does not target an individual sovereign body or collective but a concept, essentially propagating an environment in which standard conditions of victory can no longer be met. This plays out in the levels of the national terrorism alert. At the time of writing Australia had an alert level of 'medium' – which means a terrorist attack *could occur*. Interestingly, in 2004 the four-level system of low, medium, high and extreme levels replaced a system which had been in use since 1978 (Australian Government 2007). The four-level system defines the levels of alert as; Low – terrorist attack is not expected; Medium – terrorist attack could occur; High – terrorist attack is likely; Extreme – terrorist attack is imminent or has occurred. Australia has been at a medium level of alert since the system was introduced. We can assume that this four level system was installed because a level of threat was required that was more than 'low' and could express the ontological possibility of attack, in line with the slogan that we should all be 'alert but not alarmed'. Such is the politics of (in)security and uncertainty. Similar changes have been made to the British Home Office terrorism threat level system with a five level system being introduced (replacing a seven level system in this case) and threat levels being made public from 1 August 2006 (Home Office 2007).[3]

Former Federal Attorney-General Philip Ruddock during parliamentary questions in November 2005, made the following statement about the threat of terrorist attack in Australia and the proportionality of the pre-emptive measures instigated as a result:

> An attack here is feasible and could well occur. Last week I had the opportunity to meet with security chiefs in France, Spain, the Netherlands and Britain. The underlying theme in all of the discussions in which I was engaged was how we could stop terrorists before they carry out their evil deeds ... The measures that we are proposing are constrained with appropriate safeguards and are commensurate with the very significant level of threat that we face.'
>
> (Parliament of Australia 2005)

However, when the respected Australian Broadcasting Commission current affairs program *Lateline* asked 25 expert commentators from intelligence, counter-terrorism and security backgrounds whether they thought the Australian government's proposed anti-terror legislation was proportionate to the terrorist threat faced by Australia, almost two-thirds answered 'no'

(ABC Online 2005). The most concerted criticisms of Australian counter-terror measures have come from academic commentators and human rights groups. Amnesty International used the theme of the 'politics of fear' to launch its 2007 annual report. President Irene Kahn noted that governments were undermining both the rule of law and human rights and (incorporating the point about the politics of intolerance noted earlier) added that the politics of fear was 'feeding racism and xenophobia, dividing communities, intensifying inequalities and sowing the seeds for more violence and conflict' (Amnesty International 2007b).

In the precautionary society, individuals are also expected to be responsible for themselves and to be vigilant over others (Aradau and Van Munster 2007). Responsibilisation strategies in Australia have progressed from fridge magnets and advertisements on bus shelters promoting vigilance and the reporting of 'suspicious' activities to a national security hotline. Ryan (2003: 2) described the launch of Australia's anti-terror campaign, inviting the public to be 'alert but not alarmed' as 'a propagation of anxiety rather than any real attempt to gather intelligence'. The promotion of social divisions could be added to the propagation of anxiety, as another undesirable outcome of these policies. Recently, the government-funded Australian Strategic Policy Institute proposed that Australian universities should monitor students for signs of extremist tendencies (AAP 2007). This suggestion was dismissed by the chairman of the Australian Vice Chancellors Committee, who argued that universities were not an arm of the Australian intelligence services, and denied that the Australian government would never instigate such a policy. However, the proposal has been seriously canvassed in Britain, where it was described by academic groups as 'anti-Islamic McCarthyism' (ABC Online 2006b).

Security, human rights, human security

Commentators of risk, such as Johnston and Shearing, are optimistic that consensual risk reduction can act as a counter to excessive punitivism. However, they argue that a paradigm of punitive pre-emption, operating under conditions of exceptionalism, is likely to be 'increasingly effective in achieving security (by virtue of its focus on risk minimisation) but less effective in achieving justice (by virtue of its combination of retributive and anticipatory elements)' (Johnston and Shearing 2003: 96). For one thing, the costs of precautions fall unevenly on targeted individuals and groups, since 'sectional interests lurk below the surface of any claim to pursue security' (Zedner 2006: 427). Notably, precautionary regimes are justified, not by reassurances that basic human rights will be universally respected within the operation of these laws, but that the negative consequences will impact only on a minority. In marketing a sweeping new Australian anti-sedition law, the Attorney-General appealed to similar sentiments:

It is designed to protect the community from those who would abuse our democratic values and threaten our tolerant and harmonious society ... Journalists, commentators, activists, artists, performers and all those who cherish our tradition of freedom of speech and support peaceful lawful change have nothing to fear from the existing law, not from this legislation.

(Ruddock 2005)

The social costs of poorly (that is, categorically) targeted pre-emptive strategies may extend beyond official practices, stirring community responses such as mistrust and discrimination against suspect groups which serve to amplify their exclusion. Hardt and Negri (2005) acknowledge that exclusion is an inherent aspect of fear politics when they state that the assertion of power over sub-national populations receives legitimation 'not from what power is, but what power saves us from' (Hardt and Negri, 2005: 31).

These effects are not just theoretical. Research into the psychological effects of the London bombings on the general population confirmed that being Muslim was the most important indicator of developing 'substantial stress' symptoms immediately after the bombings, and was a significant risk factor for experiencing negative changes in self perception seven months later (Rubin *et al.* 2007). Qualitative research by the British Refugee Council has confirmed that members of some minority groups suffer a multidimensional sense of insecurity as a result of terrorist countermeasures (Rudiger 2007). A similar case has been made in Australia in relation to Middle Eastern minorities (Poynting *et al.* 2004). Alongside fears of a terrorist attack (which they share with the general community), participants in the Refugee Council research reported fears of racist retaliation, fear of targeting by authorities and insecurity about deportation, which they associated directly with media and government depictions of potential terrorists (see also Institute of Race Relations 2007). In fact, it was concluded that poorly targeted anti-terror measures were creating 'communities of fear', as reflected in this comment from one research participant:

... we have the whole fear, we do not feel free. We are scared over terrorism, because the terrorist does not know whom they are going to kill, we are amongst those British people, so we are scared. And the person who is next to me, to us, is also scared from us.
(Birmingham participant cited in Rudiger 2007: 14)

An official review of Australian counter-terror laws came to a similar conclusion about their potentially divisive and counterproductive effects:

Significantly, fear and uncertainty amongst Australian Muslims is not merely a result of the 'terrorist organisation' offences but a general result of the counter-terrorism laws. The most recent review of these laws, the Sheller Review, for instance, concluded that such laws have contributed to these citizens experiencing 'a considerable increase in fear, a growing sense of alienation from the wider community and an increase in distrust of authority.'

(Security Legislation Review Committee 2006, cited in Otto and Tham 2006: 11)

Anti-terrorism laws have been widely criticised for undermining human rights protections to an extent which rivals the harm they are intended to preempt. Mythen and Walklate (2006: 392) note that 'governmental policies have distanced themselves from fundamental principles of human rights and gravitated toward policies that accept a zero-sum approach that the rights of some can be forfeited to defend those of others'. Hocking (2004: 9) also notes the 'astonishing ease' with which political and legal rights, central to the rule of law, have been surrendered in the name of countering terrorism, and how these reversals of fundamental democratic protections have seemingly been welcomed by a 'tremulous' public. Lynch and Williams (2006) list a catalogue of concerns about the constitutional and human rights implications of Australian counter terror laws and ask what price is being paid for our post September 11 security. Otto and Tham (2006) express similar sentiments in a paper entitled 'The perils of countering terrorism by eroding human rights', and Australian human rights lawyer Julian Burnside (2006) turns the 'war on terror' phrase on its head in a commentary piece entitled 'The war on human rights: the climate of fear'.

Paradoxically, the previous Australian government co-opted the language of human rights to legitimise their security measures and would have national security viewed a 'human right'. Counter terror laws, according to the then Prime Minister, protect human rights by securing 'the greatest human right of all ... the right to live' (Otto and Tham 2006: 3). This sentiment was echoed repeatedly by the Federal Attorney-General at the time in statements designed to 'normalise' the denial of rights to suspect groups:

[T]his is a balancing exercise in which people's right to life and personal safety and security – which is a fundamental right that they are entitled to enjoy and governments have an obligation to protect – have to be weighed up with what steps you can reasonably take to provide that protection which doesn't unduly limit other entitlements that you expect to be able to enjoy. That balancing occurs every day of the week. People understand it in relation to road rules where they understand that your right to choose on which side of the road you'll drive is limited so that people can drive safely on roads. Here we're dealing with terrorists threats and there may well be some limits which will impact upon some, but not most of the Australian community, which will limit who you might talk to, where they might go. It doesn't seem to me that they're unreasonable if you suspect that someone is engaged in activities that might pose a significant risk to your community.

(see ABC Insiders (2005) for full transcript).

Critical commentators have questioned the efficacy of these illiberal measures in terms of security gains. In 2007, international human rights organisation Amnesty International (which includes Philip Ruddock among its 2.2 million members) concluded that: 'Ill-conceived counter-terrorism strategies have done little to reduce the threat of violence or ensure justice for victims of terrorism but much to damage human rights and the rule of law globally' (Amnesty International 2007a). In fact, the net outcome can be a reduction in security, as exceptional measures deprive citizens of the 'rudimentary security of living under the rule of law' (Gardner 2006, cited in Zedner 2007b).

While unanimous in their support for the reassertion of human rights principles, not all critical commentators are satisfied that this is a complete answer to the threats posed by the war on terror. Legal theorist Lucia Zedner indulges in some 'gentle human rights scepticism' in considering the prospects for accountability in regimes of future law, recognising the limitations of human rights principles in what are essentially political decisions (Zedner 2007b). She supports a shift away from the notion of balancing individual liberty against collective security, towards a more holistic conception of 'human security' in which security is a positive human good which is a precondition of individual liberty, rather than a threat to it:

> In place of the negative logic of defence, human security promotes concern for the basic necessities of human flourishing and the upholding of human rights. It is predicated upon the belief that the chief threats to security arise out of deprivation and frustration which together breed disorder and, at the extreme, terrorism ... In order to encompass these larger concerns, security is reconceived not as a technical, military or policing issue but as a political concept within which state security is less an end in itself than the means of securing individual liberty.
>
> (Zedner 2007a: 273)

While applauding the notion of 'human security' as a shift towards the centre and away from the liberty-security polemic, Ian Loader (with an equal measure of 'human rights scepticism') locates more promise in a 'civilised' conception of security as a collective social and political good, which stands completely outside these oppositional camps and facilitates 'democratic peace-building' (Loader 2006). Importantly, reasserting security as a *universal* public good, raises normative questions about how it is to be pursued and for whose benefit.

Conclusion: rediscovering hope?

In the Greek myth, Pandora (those who wreak destruction upon humankind through their uncontrollable curiosity seem always to be female) disobeys the instructions of the gods and, by opening the mysterious box, unleashes all the ills of the world. However, an important resource remains inside the box. That resource is hope.

In our post-September 11 world, heightened risk awareness has lifted the lid on a broad spectrum of ills created by human activity. Some observers have equated the associated politics of fear which has been the subject of discussion here, with a denial of hope. Parker (2006) claims that '[o]ver the past 10 years hope has been depleted and fear installed as the governing framework in Australian politics'; Amnesty International has argued that 'fear destroys our shared understanding and our shared humanity' (Amnesty International 2007b: preface); and Ryan (2003: 2) has written that a society based on paranoid nationalism 'diminishes the ethical bond of care and is unable to provide hope to its members'. In our contemporary world, there are no gods to contain these threats in a magical box. We must rely on the 'earthly powers' who govern us to imagine a different future:

> Imagine instead if there had been military-scale investment in creating more effective international justice and police systems and more effective dialogue with our neighbours; putting resources into programs that enable tolerance and co-existence; funding health services and mutual economic development ... It is a fundamental duty of a government to distribute hope to the people. A government has no business cultivating and exploiting fear within the population.
>
> (Parker 2006: 30)

Alternative pathways have been suggested by the commentators discussed here, which tackle the threat of terrorism while keeping hope alive. Zedner (2007a) counts human security as one of the 'resources of hope' through which 'criminology might seek to elaborate and defend a conception of justice apposite to the problems and potential of the security society' (Zedner 2007a: 271). Others see potential security benefits from 'non-coercive measures and precise offences, in a broader context of promoting tolerance and respect for diversity, and addressing pressing issues of social injustice and inequality' (Otto and Tham 2006: 4).

As with fear of crime, fear of terrorism is a messy and amorphous concept. While it no doubt has political purchase, the reasons for this remain hazy, with the available evidence suggesting it is not fear *per se* that has allowed many governments to push through illiberal counter-terrorism legislation, but a combination of fear, risk and intolerance arising from resurgent nationalism. The bio-political dynamics of a plethora of discourses concerning terror and security no doubt require further analysis. This chapter has attempted to at least map some of the interconnected domains through which these dynamics operate and to identify some alternative discourses arguing for a more hopeful, inclusive and secure future.

Notes

1 Australia's first woman Premier, who was then an Opposition federal politician.
2 In 2001 a Norwegian cargo ship the *Tampa* rescued 430 Afghan asylum seekers at sea. The federal government refused the ship permission to land on Australian territory. After the ship's captain ignored the order his vessel was boarded by Australian SAS personnel. It was reported that 70% of Australians supported the government's tough stance.
3 The UK threat levels are: critical – an attack is expected imminently; severe – an attack is highly likely; substantial – an attack is a strong possibility; moderate – an attack is possible but not likely; low – an attack is unlikely (Home Office 2007).

References

ACNielsen (2002) '71% of Australians fear a terrorist attack on Australian soil: ACNielsen survey', available at www.acnielsen.com.au/news.asp?newsID=195 (accessed 13 March 2007).

Agamben, G (2005) *State of Expectation,* Chicago, IL: Chicago University Press.

Allen, C (2006) 'Fear and politics, review of Carmen Lawrence (2006) *Fear and Politics*', Scribe, Melbourne, IPPAink27, October 2006, Institute of Public Administration, NSW.

Amnesty International (2007a) 'Report 2007: Politics of fear creating a dangerously divided world', Amnesty International Press Release 23 May 2007, available at http://news.amnesty.org/mavp/news.nsf/print/ENGPOL100092007 (accessed 1 June 2007).

—— (2007b) 'Amnesty International Report 2007: Freedom from Fear', available at http://thereport.amnesty.org.eng/Freedom-from-fear (accessed 1 June 2007).

Aradau, C and Van Munster, R (2007) 'Governing terrorisim through risk: taking precautions, (un)knowing the future', *European Journal of International Relations,* 13(1): 89–115.

Australian Associated Press (AAP) (2007) 'Unis reject spy plan to fight extremists', 13 June 2007, available at www.thewest.com.au/printfriendly. aspx?StoryName=391079 (accessed 13 June 2007).

Australian Broadcasting Corporation (ABC) Insiders (2005) 'Counter-terrorism laws a balancing exercise: Ruddock', available at www.abc.net.au/insiders/content/2005/ s1457695.htm.

Australian Broadcasting Corporation (ABC) Online (2005) Lateline Survey of Australian Security Experts, available at www.abc.net.au/lateline/content/2005/ s1492426.htm (accessed 13 March 2007).

—— (2006a) 'The World Today – Lawyers to challenge Jack Thomas control order', 29 August 2006, available at www.abc.net.au/worldtoday/content/2006/s1727023.htm (accessed 12 June 2007).

—— (2006b) 'Aus unis condemn UK moves to spy on students', 17 October 2006, available at www.abc.net.au/news/newsitems/200610/s1766501.htm (accessed 13 June 2007).

—— (2007) 'Documents show AFP, ASIO knew of Habib "rendition"', 11 June 2007, available at www.abc.net.au/news/newsitems/200706/s1948035.htm (accessed 13 June 2007).

Australian Government (2007) 'Australian National Security', available at www.ag.gov.au/agd/www/nationalsecurity.nsf/AllDocs/F2ED4B7E7B4C028ACA256FBF00816AE9?OpenDocument (accessed 10 July 2007).

Bandura, A (1990) 'Selective Activation and Disengagements of Moral Control', *Journal of Social Issues*, 46(1): 27–46.

Bauman, Z (2004) *Wasted Lives: Modernity and its Outcasts*, London: Polity.

Beck, U (1992) *Risk Society: Towards a New Modernity*, Cambridge: Polity.

—— (1996) 'Risk society and the provident state'. in S Lash *et al.* (eds), *Risk, Environment and Modernity: Towards a New Ecology*, London: Sage.

—— (2002) 'The terrorist threat: would risk society revisited', *Theory Culture and Society*, 19(4): 39–55.

Beirne, P and Messerschmidt, J (2006) *Criminology*, Los Angeles, CA: Roxbury.

Bewley-Taylor, D (1999) *The United States and International Drug Control, 1909–1997*, London: Continuum.

Bigo, D (2000) 'Liaison officers in Europe: new officers in the European security field', in J Sheptycki (ed), *Issues in Transnational Policing*, London: Routledge.

Burnside, J (2006) 'The war on human rights: the climate of fear', *New Matilda*, Wednesday, 20 December 2006, available at www.newmatilda.com/home/printarticle.asp?ArticleID=1989 (accessed 24 December 2006).

Daily Telegraph [Sydney] (2004) 'Terrorist attack fears mounting', 12 July: 4.

Ditton, J and Farrall, S (2000) *Fear of Crime*, Aldershot: Ashgate.

Dockery, M (2006) 'The immediate impact of terrorism on the wellbeing of Australians', Curtin University of Technology School of Economics and Finance Working Paper Series, Report No. 06:02, Perth, Western Australia.

Foucault, M (1991) 'Governmentality', in G Burchell and C Gordon (eds), *The Foucault Effect: Studies in Governmentality*, London: Harvester Wheatsheaf.

Freedman, L (1992) 'The concept of security', in M Hawkesworth and M Kogan (eds), *Encyclopedia of Government and Politics*, vol 2, London: Routledge, p 731.

Freely, M and Simon, J (1992) 'The new penology: notes on the emerging strategy of corrections and its implications, *Criminology*, 30: 449–70.

Furedi, F (2002) *Culture of Fear: Risk Taking and the Morality of Low Expectation*, London: Continuum.

—— (2004) '"The politics of fear": President Bush isn't the only one who plays the scare card', Spiked Online, 28 October 2004, available at www.spiked-online.com/Printable/0000000CA760.htm (accessed 27 June 2007).

—— (2005) 'Terrorism and the politics of fear', in S Hale, K Hayward, A Wahidin and E Wincup (eds), *Criminology*, Oxford: Oxford University Press, pp 307–22.

Gallup Poll, The (2007) 'The People's Priorities: Gallop's Top 10', available at www.galluppoll.com/content/?ci=24391 (accessed 10 May 2007).

Gardner, J (2006) 'What security is there against arbitrary government?', *London Review of Books*, 9 March: 19–20.

Garland, D (1996) 'The limits of the sovereign state: strategies of crime control in contemporary society', *British Journal of Criminology*, 36: 445–71.

—— (2001) *The Culture of Control*, Chicago, IL, University of Chicago Press.

Giddens, A. (1993) 'The nature of modernity', in P Cassell (ed.), *The Giddens Reader*, Stanford, CA: Stanford University Press.

Glassner, B (1999) *The Culture of Fear: Why Americans are Afraid of the Wrong Things*, New York: Basic.

Green, P and M Grewcock (2002) 'The war against illegal immigration: state crime and the construction of a European identity', *Current Issues in Criminal Justice*, 14(1): 87–101.

Hale, C (1996) 'Fear of crime: a review of the literature', *International Review of Victimology*, 4: 79–150.

Hardt, M and Negri, A (2004) *Multitude: War and Democracy in the Age of Empire*, New York: Penguin.

Holyroyd, J (2007) 'PM calls for calm after terror arrest', *The Age*, 4 July 2007, available at www.theage.com.au/news/national/pm-calls-for-calm-after-terror-arrest/2007/07/04 (accessed 4 July 2007).

Hocking, B (2004) *Terror Laws: ASIO, Counter-Terrorism and the Threat to Democracy*, Sydney: UNSW Press.

Home Office (2007) *Current Threat Level*, available at www.homeoffice.gov.uk/security/current-threat-level/?version=1 (accessed 30 August 2007).

Hudson, B (2003) *Justice in the Risk Society*, London: Sage.

Institute of Race Relations (2007) 'Community Responses to the War on Terror', IRR Briefing Paper No. 3, February 2007, London, Institute of Race Relations.

Johnston, L (2001) 'Crime, fear and civil policing', *Urban Studies*, 38(5–6): 959–76.

Johnston, L and C Shearing (2003) *Governing Security: Explorations in Policing and Justice*, London: Routledge.

Kelman, H and V Hamilton (1989) *Crimes of Obedience: Toward a Social Psychology of Authority and Obedience*, London: Yale University Press.

Lee, M (2007) *Inventing Fear of Crime: Criminology and the Politics of Anxiety*, Cullompton: Willan Publishing.

Lerner, J, R Gonzalez, *et al.* (2003) 'Effects of fear and anger on perceived risk of terrorism: A national field experiment', *American Psychological Society*, 14(2): 144–50.

Loader, I (2002) 'Policing, securitization and democratization in Europe', *Criminal Justice*, 2(2): 125–53.

—— (2006) 'Civilizing security', The 2006 John Barry Memorial Lecture, University of Melbourne, 23 November 2006, available at www.criminology.unimelb.edu.au/barrylecture/barry_lecture_2006.pdf (accessed 28 June 2007).

Lupton, D (1999) *Risk*, London: Routledge.

Lynch, A and G Williams (2006) *What Price Security?: Taking stock of Australia's Anti-Terror Laws*, Sydney: UNSW Press.

Malloch, M and E Stanley (2005) 'The detention of asylum seekers in the UK: representing risk, managing the dangerous', *Punishment and Society*, 7(1): 53–71.

McCulloch, J (2004) 'The neo-liberal fear factory: or how Howard plans to win the election', *Arena Magazine* (June/July): 71.

McCulloch, J and B Carlton (2006) 'Preempting justice: suppression of financing of terrorism and the "War on Terror"', *Current Issues in Criminal Justice*: 397–412.

Mythen, G (2007a) 'Cultural victimology: are we all victims now?', in S Walklate (ed), *Handbook on Victims and Victimology*, Cullompton: Willan Publishing.

Mythen, G (2007b) 'The postmodern terrorist risk: plus ça change, plus c'est la même chose?', in T Owen and J Powell (eds), *Reconstructing Postmodernism: Critical Debates*, New York: Nova Science Publications.

Mythen, G and S Walklate (2006) 'Criminology and terrorism: which thesis? risk society or governmentality?', *British Journal of Criminology* 46: 379–98.

Nixon, S (2006) 'Terrorism top worry of increasingly fearful flyers', *Sydney Morning Herald*, 25 January 2006, available at www.smh.com.au/news/national/terroris-top-worry-of-increasingly-fearful-flyers/2006/01/25 (accessed 13 March 2007).

O'Malley, P (1992) 'Risk, power and crime prevention', *Economy and Society*, 21: 252–75.

—— (2001) 'Risk, crime and prudentialism revisited', in K Stenson and R Sullivan (eds), *Crime, Risk and Justice*, Cullompton: Willan Publishing.

—— (2004) 'The uncertain promise of risk', *The Australian and New Zealand Journal of Criminology*, 37(3): 317–23.

Otto, D and J-C Tham (2006) 'The perils of countering terrorism by eroding human rights', *Human Rights 2006: The Year in Review Conference*, Melbourne: CB Malthouse.

Parker, M (2006) 'A grave new world', *Sydney Morning Herald*, 2–3 September 2006, News Review, p 30.

Parliament of Australia (2004) 'House of Representatives Official Hansard No 6, 2004', Tuesday, 30 March 2004, available at www.aph.gov.au/hansard/reps/dailys/dr300304.pdf.

—— (2005) 'Questions without notice: national security', *Hansard*, 1 November 2005, p 7.

Prewitt, K, E Alterman *et al.* (2004) 'The politics of fear after 9/11', *Social Research* 71(4): 1129–46.

Poynting, S., G Noble, P Tabar and J Collins (2004) *Bin Laden in the Suburbs: Criminalising the Arab Other*, Sydney: Sydney Institute of Criminology.

Robinson, E (2006) 'Using our fear', *Washington Post*, Friday, January 27, 2006, p A23.

Rose, N (1990) *Governing the Soul*, London: Routledge.

Rothe, D and Muzzatti, SL 2004. 'Enemies everywhere: terrorism, moral panic, and US civil society', *Critical Criminology* 12(3): 327–50.

Rubin, G, C Brewin *et al.* (2007) 'Enduring consequences of terrorism: 7-month follow-up survey of reactions to the bombings in London on 7 July 2005', *British Journal of Psychiatry*, 190: 350–6.

Rudiger, A (2007) *Prisoners of Terrorism? The Impact of Anti-Terrorism Measures on Refugees and Asylum Seekers in Britain, February 2007*, London: Refugee Council.

Ruddock, P (2005) 'Freedom of speech protected', Attorney-General's Department Media Release, 31 October 2005, available at www.nttf.gov.au/agd/WWW/MinisterRuddockHome.nsf/Page/RWPEAF63E84CDA0D89ECA2570CA007F5F6F (accessed 12 June 2007).

Ryan, M. (2003). 'Be Australian – be afraid?' *Arena Magazine.* 63, February–March.

Sassen, S (1996) *Sovereignty in an Age of Glablisation,* New York: Columbia University Press.

Scherer, K, T Wranik, J Sangsue, V Tran and U Scherer (2004) 'Emotions in everyday life: probability of occurrence, risk factors, appraisal and reaction patterns', *Social Science Information,* 43(4): 499–570.

Security Legislation Review Committee (2006) *Report of the Security Legislation Review Committee,* Commonwealth Parliament.

Simon, J (1997) 'Governing through crime', in L Friedman and G Fisher (eds), *The Crime Conundrum: Essays on Criminal Justice,* Boulder, CO: Westview Press, pp 171–89.

Valverde, M (2001) 'Governing security, governing through security', in P Daniels, P Macklem and K Roach (eds), *The Security of Freedom: Essays on Canada's Anti-Terrorism Bill,* Toronto: University of Toronto Press, pp 83–92.

Webber, F (2004) 'The war on migration', in P Hillyard, C Pantazis, S Tombs and D Gordon (eds), *Beyond Criminology: Taking Harm Seriously,* London: Pluto Press.

Weber, L (2007) 'Policing the virtual border: punitive preemption in australian offshore migration controls. forthcoming in 2008', *Social Justice* (Special Issue on Transnational Criminology) 34(2).

Welch, M (2003) 'Trampling human rights in the war on terror: implications to the sociology of denial', *Critical Criminology,* 12: 1–20.

Zedner, L (2000) 'The pursuit of security', in T Hope and R Sparks (eds), *Crime, Risk and Insecurity,* London: Routledge.

—— (2006) 'Neither safe nor sound: the perils and possibilities of risk', *Canadian Journal of Criminology and Criminal Justice,* 48(3): 423–34.

—— (2007a) 'Pre-crime and post-criminology?', *Theoretical Criminology,* 11(2): 261–81.

—— (2007b) 'Preventive justice or pre-punishment? the case of control orders', *Current Legal Problems,* Vol. 60, Oxford: Oxford University Press.

Chapter 6

Being feared

Masculinity and race in public space[1]

Kristen Day

Introduction

> Other persons never see the world from my perspective, and in witnessing the other's objective grasp of my body, actions, and words, I am always faced with an experience of myself different from the one I have.
>
> (Young 1990a: 231)

I began this study to better understand men's experiences of public space. For several years, I have studied women's fear in public space. By 'public space', I refer loosely to that category of generally accessible places outside of the home, which are used on a temporary basis (after Franck and Paxson 1989). It is possible to say, without exaggeration, that fear in public space is a common experience for many women in the US, one with profound impacts for women's lives. I have investigated the implications of fear for different groups of women, including mostly white college students in the Midwest US; and for black, white, and Latina women of varied ages in Orange County, California. I examined fear as it shaped women's use and experience of college campuses and of public spaces like bookstores and coffee shops. I have been especially interested in fear as a form of social control over women's use of public space, and in the intersections between the location and meaning of fear and women's race and class identities (Day 1994, 1995, 1997, 1999a, 1999b, 1999c).

That women chiefly feared men (rather than other women) was so universal among women I interviewed as to almost pass without mention. Increasingly, however, I wondered about men's reactions to being feared. Were men in public spaces conscious of being feared by women? Did men notice the signals of fear that women reported – the quickened steps, furtive glances, and keys held ready to wield as weapons? If so, what did men make of this? How were men's behaviours and their perceptions – of public spaces, of women, and of themselves – influenced by being the objects of others' fear?

In this chapter, I adopt a social constructionist approach to investigate men's experiences of being feared in public spaces. In geography and related fields, social constructionism involves the 'interrogation of the formation of sociospatial meaning' (Bonnett 1996: 872). I apply this perspective to examine men's experiences of being feared and their interpretations of these experiences, and the consequences of being feared for men's lives.

Researchers have long studied fear and its negative impacts for those who fear (see Koskela 1997; Pain 1991; Valentine 1990, 1992). The experience and implications of being feared have received less attention, however, apart from some powerful personal accounts (see Ellis 1995; Kelley 1988) and a broader geographical literature on exclusion (see Iveson 2003; Sibley 1995, 2001). This chapter examines men's experiences of being feared in public spaces, drawing on findings from interviews with 82 undergraduate male students at the University of California, Irvine. Male college students were selected for the study because this group was readily accessible and, as importantly, because it is high school and college-age men who are typically linked with danger in the media and in crime statistics. It is these young men who are most often feared, according to existing research (discussed later).

A pilot study revealed wide divergence in young men's experiences of being feared in public spaces. Not surprisingly, men's experiences of being feared were shaped by their racial identities and by the meanings assigned to these identities. Much research on women's fear treats men as a fairly homogeneous group, beyond noting that it is certain types of men (young and black or Latino) that women especially fear (see Day 1999a, 1999c; Gordon and Riger 1989; Koskela 1997). However, by ignoring men's specific identities, we miss the fact that women's and men's identities are not distinct but interdependent. They are constructed interactively, including through the use of public space (Jackson 1991; Ruddick 1996). Thus, I sharpened the focus of the study to deal less with 'men' as an undifferentiated group, and more with the role of racial identity in men's experiences of being feared.

As I argue in this chapter, the experience and interpretation of being feared (or not feared) in public space intersects with men's construction of gender and race identities, and the ways that men assign racial meanings to public places. As such, the question of how men experience being feared acquires broad societal significance. In this chapter I expand our understanding of a key mechanism (that is, fear) by which race privilege and exclusion are maintained and justified, and propose strategies for challenging fear and exclusion.

The social construction of race in research on place

The term 'social constructionist' encompasses a broad range of research, which examines how various categories of meaning, such as race, are constructed (Bonnett 1996). Such research rejects the notion of categories like race as 'natural':

Social construction theory argues that many of the categories that we have come to consider 'natural', and hence immutable, can be more accurately (and more usefully) viewed as the product of processes which are embedded in human actions and choices ... [and later] The social construction perspective works by identifying the components and processes of category construction. The resultant knowledge can then be used to reconstruct categories in ways which allow their inherent power to be used in the pursuit of equality.

(Jackson and Penrose 1993: 2–3)

Nash (2003) expands further, describing social constructionism as:

anti essentialist perspectives on race which seek to deconstruct race as a 'naturalized' hierarchy of biologically distinctive human groups, while exploring processes of racialization which place individuals and groups within racial categories and have material effects in terms of the unequal distribution of power and wealth.

(Nash 2003: 639)

Bonnett (1996) provides a framework that situates social constructionism as the most recent of several contemporary geographical approaches to the study of race, and the prevailing approach in geography today. Bonnett distinguishes social constructionism from earlier approaches to the study of geography and race, in which race is treated as a real and fixed characteristic.

In contrast with earlier approaches, social constructionists typically examine racism and its geographical ramifications, rather than 'race' *per se* (Bonnett 1996). Social constructionist research often investigates how places are assigned racial meanings (Nash 2003). Studies also explore how racial groups make decisions within the context of racially interactive processes such as discrimination and assimilation. Social constructionist research acknowledges that race is often constructed in ways that make the current arrangements of power appear 'natural' (Bederman 1995; Nash 2003). Researchers interrogate the reasons and conditions under which race is constructed to support these inequitable arrangements (Miles 1989; in Jackson and Penrose 1993).

Social constructionists do not interrogate all categories with equal vigour. As Bonnett (1996) argues, social constructionists often exempt from critique such 'progressive' categories as equality and racism, trying instead to fix the meanings of these categories to support the researchers' political goals. A more useful approach would interrogate the meanings of categories such as race privilege and fear.

Fear in public spaces is a key mechanism through which race privilege is constructed. Fear of racialised others serves to maintain and justify exclusion and race oppression. As I discuss, men's experiences of being and not being feared in public spaces, and their interpretations of those experiences, contribute to the construction of men's racial identities and to men's understandings of race and racism more broadly. In interpreting their experiences of being feared, men attempt to negotiate the boundaries of exclusion that are tied to identity. They exercise control over how they are perceived by others and seek opportunities for themselves. In their efforts, young men may deny, rationalise, accommodate, or resist others' fear in public spaces, each of which has implications for the maintenance of race privilege. The following sections explore these themes in greater detail.

Methods

Findings derive from interviews of 82 male college students at the University of California, Irvine. Students received course credit, typically in large introductory courses, for participating in the study. The men I interviewed ranged in age from 18 to 36 years, with a median age of 20 years. My intention was to examine the intersections of men's racial/ethnic identities and their experiences of being feared. In a one-page survey that accompanied interviews, male students were asked to identify themselves in terms of their racial/ethnic identities. A wide array of overlapping and disjointed categories of racial/ethnic/geographical identifies were offered, to accommodate the disparate ways men might conceive of their identities. Men were invited to describe themselves using all categories that fit their definitions of their own racial/ethnic identities, and to add other categories as needed. In response, men identified themselves as Asian/Asian American (24), white/Anglo/ Caucasian (15), Hispanic/Latino/Chicano (11), Middle Eastern (8), black/ African-American/African (4), Pacific Islander (4), South Asian/Indian (3), and other (4). Nine additional participants identified themselves as belonging to multiple groups.

Prior to beginning this study, an undergraduate research assistant completed a pilot study involving brief, in-person interviews with 18 male students. For the study itself, I conducted semi-structured interviews with all participants. Interviews lasted 30–45 minutes on average. All interviews were tape-recorded, transcribed verbatim, and analysed through qualitative content analysis involving iterative stages of detailed coding and interpretative memos (after Patton 1990).

In the interviews, men were asked about their feelings of fear and safety in public spaces, and their experiences of being feared by others. In particular, they were asked whether and where they had ever experienced fear in public space, and where and when they felt safe. In interviews, I asked men to respond to a series of hypothetical scenarios, which they could choose to interpret as instances in which strangers were or were not fearful of them. Each scenario was designed so that it might have multiple interpretations. I read the scenarios to the men in a neutral voice, and then asked for their possible interpretations. For example, one scenario asked each man to imagine that he and a group of his friends entered an elevator at a shopping mall, after which the sole occupant – an older, Asian American woman – immediately left the elevator. Men were asked to provide possible interpretations of each scenario. They were also asked whether any such experience had ever happened to them and, if so, how they had interpreted it. I then asked men directly whether they might have interpreted the scenario in the interview as an instance in which the stranger described was afraid of them, and asked men to explain their interpretations. Other interview questions asked men to discuss any times they had been conscious of being feared by strangers in public spaces and their interpretations of those experiences. Findings speak most centrally to the experiences of college-age men in postsuburban Southern California. Many findings are also relevant to the experiences of college-age men elsewhere in the US and in other Western countries.

The fact of being interviewed by a white woman in her mid-thirties had bearing on the information men divulged, and the ways they chose to present themselves as men during interviews. In interviews, I introduced myself by first and last name, and stated that I was interested in men's uses of and feelings about public spaces. Throughout interviews, I did not attempt to encourage men to answer in particular ways, and was accepting of all responses. To some men, I may have appeared to be a professor (which I was) or authority figure, and their responses may have been guided by trying to give the 'right' or 'politically correct' response. For others, my apparent age may have indicated more of a 'peer-group' status, and their responses may have been intended to impress, shock, or solidify that connection. Men who identified themselves and me as white may have neglected to address the significance of white race identity in their experiences in public spaces, assuming that we had similar understandings that required no elaboration. At the same time, some men of colour may have elected to minimise the significance of racism in their lives to avoid being labelled as 'whiners' who blamed racism for their troubles (Feagin 1991), or to spare my feelings of guilt for their experiences. In general, my stranger status and my reluctance to proffer my own views on race likely tempered men's responses on these sensitive topics.

The context

Orange County, the site of this study, is located in Southern California, midway between Los Angeles and San Diego. Outsiders know Orange County for its affluence and its conservative politics. Originally more of a suburb of Los Angeles, Orange County often prefers to think of itself as separate and superior to Los Angeles in terms of safety, prosperity, and quality of life (Soja

1992). This distinction is blurring somewhat as Orange County becomes more highly urbanised. In the national and regional imagination, however, Orange County remains linked with archetypical suburban living, political conservatism, and shopping malls for the well-heeled (Blakely and Snyder 1997; McGirr 2002; Soja 1992; Sorkin 1992).

Orange County residents are diverse overall, but communities are segregated. According to census data from 2000, of the nearly three million Orange County residents, 65 percent are white, 14 percent are Asian American, and 2 percent are black (US Bureau of the Census 2000). Fifteen percent of residents identify themselves as some other race. Additionally, 31 percent of residents identify themselves as Hispanic or Latino. Residents are unevenly divided into the less populated, wealthier, and 'whiter' South County, and the poorer, more populated, and more racially and ethnically diverse North County.

The city of Irvine sits in the centre of postsuburban Orange County. Incorporated in 1971, Irvine (population 143,000) is one of the largest planned communities in the US. Irvine residents identify themselves as white (65 percent), Asian (32 percent), and black (2 percent); seven percent of Irvine residents are Hispanic (US Bureau of the Census 2000). Irvine is an affluent city. Residents' median household income was over US$72,000 in 2000. The city is known for its strict control over urban design and for its reputation as one of the safest cities of its size in the nation (Garvin 1996; Kelley 1994; Savageau and Loftus 1997; Soble and Kelley 1992; Soja 1992; Watson 1992).

The University of California, Irvine (UCI), serves a population of approximately 23,000 students. As a group, UCI students are racially, ethnically, and linguistically diverse. Students identify themselves as Asian American (44 percent), white/Caucasian (27 percent), Chicano(a)/Latino(a) (11 percent), African American/black (2 percent), and Native American (less than 1 percent) (UCI Analytical Studies and Information Management 1999). (Approximately 11 percent of students registered as 'other' or registered no racial/ethnic affiliation.) Seventeen percent of UCI students are not US citizens, and many are first-generation immigrants. Many students commute to campus from throughout Los Angeles and Orange counties. Conservative students on campus are vocal (see, for example, Swingle 2005). UCI is the college of choice for many immigrant families who want their sons or daughters to live at home while in school. It may be that, as college students, many men in this study had socially liberal attitudes about race, and yet the characteristics of the student population and the local context may temper this liberalism.

Living in a diverse, highly urbanised region – perched on the Pacific Rim, two hours from Mexico – Orange County residents share a certain consciousness of race with other Southern Californians. Strained relations between groups are revealed in past reactions to the OJ Simpson trials and the Rodney King beating, heated battles over Affirmative Action in the University of California and the state of California, and recent clashes over immigrant rights and punitive anti-immigrant legislation. Orange County residents may be especially conscious of racial diversity and racial tension, compared with Americans in many other places.

Who is feared in public space?

Extensive research on fear of crime identifies who is most fearful in public space, which includes those who are more socially vulnerable, such as older adults, women, low-income groups, and people of colour (see Box *et al* 1988; Garofalo and Laub 1978; Gordon and Riger 1989; Madriz 1997; Pastore and Maguire 2000; St John and Heald-Moore 1995, 1996; Skogan 1995; Skogan and Maxfield 1981; Vander Ven 1998). Research also identifies who is feared. According to these studies (and consistent with expectations), men are overwhelmingly more feared than are women. Young men and men of colour are especially the targets of fear, though findings vary with neighbourhood composition (see Chiricos *et al.* 1997; Day 1999c; Mahoney 1995; St John and Heald-Moore 1995; Taylor and Covington 1993). Men are frequently feared in outdoor, public places (Day 1999c; Valentine 1990). The remainder of the chapter explores these experiences of being feared from men's perspectives.

Men's experiences of being feared in public spaces

Who was feared?

Slightly more than half of the male students in this study said that they had been feared in public space (including 45 of 82 men, or 56 percent). Awareness of being feared differed by men's self-identified racial/ethnic groups (see Table 6.1).[1] Although their numbers were small, most black and Hispanic men in the study said that they had experienced being feared in public spaces (100 percent and 82 percent, respectively). White and Asian men less often reported that they had been feared (53 percent and 52 percent, respectively). Men who identified with multiple and/or other racial/ethnic groups were also less likely to report having been feared (42 percent). (This number includes men who identified themselves as belonging to more than one racial group, and those who identified themselves as Middle Eastern, Pacific Islander, South Asian/Indian, and 'other' groups.)

The experience of fearing others in public space resonates strongly with women as a gender-related issue. Most men in the study did not, however, differentiate being feared by women from being feared by other groups, such as by older men or children. Thus, men experienced being feared primarily

Table 6.1 Male students varied in their experiences of having been feared in public spaces, linked to their self-described racial identities

	Aware of having been feared by others in public space	Not aware of having been feared by others in public space	No response	Total
Anglo/White/ Caucasian men	8 (53%)	4 (27%)	3 (20%)	15 (19%)
Asian/Asian American men	12 (52%)	10 (43%)	1 (4%)	23 (29%)
Black/African American men	4 (100%)	0	0	4 (5%)
Hispanic/ Chicano/Latino men	9 (82%)	0	2 (18%)	11 (14%)
Multiple and other racial groups	8 (42%)	7 (37%)	4 (21%)	19 (24%)
Total	45 (56%)	23 (29%)	12 (15%)	82 (100%)

in terms of their own gender and racial identities, not necessarily in terms of the gendered meanings of fear for women.

Recalling places when they were aware of being feared, men listed shopping malls, bars, and grocery stores, city streets, and the campus itself. Men described their awareness of being feared in upscale shopping malls or jewellery stores, where we might expect teenage men to be more conscious of their 'outsider' status. Some men described having been feared in particular cities such as Newport Beach, Los Angeles and Monterey Park. These cities often carried racialised meanings that are locally recognised. Newport Beach, for example, is regarded as an affluent 'white' city. Los Angeles is synonymous with 'diversity' for many (especially for people in Orange County), and Monterey Park is known as a thriving Chinese community. It may be both that men are more often feared in places where they 'stand out' in terms of race and class, and that young men are more conscious of others' reactions to them in such settings.

Almost one-third of the men in the study were not aware of having personally been feared in public spaces. (Another 15 percent of men provided no clear indication of whether or not they had been feared.) Men did, however, generally believe that many women were fearful in public spaces, including in the public spaces of Irvine and UCI (Day 2001). Several possible explanations can be posited for some men's lack of awareness of being feared. First, being feared may be so commonplace that it does not register in the memories of young men. Men's interview responses suggest that this is sometimes the case.

Being feared is not commonplace for all men, however. In fact, several men seemed to find it strange to think that women would fear them in public spaces. Interviews asked men to explain various scenarios in which women displayed behaviour in public spaces that could be read as fearful. One scenario, for example, describes a woman alone at an automatic banking machine, who becomes nervous as the interview respondent joins the line behind her. She hurriedly leaves after finishing her banking. Men were asked whether they had ever experienced such situations in real life. Some men denied any such experiences. They described the women's reactions in these scenarios not as legitimate, but as 'weird' or 'odd':

> Okay, I would just go, uh, 'You're weird'. ... Like, if she really started freaking out or something, you know, I would go, 'Look, um, I'm not gonna do anything to you so, you know, you calm down. I'm just trying to get my money. Go get your money. Everything is fine'. ... I would just think that she's a little too paranoid. Just a little too paranoid.
>
> (White/Anglo/Caucasian man, age 18)

> I mean, myself, I'd probably ignore it. I'd kinda interpret it as maybe she was uncomfortable around me. She felt like I was going to grab her purse or something, if I looked scary ... . It wouldn't affect my feelings. It would probably just make me think that she just had some mental problem. Maybe she was just insecure.
>
> (White/Anglo/Caucasian man, age 19)

Some men may be unaware of being feared in public spaces, especially by women, because these men have not themselves been feared. This explanation is most plausible for men who do not have the physical characteristics (of race, size, and appearance) that women fear most. And yet, the prevalence of women's fear in public spaces[2] makes it unlikely that the college-age men in this study were not feared by women in public spaces at least occasionally.

More likely, it seems, is that many men in this study were not aware of being feared in public spaces because such awareness may be inconsistent with their identities as men. To understand men's responses, we must consider men's racial and gender identities and the ways in which these identities interact with men's interpretations of being feared. Men's own racial identities are shaped by their attempts to deny, rationalise, accommodate, and resist being feared by strangers in public spaces. Exchanges in public places matter at the local, 'micro scale' of the space itself and at the broader 'macroscale' of the city and region (Ruddick 1996).

The following sections look at common experiences of being feared among men, which often overlapped with specific racial identities. I look, in particular, at the experiences of male students who identify themselves as white, Asian, and Latino.[3] I do not intend to suggest that all men who identify with a particular racial group (or are identified as such by others) shared similar experiences, or that such experiences[3] are exclusive to men in that group. Additionally, individual men sometimes drew on more than one explanation to account for different experiences. Men's experiences of being feared reflected complex intersections of personal characteristics – racial identity, as well as age, physical appearance, background, and so on – and broader factors such as geography and history, which create the context in which men negotiate public space.

Race privilege and 'individualism'

I asked men in the study to offer explanations for why they had or had not experienced being feared by others, and especially by women, in public spaces. Many men attributed their experiences to their own characteristics as individuals. This explanation was the most common one among men who identified themselves as white. Men in other racial groups also often explained their experiences in this way. For example, men explained that women did not fear them in public spaces because they (these men) were 'nice guys' or had 'good personalities', 'nice smiles', or even 'good karma'. When they were feared, these men frequently offered as explanations their identities as (unracialised) fear-inducing 'teens'. Men often cited their own behaviour or features of their appearance not tied to race (size, clothing, hair) to explain others' fear or lack of it.[4] Men drew on their identities as individuals to explain their experiences of being feared or not feared in various public places – shopping malls, Disneyland, city streets, and others. In their explanations, men often assumed that strangers regarded them as 'individuals' in public spaces, and not as representatives of racialised groups. In this section, I focus on the experiences of those men who identified themselves as white:

> Mainly, well, at least most people tell me this, but – I don't look like a person that's going to come out and, you know, scare someone or scare them away... [it's my] conservative kind of dressing. Not a wild hairdo or something. Nothing to scare people away. Yeah, I'd say, more conservative dressing.
>
> (white/Anglo/Caucasian man, age 19).

> My face, my – I don't, I can't explain, I'm trying to think – personality, the way I act around people ... . It's just, it's not very threatening at all.
>
> (white/Anglo/Caucasian man, age 18)

The meanings associated with individual characteristics such as body shape and size, dress, physical stance, and facial expression, clearly played into men's perceptions of how they were regarded by others. Men's responses sometimes reveal an awareness of how their physical bodies – as men – shape their relationship with the broader world. So, for example, shorter men sometimes remarked that their height made them less fear-inspiring to others. These responses are consistent with the scholarly literature on embodiment (see, for example, Brownmiller 1984; Butler 2004; Connell 1987, 2000; Deegan 1987; Gardiner 1995). 'It is the ordinary, purposive orientation of the body as a whole towards things and its environment that initially defines the relation of a subject to its world' (Young 1990b: 143). This orientation varies with socio-historical circumstances (Young 1990b). For instance, the common characteristics of how young, white, middle-class men typically move, walk, take-up space in the US in the twenty-first century are not the same as they might have been 200 years ago. Social institutions and discourses give meanings to men's bodies (such as feared or safe), but men also have agency in the social practices and the material diversity of their bodies (Connell 2000). Thus, men can, to some extent, elect to present their bodies in ways that are more or less likely to elicit fear in public space (see Day 2001; Katz 1988).

Men's explanations of 'individualism' as a reason for being or not being feared were also consistent with the tendency of many US men – especially men privileged by race or ethnicity, class, sexuality, and so on – to see themselves as 'the norm', rather than as representing a particular perspective tied to gender, racial identity, and so on (Kimmel and Messner 1998). Whiteness, especially, allows one's perspectives and behaviour to remain unmarked (Frankenberg 1993; Mahoney 1995). A few men in the study acknowledged the role of white race identity in their experiences of being feared:

> I don't want to get myself into a confrontational situation with other people, so I guess I just assume that they would perceive that about me ... I mean, just body language. And I'm Caucasian, and I think maybe people have more fears of minorities.
>
> (white/Anglo/Caucasian man, age 36)

For white people and others privileged by race, attributing one's experiences in public spaces to 'individual' characteristics (personality, etc.) can be part of a broader resistance to acknowledging the privileges associated with race (Lipsitz 1998; Mahoney 1995). Race prejudice is easy to spot (especially in others), yet race privilege often remains invisible. The experience of being feared in public spaces therefore becomes a problem for some racialised others, not a privilege for oneself. A few men in the study, recognising their own race privilege, shifted the discussion of their own experiences of being feared to talk instead about discrimination against friends in other racial groups. Such tactics can sometimes have the effect of distancing oneself from the issue:

We were at Soup Plantation one time, which is a soup restaurant right there. And there was an Asian fight. And we were all sitting there eating, and the police came. And the Asians all took off, and we were there sitting with our food. And the police came, like, and they pulled their guns. And they pulled their guns over me like this, like four of us and me. And three of my friends are pretty dark, and I'm light skinned. So they pull them on them – 'Get on the ground! Get on the ground!',

(Middle Eastern man, age 18)

If I dressed in something flashy, and I went to a store, people kind of tend to look at me ... . Just that they don't know, or they might generalize. Maybe just, yeah, if they didn't know. For security reasons. I'm not sure. You know, like, with – my friend's African American. He just gets looked at. Just – I go with him, and he's the first one they look at ... I don't get looked at as much. I mean, yeah, just like a couple times that they really looked at – but with him, I mean, he's mentioned it, and I've seen it too. I've seen those other people. They always tend to look at African Americans, seems like, through all the ethnicities. They look at that. I've noticed that.

(Asian/Asian American man, age 20)

Many white people, in particular, find it hard to see that the construction of whiteness allows white people to not be feared in public spaces – to move freely, to interact easily with strangers, to escape habitual surveillance:

The privilege that facilitates mobility and comfort in ordinary life is particularly difficult for whites to see. Opening a bank account appears routine, as does air travel without police stops, or shopping without facing questions about one's identification – unless the absence of suspicion is a privilege of whiteness.

(Mahoney 1995)

By locating the problem of being feared in other people (as racist actors or racialised victims), white people may maintain their own race privilege without drawing attention to it. Of course, not all constructions of whiteness connote safety. For people of colour, whiteness can signal danger of hate crime or harassment (see hooks 1995). The question remains about whether and when white people are aware of such associations between whiteness and danger.

Acknowledging the role of race in fear: 'Safe' but stigmatised Asian masculinity

As with white men, roughly half of the men in the study who identified themselves as Asian or Asian American men, had not experienced being feared by women in public space. Compared to the white men in the study, however, these Asian American men more often connected their experiences of being and not being feared to their racial identities:

> I would say, I mean, they would consider me kind of like, a 'blah' person whose sort of, you know, he's just there and he's not going to harm me ... . You know, nothing special, nothing harmful, just there ... . I think mainly it's because of my race.
>
> (Asian American/Asian man, age 19)

> It [being feared] wouldn't occur in Westminster or where it's predominantly Asian. But I think like in middle-class neighborhood that's predominantly white, it's kinda like there's a perception of a little more danger, because I'm a different race and because I'm young.
>
> (Asian/Asian American man, age 20)

In fact, the marking of the city of Irvine and UCI as 'Asian' or 'white and Asian' places is closely linked to the perceived safety of these spaces (Day 2001).

Some men's responses reflected a consciousness of how Asian masculinity is frequently constructed as 'safe' in the US. For much of the last century, a dominant US stereotype has characterised Asian men as weak, dutiful, asexual or homosexual, and feminised (Chen 1996; Chua and Fujino 1999; Newsweek 2000).[5]

The feminised notion of Asian masculinity traces its roots to US laws from the 1850s to 1930s, which prevented Chinese women from coming to the US and which banned intermarriage between Chinese and white people (Cheng 1999; Chua and Fujino 1999; Espiritu 1988). The resulting society of Chinese 'bachelors' bolstered the idea of Chinese men as asexual. Widespread employment of Chinese, Japanese, Korean and Filipino men in domestic positions and 'women's' occupations (including laundry and cooking) further supported feminised constructions of Asian masculinity in the US. These stereotypes were reinforced by the smaller (that is, more feminine) size of many Asian men compared with white men, and by the 'feminine' styles of hair and clothing among some Asian men early in the 1900s (Cheng 1999; Chua and Fujino 1999).

This feminised masculine identity may exempt some Asian men from associations with danger in public spaces. Ironically, the experience of not being feared may be demasculinising for some Asian American and other men, as to be regarded as 'safe' may suggest that one is inadequately 'manly' to constitute a threat to women (Chua and Fujino 1999; Westwood 1990). For example, in one interview, a man who identified himself as Asian American, told of walking with a female friend at night after class, when the woman encountered catcalls from a stranger. The man was embarrassed, feeling that his small size diminished his stature as a 'protector' of his friend. The woman resolved the situation by rebuking the harasser herself.

Today, the 'safeness' of Asian identity in the US is further supported by stereotypes of Asians as smart and well-educated. Newsweek magazine describes Asian American men as the ' newest trophy boyfriends' because of their image as 'future internet millionaires' (Newsweek 2000). Because of successes in education and earning, Asian Americans are often regarded as more similar to whites than to 'minority' groups such as blacks and Latinos (Chen 1996; Kobayashi 1994, in Ruddick 1996). As with white men, economic power and status may translate into an extra measure of privilege for many Asian American men in public space. Characterisations of Asian men as safe 'model minorities' can be used to justify discrimination against other 'troublemaker' groups, especially black men.

Rationalising race-based fear: The myth of limited exposure between 'opposite' groups

Several men who identified themselves as Asian or Asian American told stories of being feared by people in public spaces where there were 'few Asians'. These men thus characterised places (cities, regions of the country, etc.) in terms of their 'Asianness'. Most often, these men reported fear by white people in these locations, rather than by other racial groups. Men often explained white people's fear as a result of limited exposure to Asians:

> I went to San Luis Opisbo, where the majority of the race is not Asian. And I went there and I guess a lot of people were like staring, cause they'd never seen – I got a feeling – that much Asians, or so I guess.
> (Asian/Asian American man, age 20)

> There was this old lady. And then – it was really out of state, Oregon or somewhere, because me and friends were going up there. And then, I was at a gas station and then we went into the shop to buy some drinks or whatever, and she was standing there. And then I was standing right behind her. And then she, it might just be my, just being around. She was kind of nervous, looked at me 'cause maybe I'm Asian or something ... . I mean, in California, there are a lot of Asians here, so that's not really an issue. But up there, there's like, you know, something like [I'm a] foreigner type of thing ... . I mean, she was racist, I guess, but I did

not think of it as a hatred. But it's just something, you know, out of her normal thinking parameter, that's what I thought.

(Asian/Asian American man, age 25)

This 'limited exposure' explanation for fear has some utility for explaining race-based fear (see Merry 1981), but it is also problematic. In tying fear to unfamiliarity with racialised others, the 'limited exposure' explanation positions two groups as opposite, reinforcing a 'binary' division of urban space and cultural groups (Sibley 2001; Soja 1996) that is rooted in fundamentalist Western distinctions between nature and nurture, pure and impure (Nash 2003; Sibley 1995). Such dualistic thinking obscures the complexities of cultural identities. This thinking also suggests that mistrust between opposite groups is to be expected. Thus, animosity between cultural groups is posited a naturalised condition – 'human nature' – implying that such antagonisms are fixed rather than constructed (Nash 2003).

Further, by positing groups as 'naturally' opposite but equivalent, we obscure the real differences that exist between groups in terms of power to act on their fears (Jackson 1994). White people are not equivalent to other groups in this regard. White people's fear of Asian Americans (and of Latinos and blacks) has much more serious consequences than does the reverse, including implications for legal justice, exposure to violence, and access to resources.

Binary thinking reflects a concern with order and conformity, and a desire to keep unlike groups separate through boundaries between imagined safe and dangerous spaces (Sibley 1995, 2001). Fear of different 'strangers' is controlled by segregation into like-bodied communities (Sibley 2001). Thus, people of colour have been historically excluded from privileged white neighbourhoods and concentrated into poor neighbourhoods that are stigmatised by race and plagued by disinvestment and unemployment (Mahoney 1995; Sibley 1995). White neighbourhoods (and white people) are then regarded as 'naturally' good and safe, and non-white neighbourhoods and individuals become 'naturally' suspect (Mahoney 1995).

Learning to be feared: Moving between safe and feared identities

Most men in the study who identified themselves as Latino also reported having been feared in public spaces. These men frequently described being feared by people they characterised as white or Asian American, in places that included upscale stores or 'white' or 'Asian' cities or districts (see also Mahoney 1995). Here, the very presence of some men of colour is characterised as deviant and 'out of place' (Davis 1990; Iveson 2003; Sibley 1995):

I feel that there's still a large, a lot of racism, among the races in general. Because where I lived in Los Angeles, I was very comfortable and I would go to, you know, the small Oriental communities. And I would go there, and I would always – especially among the first generation, the first immigrants that come here – they're very much, always seem 'reserved' – but the word is 'snobbish' and against my culture and my people. They are very much wary of them ... [In] Irvine, specifically, that's where I spend a lot of time, I haven't had that happen to me yet. But if I go back to Alhambra or somewhere back there, then I'm gonna get it whether I'm with my friends or without.

(Hispanic/Latino/Chicano man, age 19)

The smaller number of men in the study who identified themselves as Latino (11) makes interpretation of their experiences more speculative.

Unlike the Asian American men described earlier, Latino men in the study did not typically attribute others' fear to limited exposure to Latinos. Instead, men who identified as Latinos, often ascribed others' fear to negative stereotypes about Latinos. These stereotypes, based in the media and popular culture, characterise Latinos as a single group. Differences between cultures and between US 'minority' groups and new immigrants are typically ignored (Olivarez 1998). Stereotypes of Latino men emphasise 'machismo' and dominance of women, while younger Latino men are portrayed as gang members or gangster 'wannabes' (Zinn 1988).

Stereotypes apply to Latinos and to those who look Latino. More than one non-Latino man in the study reported that he was sometimes feared because he looked Latino. Comments referred not only to hair and skin colour, but also to comportment, stance, and dress – all according meaning in our contemporary context, as discussed earlier (see Butler 2004; Connell 1987, 2000; Day 2001; Day et al. 2003; Katz 1988; Young 1990b).

It may also be that some non-Latino men prefer to link others' fear to mistaken 'Latino' identities, rather than to attribute others' fear to their own racialised identities. Doing so might allow men to minimise the perceived prejudice directed at them as individuals and as a group. This could be especially true in the current US climate of fear of Middle Eastern men. Findings from the study do not allow us to examine this possibility more directly.

Several Latino men noted that they were not feared in 'diverse' places like Los Angeles where, they asserted, their race identities and their appearances (clothing, manners, etc.) were less 'visible' (Westwood 1990) and did not automatically signal danger. The issue is not so much whether Latino men are more visible in Los Angeles than elsewhere, but rather how Latino male bodies are 'read' by different 'viewers'.[6] Men's responses reflected their sensitivity to how their bodies are perceived by others – as young men and as members of racialised groups (see also Brownmiller 1984; Deegan 1987;

Gardiner 1989, 1990, 1995) – and to how the meanings of these embodied identities vary with place.

The meanings and markers of feared racial groups are fluid over space and time. For some Latino men, being the object of prejudicial fear seemed to be a new experience upon coming to UCI, Irvine, and southern Orange County. Many Latino students come to UCI from Los Angeles or northern Orange County, where Latinos often make up the majority in neighbourhoods and schools. As students in the prestigious University of California (UC) system (only the top 12 percent of California students attend UC universities), some Latino men in this study described themselves as the 'smart kids' in their former schools and communities. Being marked now as 'dangerous' in upscale, white-identified Irvine was unsettling. A few men (Latino men and others) described how their identities and behaviour changed over time and even throughout the day as they moved between communities (see also hooks 1992):

> It was my first year here. I have friends from LA. They kinda tend to look like gang members. So I brought them here once for a party. It was like a dorm party or something. And this girl asked me if they were like safe to be with, because she had kind of a feeling, well, she asked me, she goes 'Are you guys like gang members? You know, 'cause we don't really like go out with gang members'. Cause she thought we were gang members just because my friends were dressed like that. And that's, I think that was, she was, I think she was scared. A lot of people there were also scared, because some of my friends have tattoos and stuff ... I mean, back home, when I hang around with them, people are not really scared because they're used to seeing guys like that, you know, in the streets.

Later, the same man described why people fear him less now:

> Maybe because my speech has improved. Because, I mean, I learned slang in the streets over there, and I kinda used more slang, and I kinda tend, I think I'm more educated verbally, like vocabulary-wise ... . And my dress, now I work here at the Student Center. I wear a tie, I tend to dress better now. And before I used to wear baggy shirts, baggy pants, and now I don't do that anymore. I assimilated to, I guess, my surroundings ... . The way I used to portray myself to like women, and I'd say like 'What's up? What's going on?' this and that, it was more like, I don't know, I guess they were scared of that, just my image. But now, it's like, 'Oh, how are you doing?' you know, and they're not as scared'.
>
> (Hispanic/Latino/Chicano man, age 22)

Men themselves may change in response to their experiences of being feared (Root 1997).

The experience of being feared in public space may play a role in young men's initial formation of racialised identities, though findings from this study do not explore this process directly. Tse (1999) posits a model of ethnic identity formation in which individuals move from: (1) unawareness of ethnic identity; to (2) ambivalence towards or evasion of ethnic identity; to (3) emergence of ethnic identity, tied to a growing sense of not belonging to the dominant group or of not wanting to belong; to (4) identification with a specific racial group (see also Root 1997; Tse 1999). It is during their teens and early twenties, when they are most likely to be feared by strangers in public spaces, that men often deal with questions of racial identity.

It may be, then, that the experience of being feared in public spaces (and the associated anger or shame) may prompt some men to consider further their racial identities or their racial group affiliation (see also Root 1997). In this way, young men negotiate their identities as they struggle to circumvent barriers that exclude them from privileged groups and places (see Sibley 1995).

Likewise, in some instances, a decision not to interpret others' fear in public space as racially motivated could reflect men's desire not to see themselves as excluded, or their desire not to see the world as rife with discrimination and prejudice. In interviews, many men carefully outlined how they would assess whether another's reaction constituted fear and whether they would interpret such fear as race prejudice (see also Feagin 1991). In this way, men constructed definitions of racism that exempted some conditions under which fear of men of colour could be legitimately feared. Men often eliminated situations that were 'justifiably' scary (dark, night, remote, etc.), as situations where another's display of fear would not constitute race prejudice. For example, one hypothetical scenario described a woman walking alone on campus at 9 o'clock at night. The woman in the scenario quickens her pace when she notices a man behind her. In interviews, several men claimed that they would not judge the woman's fear in this situation to be race prejudice, because of the context: dark, night time, and being alone:

> I mean, to each their own. That – just watch your own back and be cautious – that's fine. I wouldn't be offended by that, that's different. You know, it's late at night, you know, nobody's really around, and you have the impression somebody might be following you ... . She doesn't know why I'm on campus, I could be, you know, I could be a night stalker for all she knows'.
>
> (Middle Eastern man, age 18)

> I don't think it would be prejudice, you know, not really ... . I could have very easily been someone who was going to attack her, so especially in

the evening, no one else around, where she can feel vulnerable like I said, so. There's a real reason to be nervous of someone, especially if I'm catching up, you know, real close to her, kinda walking fast.

(Native American and white/Anglo/Caucasian man, age 19)

Thus, some young men may attempt to distance themselves from racial prejudice and avoid foreclosure on opportunities by rationalising others' fear. Such responses leave open the possibility that discrimination can happen, especially to other people.

Making exceptions for 'safe' middle-class men

Men of colour may also attempt to forefront their class status to challenge exclusion that is tied to race. Writings on men's experiences of being feared in public spaces include personal accounts by middle-class and upper-class, professional black and Latino men (Ellis 1995; Estavillo 1996; Kelley 1988; Staples 1986). In these stories, professional men (including some highly distinguished individuals) are mistaken for thugs or criminals by strangers who refuse to pick them up in taxis, scrutinise them in shops or movie theatres, or otherwise react in ways that automatically associate men's racialised bodies with danger. The authors rely on signs of middle-class status (professional dress, refined manners, even whistling classical music) to avoid rousing prejudicial fear among other middle-class strangers in public space (see Feagin 1991).

These authors typically interpret being feared as an affront to their middle-class or professional status. In their stories, it is the idea that they are 'successful' that especially rankles. The authors' chagrin at their treatment, while understandable, does not challenge the stereotype of racialised black or Latino men as dangerous (see also Sibley 1995). Instead, it attempts to redraw the boundaries around the stereotype to exempt middle-class individuals. As resistance, these reactions fall short by leaving intact the association between poor or working class, racially stigmatised men and danger (see also Bashi and McDaniel 1997; Olivarez 1998).

Conclusions

Being feared in public space has significant implications for individual men and for society. A story by Audrey Lourde (1984) reveals the emotional consequences of being feared for people of colour. In the story, Lourde (a black woman) tells of being a small child on a bus, and realising that she was despised by the white woman wedged in the seat beside her. Ruddick (1996) retells this story to show how experiences of race prejudice and fear in public spaces can 'deeply scar the psyche, inscribing into the very bodies of people their understanding of themselves and their place in a racialised hierarchy'

(Ruddick 1996: 136). For men, not being targeted by such fear is part of the 'right to public space' (Iveson 2003).

Fear of racialised others is rooted in the dualism of culture versus nature, masculine versus feminine. This dualism underlies racist views that distinguish white people from 'savages' (Nash 2003), and that seek safety by drawing boundaries that exclude unlike, 'dangerous' others (Sibley 1995). Young men of colour often interact with this urge towards exclusion by attempting to negotiate their identities in ways that minimise perceived differences and that stretch boundaries to include themselves. Responses to fear may thus undermine a potential solidarity between marginalised groups, such as between people of colour across class lines and between members of different cultural groups.

Race-based fear has consequences for those who fear as well, in the form of expanded race privilege, especially for white people. It matters little whether fear, when expressed by individuals in public spaces, is 'intended' to be prejudicial. The effects are the same regardless of intent (Lipsitz 1998).

Fear of crime in public spaces is frequently framed as a 'women's' problem. Women's fear is, unfortunately, often warranted. The reality of violence against women in US public spaces coexists with the reality that fear often functions to exclude racialised others. It is too simple to portray all women as victims in this equation and all men as aggressors. We must work, instead, to increase women's real and perceived safety whilst acknowledging that women and men occupy a range of positions in these relationships.

Fear that underlies public decision making is even more burdensome than that expressed by individuals. The characterisation of (some) racialised men as dangerous underlies discriminatory public policies, and justifies the inequitable distribution of resources in the US. For example, current US policies related to 'homeland security' stoke and harness fear of Arab men and of Mexican immigrants, to advance the business and political interests of an elite minority (Saito 2003).

Results of this study suggest directions for tackling questions of fear, race, and gender that jeopardise equality for women and for men. First, we can reconstruct masculine identities by challenging associations of some men of colour with danger. Sustained efforts are needed to reveal the discrimination inherent in linking black and Latino men (and now Middle Eastern men) with danger. The media play an important role in these efforts. At the same time, we must interrogate public policies and spending programmes that are rooted in stereotypes of who is 'dangerous' and who is 'safe,' including policies that guide economic development, infrastructure planning, and law enforcement.

Young (1990a) suggests one possibility in her description of the 'city of difference' – urban space that acknowledges difference and that seeks not homogeneous 'community', but rather acceptance of co-presence and unassimilated otherness. These urban spaces defy binaries, and encourage decreased border maintenance and lessened preoccupation with the separation into pure and impure (Sibley 2001). The postsuburban geography of places like Orange County – neither city nor suburb, centreless, peripheryless, with liminal spaces at the borders of cities and counties – offers this potential for multiplicity, at least in principle, if individuals and groups can overcome the urge to fortress and exclude (Davis 1990).

For the individual or group socialised into believing that the separation of categories is necessary or desirable, the liminal zone is a source of anxiety. It is a zone of abjection, one that should be eliminated in order to reduce anxiety, but this is not always possible. Individuals lack the power to organise their worlds into crisp sets and so eliminate spaces of ambiguity (Sibley 1995: 33)

Supportive policies would help to blur these boundaries by supporting public life over private retreat. Sibley (2001) includes here such interventions as investment in public transportation rather than private transportation systems, and support for residential development in city centres instead of in private enclaves. When exclusion is supported, it should be to foster public spaces that afford sanctuary to marginalised groups (Iveson 2003), and not to protect power by excluding feared others.

Acknowledgements

I would like to thank the Committee on Cultural Diversity, University of California, Irvine, for their support of this project. I am grateful for excellent research assistance from Daisy Carreon, Sarah-Jayne Macey, Arlene Magturo, Charla Ruby Malamed, Doan Nguyen, Cheryl Stump, and Lihn Truong. I especially acknowledge the contributions of Katherine Fookes, who conducted the pilot study for this chapter as her undergraduate honours thesis.

This article was first published in (2006) *Environment and Planning A*, 38: 569–86 and is reproduced here by kind permission of Pion Limited, London

Notes

1 Throughout, I refer to men by the racial or ethnic categories the men themselves identified with. This practice acknowledges that, although categories such as race are not 'real' and do not exist as fixed categories, people behave as if categories are real (see Jackson and Penrose 1993).
2 Especially at night, in particular kinds of places, among older women and women of colour (Gordon and Riger 1989; Valentine 1990, 1992),
3 To date, most research and writing on men's experiences of being feared in public spaces has examined the experiences of black men (see Bederman 1995; hooks 1992; Kelley 1988; Marable 1997; Westwood 1990). Race factors strongly into black men's experiences of fear and safety. The limited number of people who

identify as black both at UCI and in Orange County – 2 percent, in each instance – makes it difficult to speak directly to black men's experiences of being feared in the Irvine/Orange County context. (Only four men who participated in this study identified themselves as black/African American. All four had been feared in public spaces.) I refer the interested reader to the existing literature on black men's experiences of being feared.

4   Such cues may sometimes be intended to provoke fear (see Day 2001; Katz 1988).

5   An opposing construction identifies Asian men as sinister villains and rapists (see Chen 1996; Chua and Fujino 1999). Some men in the study utilised this more sinister Asian identity and its contemporary, Southern California 'gangster' manifestation (see Day 2001).

6   Butler (2004) makes the same point in discussing the meaning of Rodney King's black body to jurors in the trial of King's police assailants.

References

Bashi, V and McDaniel, A (1997), 'A theory of immigration and racial stratification', *Journal of Black Studies*, 27: 668–683.

Bederman, G (1995) *Manliness and Civilization*, Chicago, IL: University of Chicago Press.

Blakely, EJ and Snyder, MG (1997) *Fortress America: Gated Communities in the United States*, Washington, DC: Brookings Institution Press.

Bonnett, A (1996) 'Constructions of "race", place and discipline: geographies of "racial" identity and racism', *Ethnic and Racial Studies*, 19: 864–83.

Box, S, Hale, C and Andrews, G (1988) 'Explaining fear of crime', *British Journal of Criminology*, 28: 340–56.

Brownmiller, S (1984) *Femininity*, New York: Linden Press.

Butler, J (2004) 'Endangered/endangering: schematic racism and white paranoia', in S Salih (ed), *The Judith Butler Reader*, Malden, MA: Blackwell; reprinted from R Gooding-Williams (ed) (1993) *Reading Rodney King/Reading Urban Uprising*, New York: Routledge, pp 15–22.

Chen, CH (1996) 'Feminization of Asian (American) men in the US mass media: an analysis of The Ballad of Little Jo', *Journal of Community Inquiry*, 20(2): 57–71.

Cheng, C (1999) 'Marginalized masculinities and hegemonic masculinity: an introduction', *Journal of Men's Studies*, 7: 295–315.

Chiricos, T, Hogan, M and Gertz, M (1997) 'Racial composition of neighborhood and fear of crime', *Criminology*, 35: 107–31.

Chua, P and Fujino, DC (1999) 'Negotiating new Asian American masculinities', *Journal of Men's Studies*, 7: 391–413.

Connell, RW (1987) *Gender and Power. Society, the Person and Sexual Politics*, Cambridge: Polity Press.

—— (2000) *The Men and the Boys*, Cambridge: Polity Press.

Davis, M (1990) *City of Quartz. Excavating the Future in Los Angeles*, London: Verso.

Day, K (1994) 'Conceptualizing women's fear of sexual assault on campus: a review of causes and recommendations for change', *Environment and Behavior*, 26: 742–65.

—— (1995) 'Assault prevention as social control: women and sexual assault prevention on urban college campuses', *Journal of Environmental Psychology*, 15: 261–81.

—— (1997) 'Better safe than sorry? Consequences of sexual assault prevention for women in public space', *Perspectives on Social Problems*, 9: 83–101.

—— (1999a) 'Embassies and sanctuaries: women's experiences of race and fear in public space', *Environment and Planning D: Society and Space*, 17: 307–28.

—— (1999b) 'Introducing gender to the critique of privatized public space', *Journal of Urban Design*, 4: 155–78.

—— (1999c) 'Strangers in the night? Women's fear of sexual assault on urban college campuses', *Journal of Architectural and Planning Research*, 16: 289–312.

—— (2001) 'Constructing masculinity and women's fear in public space in Irvine, California', *Gender, Place and Culture*, 8: 109–28.

Day, K, Stump, C and Carreon, D (2003) 'Confrontation and loss of control: masculinity and men's fear in public space', *Journal of Environmental Psychology*, 23: 311–22.

Deegan, MJ (1987) 'The female pedestrian: the dramaturgy of structural and experiential barriers in the street', *Man-Environment Systems*, 17: 79–86.

Ellis, T (1995) 'How does it feel to be a problem?', in D Belton (ed), *Speak My Name. Black Men on Masculinity and the American Dream*, Boston, MA: Beacon Press, pp 9–11.

Espiritu, YL (1988) 'All men are not created equal: Asian men in US history', in MS Kimmel and MA Messner (eds), *Men's Lives*, 4th edn, Boston, MA: Allyn and Bacon, pp 35–44.

Estavillo, JL (1996) 'Pathos, bathos and Mexiphobia', *The Massachusetts Review*, 37: 355–64.

Feagin, JR (1991) 'The continuing significance of race: anti black discrimination in public places', *American Sociological Review*, 56: 101–16.

Franck, K and Paxson, L (1989) 'Women and public space', in I Altman and E Zube (eds), *Public Places and Spaces*, New York: Plenum, pp 121–46.

Frankenberg, R (1993) *White Women, Race Matters: The Social Construction of Race*, Minneapolis, MN: University of Minnesota Press.

Gardiner, CB (1989) 'Analyzing gender in public places: rethinking Goffman's vision of everyday life', *American Sociologist*, 20: 42–56.

—— (1990) 'Safe conduct: women, crime, and self in public places', *Social Problems*, 37: 311–28.

—— (1995) *Passing By: Gender and Public Harassment*, Berkeley, CA: University of California Press).

Garofalo, J and Laub, J (1978) 'The fear of crime: broadening our perspective', *Victimology: an International Journal*, 3: 242–53.

Garvin, A (1996) *The American City: What Works, What Doesn't*, New York: McGraw-Hill.

Gordon, MT and Riger, S (1989) *The Female Fear: The Social Cost of Rape*, Urbana, IL: University of Illinois Press.

hooks, b (1992) *Black Looks. Race and Representation*, Boston, MA: South End Press.

—— (1995) *Killing Rage*, New York: Henry Holt.

Iveson, K (2003) 'Justifying exclusion: the politics of public space and the dispute over access to McIvers Ladies' Baths, Sydney', *Gender, Place and Culture*, 10: 215–28.

Jackson, P (1991) 'The cultural politics of masculinity: towards a social geography', *Transactions of the Institute of British Geographers*, 16: 199–213.

—— (1994) 'Constructions of criminality: police–community relations in Toronto', *Antipode*, 26: 216–35.

Jackson, P and Penrose, J (1993) *Constructions of Race, Place and Nation*, London: University Press.

Katz, J (1988) *Seductions of Crime. Moral and Sensual Attractions in Doing Evil*, New York: Basic Books.

Kelley, D (1994) 'Simi Valley tops list of safest US cities', *Los Angeles Times*, 2 May, pp A3, 27.

Kelley, RDG (1988) 'Confessions of a nice Negro, or why I shaved my head', in MS Kimmel and MA Messner (eds), *Men's Lives*, 4th edn, Boston, MA: Allyn and Bacon, pp 378–84.

Kimmel, MS and Messner, MA (1998) 'Introduction', in MS Kimmel and MA Messner (eds), *Men's Lives*, 4th edn, Boston, MA: Allyn and Bacon, pp xiii–xxii.

Kobayashi, A (1994) 'Coloring the field: gender, "race", and the politics of field work', *The Professional Geographer*, 46: 73–80.

Koskela, H (1997) '"Bold walk and breakings": women's spatial confidence versus fear of violence', *Gender, Place, and Culture* 4: 301–20.

Lipsitz, G (1998) *The Possessive Investment in Whiteness: How White People Profit from Identity Politics*, Philadelphia, PA: Temple University Press.

Lourde, A (1984) *Sister Outsider*, Freedom, CA: Crossing Press.

McGirr, L (2002) *Suburban Warriors: The Origins of the New American Right*, Princeton, NJ: Princeton University Press.

Madriz, E (1997) 'Latina teenagers: victimization, identity, and fear of crime', *Social Justice*, 24: 30–46.

Mahoney, MR (1995) 'Segregation, whiteness, and transformation', *University of Pennsylvania Law Review*, 143: 1659–84.

Marable, M (1997) 'The black male: searching beyond stereotypes', in MS Kimmel and MA Messner (eds), *Men's Lives*, 4th edn, Boston, MA: Allyn and Bacon, pp 18–24.

Merry, SE (1981) *Urban Danger: Life in a Neighborhood of Strangers*, Philadelphia, PA: Temple University Press.

Miles, R (1989) *Racism*, London: Routledge.

Nash, C (2003) 'Cultural geography: anti-racist geographies', *Progress in Human Geography*, 27: 637–48.

Newsweek (2000) 'Why Asian guys are on a roll', 135(8): 21 February, p 50.

Olivarez, S (1998) 'Studying representations of US Latino culture', special issue: Constructing (mis)representations, *Journal of Communication Inquiry*, 22: 426–37.

Pain, R (1991) 'Space, sexual violence and social control: integrating geographical and feminist analyses of women's fear of crime', *Progress in Human Geography*, 15: 415–31.

Pastore, AL and Maguire, K (eds) (2000) 'Sourcebook of criminal justice statistics', available at www.albany.edu/sourcebook/ (accessed July 13, 2003).

Patton, MQ (1990) *Qualitative Evaluation and Research Methods*, Beverly Hills, CA: Sage.

Root, M (1997) 'Multiracial Asians: models of ethnic identity', *Amerasia Journal*, 23: 29–42.

Ruddick, S (1996) 'Constructing difference in public spaces: race, class, and gender as interlocking systems', *Urban Geography*, 17: 132–51.

St John, C and Heald-Moore, T (1995) 'Fear of black strangers', *Social Science Research*, 24: 262–80.

—— (1996) 'Age, racial prejudice and fear of criminal victimization in public settings', *Sociological Focus*, 29: 15–31.

Saito, N (2003) 'Whose liberty? Whose security? The USA Patriot Act in the context of COINTELPRO and the unlawful repression of political dissent', *Oregon Law Review*, 14: 1057–1128.

Savageau, D and Loftus, G (1997) *Places Rated Almanac 1997*, 5th edn, New York: Macmillan.

Sibley, D (1995) *Geographies of Exclusion: Society and Difference in the West*, London: Routledge.

—— (2001) 'The binary city', *Urban Studies*, 38: 239–50.

Skogan, WG (1995) 'Crime and the racial fears of white Americans', *Annals of the American Academy of Political Science*, 539: 59–71.

Skogan, WG and Maxfield, MG (1981) *Coping with Crime*, Beverly Hills, CA: Sage.

Soble, R and Kelley, D (1992) '2 Ventura cities are safest of their size in US', *Los Angeles Times*, 29 April, p A22.

Soja, E (1996) *Thirdspace*, Oxford: Blackwell.

Soja, EW (1992) 'Inside exopolis: scenes from Orange County', in M Sorkin (ed), *Variations on a Theme Park: The New American City and the End of Public Space*, New York: Hill and Wang, pp 94–122.

Sorkin, M (1992) 'See you in Disneyland', in M Sorkin (ed), *Variations on a Theme Park: The New American City and the End of Public Space*, New York: Hill and Wang, pp 205–32.

Staples, B (1986) 'Just walk on by: a black man ponders his power to alter public space', *Ms. Magazine*, 55: 84.

Swingle, J (2005) 'Socialist ecology at UC Irvine. Accuracy in Academia', available at www.academia.org/news/socialist ecology.php (accessed January 9, 2005).

Taylor, RB and Covington, J (1993) 'Community structural change and fear of crime', *Social Problems*, 40: 374–95.

Tse, L (1999) 'Finding a place to be: ethnic identity exploration of Asian Americans', *Adolescence*, 34: 121–38.

UCI Analytical Studies and Information Management (1999) 'University of California, Irvine, Student Characteristics Summary, Spring 1999', available at www.oas.uci.edu/scs/ (accessed August 1, 1999).

US Bureau of the Census (2000) available at http://factfinder.census.gov/ (accessed July 13, 2003).

Valentine, G (1990) 'Women's fear and the design of public space', *Built Environment*, 16: 288–303.

—— (1992) 'Images of danger: women's source of information about the spatial distribution of male violence', *Area*, 24: 22–9.

Vander Ven, TM (1998) 'Fear of victimization and the interactional construction of harassment in a Latino neighborhood', *Journal of Contemporary Ethnography*, 27: 374–99.

Watson, R (1992) *Irvine at 20: Planning Ahead*, Irvine, CA: Irvine Company.

Westwood, S (1990) 'Racism, black masculinity, and the politics of space', in J Hearn and D Morgan (eds), *Men, Masculinities and Social Theory*, Sydney: Allen and Unwin, Sydney, pp 55–71.

Young, IM (1990a) *Justice and the Politics of Difference*, Princeton, NJ: Princeton University Press.

—— (1990b) *Throwing Like a Girl and Other Essays in Feminist Philosophy and Social Theory*, Bloomington, IN: Indiana University Press, Bloomington.

Zinn, MB (1988) 'Chicano men and masculinity', in MS Kimmel and MA Messner (eds), *Men's Lives*, 4th edn, Boston, MA: Allyn and Bacon, pp 25–34.

Chapter 7

Untangling the web

Deceptive responding in fear of crime research

Robbie M Sutton and Stephen Farrall

Ask a layperson for an explanation for the criminal, generous, successful or futile actions of others, and it is very likely that he or she will refer you to psychological causes (Heider 1958; Sutton and McClure 2001). The kids busted up the shop because they were *bored*, or because they had no *respect* for authority; auntie does not go out at night because she's *afraid* to. These kinds of explanations appear, cheerfully, to ignore a profound epistemological problem: the psychological states and properties that people impute to each other cannot directly be observed or verified. Nor, for that matter, can we directly observe or verify other people's claims about their own psychological states.

For Ryle (1949) this was the 'problem of other minds', and it has occupied philosophers at least since Descartes (1637/1960). More recently, sceptical thinkers have found internal, psychological constructs too slippery and inscrutable to be fitting subject matter for social science (for example, Skinner 1965). Unfortunately, the paradigms that resulted from this 'eliminativism' turned out not just to be sceptical but sterile, and ultimately unsuccessful (for example, Chomsky 1967). A comprehensive understanding of the social structures that people construct and inhabit is not likely to be achieved unless we take into account the way people think, feel, and make meaning out of the events that unfold within these structures. Therefore, despite the thorny problems involved, social scientists generally attempt to describe the interior as well as the exterior landscapes of human life.

In theory, the fear of crime is a striking example of an interior, but socially important process. Familiarly, politicians appeal to the fear of crime in order to justify, attack, or defend policies (Harris 1969; Loo and Grimes 2004). Further, changes in the fear of crime are tracked in the service of public policy (for example, Dodd *et al.* 2004). Theoretically, criminologists have described the fear of crime as both an outcome (for example, Warr and Stafford 1983) and a cause (for example, Putnam 1995) of low social cohesion (see Woldoff 2006, for a recent review). Fear of crime has also been characterised as a means of social control, as in Brownmiller's (1975) provocative claim that men use rape, and the fear of rape, to subjugate women.

In practice however, as this book demonstrates, the study of the fear of crime is wracked with the conceptual, epistemological and methodological difficulties that attend the study of 'other minds'. For example, do the mental and emotional states that people report in fear of crime surveys really comprise 'fear' (Farrall *et al* 1997; Farrall 2004)? In general, are people able to report their fears accurately, given that attitudes and emotions can remain hidden from conscious awareness for much of the time (Wilson *et al.* 2000)? Are people's expressed fears really representative of their inner experience or are they symbolically loaded with unease about society in general (Farrall *et al.* 2007; Jackson 2004)?

This chapter is concerned specifically with another problem that bedevils survey research: even if we assume that people are more or less able to report their emotions and attitudes, they may not be *entirely* willing to do so. For various reasons, respondents may be motivated[1] to report high or low levels of fear, and their reports of fear may be altered as a result. If survey responses are a 'window to the mind', these motivators are likely to warp the glass, producing a distorted picture of what is going on inside.

As will become clear, we are not suggesting that respondents are deliberately setting out to pull the wool over researchers' eyes. Even respondents who consciously – and conscientiously – strive for honesty in their responses may be subject to conflicting motivational pressures. For example, honesty may conflict with the desire to portray oneself in a particular light, or express one's views about social disorder. Respondents who have these conflicting motivations may or may not be consciously aware of them, and therefore may or may not experience the survey as dilemmatic. As we shall see, even respondents whose responses are heavily influenced by these conflicting motivations may perceive their responses as perfectly honest. Throughout this chapter therefore, when we use terms that imply that participants are *motivated* to provide distorted answers, are *attempting* to portray a distorted image of themselves and suchlike, we do not mean to connote that they are conscious of their motivations. Our position here is consistent with recent developments in psychology which stress that much, and indeed probably most, human behaviour is motivated by goals, situational pressures, and ideologies of which people are not aware (for example, Bargh and Chartrand 1999; Förster *et al.* 2007: for a sample of recent work on unconscious goal pursuit see Forgas *et al.* 2005)

This chapter deals with the impact of what we call *deceptive responding* in fear of crime research. In the pages below, we first explain what we mean by deceptive responding. In a kind of 'case study' of its importance, we then discuss the role that deceptive responding may have played in the widely documented, but somewhat paradoxical, finding that women report higher levels of fear than men (for example Hale 1996: 96–100). In this discussion, we review some of our own recent findings, and present some new research findings concerning gender stereotypes and the fear of crime.

In a final section, we step outside the domain of gender and consider other ways in which deceptive responding may affect the results of surveys which investigate the fear of crime.

Deceptive responding

Deceptive responding occurs when, independently of their experienced fear levels, respondents are motivated (consciously or unconsciously) to report either high or low levels of fear. To some extent, this process decouples the lived-reality of anxiety about crime and reported fear levels, causing reported fear levels to be higher or lower than they otherwise would be. The motives that people might have to present their fears in a certain light can be considered under the umbrella of *impression management* (Goffman 1959). Much of the time, people desire the approval of others and want to be liked (Leary and Baumeister 2000). Thus, for much of the time, many people strive to portray themselves as likeable, decent, and competent, and avoid portraying themselves as deviant. In surveys, this results in *social desirability bias*, where respondents' answers are skewed by the human desire to foster a particular impression of themselves in others (Tourangeau *et al.* 2000). Deceptive responding in surveys can therefore be seen as a special case of the impression management that is ubiquitous in everyday life. We reiterate that in many cases, participants whose answers are distorted by deceptive responding will not be aware of their impression management motives, nor the impact of those motives on their responses. Indeed, research suggests that an element of self-deception regularly accompanies the provision of distorted responses to others (Paulhus 1991).

Researchers, unless they take account of the possibility of deceptive responding, are bound by theories of measurement, and statistical procedures, to interpret reported fear levels as 'signal plus noise' (Paulhus 1991; Schwarz *et al.* 1998). In this schema, the 'signal' is the respondents' true fear level, and everything else is essentially 'random noise' that causes non-systematic fluctuations in reported fear. Deceptive responding, however, threatens to violate this assumption because it is capable of shifting reported levels of fear upward or downward in a systematic, non-random fashion.

In particular, serious problems arise from deceptive responding when it is related to a third variable, such as gender or political preference. For example, suppose that right-wingers presented themselves as afraid of crime, or men presented themselves as unafraid of crime. Researchers who trust in the fidelity of respondents' answers, assuming any 'measurement error' to be random, may be led to conclude that right-wingers are more afraid of crime than left-wingers, and women are more afraid of crime than men: *even if there are, in fact, no differences in the levels of fear privately experienced by those groups.*

Similarly, the notion of deceptive responding does not entail that any individual respondent provides responses that are demonstrably at odds with their experiences of fear. The intensity of such emotions are not arranged conveniently on the 'very fearful', 'quite fearful' etc. codes commonly offered to respondents. Respondents, unless they refuse to answer the question, are therefore required to engage in an informal, imprecise conceptual mapping of their experiences to the responses that are available to them. In order to do this, they are inevitably required to cast their minds back to situations that they may not recall very clearly and across which their thoughts and feelings about crime may have varied widely (Farrall *et al.* 2006: 7–8). Respondents are not helped greatly by common survey practices. For example, prior research has suggested that closed-ended fear of crime questions (when compared to open-ended questions) may consistently produce higher levels of fear (Farrall *et al.* 1997: 671; Yin 1982), in keeping with research on other topics (for example Belson 1986, on confectionary purchase). Even when confronted with simple yes/no questions, respondents need to decide whether these thoughts and feelings qualify as 'fear', 'anxiety', 'apprehension' or whatever the question asks them about.

When responses on a longer, graded n-point scale are required, respondents need to decide how much is 'very much', how rarely is 'hardly ever', and so on. Of course, qualifiers such as these leave a lot of room for interpretation. Thus, even very biased respondents may be entitled to believe that their responses are accurate reflections of their own experience. Who – whether researchers, or their critics – is to say that an individual's responses are wrong? Probably, it would be fairer to say that a spectrum of possible responses is permitted by the imprecise relation of the response format to private experience, and that responses will tend to gravitate to the end of the spectrum that facilitates individuals' impression management goals. This process, perhaps, is more akin to putting a particular 'spin' on the truth than actually telling mistruths. By analogy, respondents may have imperfect access to the 'true' number of sexual partners they have had, because of definitional ambiguity and imperfect memory. This uncertainty gives them leeway to report a self-serving estimate that does not necessarily conflict with their sincere understanding of the correct number (Tourangeau *et al.* 2000: 234).

In sum, deceptive responding in fear of crime surveys may, but need not be, dishonest. It need not even be demonstrably false. Simply, it is responding that is influenced, independently of the levels of fear that people privately experience, by their motivation (deliberate or otherwise) to cast themselves in a certain light. Given that deceptive responding implies neither deceit nor even falsity, how can we tell when respondents are doing it? How can be quantify its effects? Without a method for doing this, the concept of deceptive responding would contribute only an unhelpful – and unsubstantiated – caveat that inevitably, but ineffably, data from fear of crime surveys cannot be trusted. Another, related question is what, if any, potentially misleading conclusions has deceptive responding generated? With the hope of providing some answers to these questions, we turn now to our recent research on the role of socially desirable responding in the observed gender differences in reported fear of crime.

Deceptive responding in fear of crime surveys: The case of gender

Across a wide variety of survey and interview methods, women, in general, report higher levels of fear than do men (Hale 1996: 96–100). In contrast to this gender difference in reported fear, men appear to be more likely, objectively, to become the victims of many of these crimes (for reviews see Goodey 1997; Hale 1996; Sutton and Farrall 2005). This apparent discrepancy has been termed the 'risk-fear' or 'victimisation-fear' paradox (for example, Smith and Torstensson 1997). For some years, this paradox stumped criminologists, and became just another of the bewildering findings from this body of work. However, one possible explanation for this paradox refers to the possibility of deceptive responding in surveys and open-ended interviews. Stereotypically, men are expected to experience lower levels of fear, in part because emotional vulnerability is not readily compatible with traditional notions of masculinity (Bem 1981; Goodey 1997). For this reason it has been suggested that men may 'downplay' their fear of crime in surveys and interviews (Goodey 1997; Hale 1996; Stanko and Hobdell 1993). The characteristics of hegemonic masculinity are seen to prevent, inhibit or discourage men from disclosing their fears and consequently boys learn from an early age to hide their feelings of vulnerability (see also Gadd and Jefferson, Chapter 8, in this book). On the other hand, reporting heightened levels of fear of crime is likely to be less problematic for women. Indeed, some degree of fear may be entirely consistent with more traditional femininities, and may be expected and even rewarded in certain contexts (for example, Bem 1981; Brownmiller 1975; see also Rudman and Fairchild 2004).

Theoretically, therefore, we have a case in which deceptive responding may have had a material impact on the results of fear of crime surveys, potentially misleading researchers into the conclusion that women are more fearful than men. Sutton and Farrall (2005) attempted to explore this possibility so by using a so-called 'lie scale' (Barrrett and Eysenck 1992), designed to measure the extent to which each participant is providing socially desirable, but less than candid, responses. Lie scales ask participants to indicate whether statements like 'I have never stolen anything' and 'I don't gossip about other people's business' are true for themselves. The more implausible but superficially desirable responses each participant provides, the more the researcher can be confident that he or she is providing distorted responses with the aim of creating a good impression.

Sutton and Farrall's (2005) results showed that men who scored highly on lie scales reported significantly *lower* levels of fear of crime. This suggested that men who were more concerned to distort their answers to conform to perceived social expectations were more likely to downplay (that is, under-report) their fears. In contrast, women's lie scores were unrelated to their reported fear levels. These findings suggest that at least some of the tendency for men to report lower levels of crime than women stems from a social desirability bias. Further, using statistical regression Sutton and Farrall (2005) showed that men who score zero on the lie scale would be expected to report *more* fear than similarly honest women. These findings therefore promised to resolve the victimisation-fear paradox insofar by showing that it is likely to depend on asymmetries in socially desirable responding.

One limitation of Sutton and Farrall's (2005) research concerns the drawbacks associated with lie scales. For example, scores on lie scales tend to conflate deceptive responding with self-deception, (low) social skills, and a chronic desire to please, which has been characterised as a variable in its own right (McCrae and Costa, 1983; see also Paulhus, 1991). Further, because Sutton and Farrall (2005) employed a correlational, cross-sectional research design, we cannot be sure that reported fear of crime was really the outcome of deceptive responding. Perhaps, men who are fearful are motivated to be honest; perhaps some other, unmeasured third cause produces a spurious correlation between lie scale and fear scores.

Further research conducted by Sutton *et al.* (2007) does much to alleviate these methodological concerns. Rather than relying on a lie scale, they assigned men and women, at random, one of two 'instructional sets'. In the 'honest' set of instructions, respondents were asked to provide totally honest and accurate responses to the fear of crime questions that follow. In the 'fake good' instructions, respondents were asked to provide responses that cast them in a favourable light. Manipulations of instructional set are commonly used to validate scales of measurement – ideally, response scales, and relationships between them, should be unaffected by such manipulations (Scandell and Wlazelek 1999; Martin *et al.* 2002; Zickar and Robie 1999).

As it turned out, Sutton *et al.* (2007) observed a statistically significant effect of instructional set for both men and women. As expected, the 'fake good' instruction caused men to minimise their fears relative to those reported under 'be honest' instructions. In contrast, the 'fake good' instruction caused women to *exaggerate* their fears relative to women given the 'be honest' instructions. The results therefore extended Sutton and Farrall's (2005) findings by showing that gender differences in reports of fear of crime may emerge because of gender-typified, deceptive responding by women as well as by men. Deceptive responding may have been detectable among women in the Sutton *et al.* (2007) study simply because the effects of the instructional set manipulation on reported fear were much stronger than were the associations between lying and fear that were observed by Sutton and Farrall (2005). Crucially, Sutton *et al*. (2007) also extended their previous research by showing that it is possible to uncover the effects of deceptive responding without having to rely on correlations between reported fear and lie scales.

This line of research has therefore shown that there is at least one case in which deceptive responding can indeed be deceptive in the sense that it has the capacity to lead researchers into inaccurate conclusions. Specifically, deceptive responding may account for or at least augment the observed gender difference in fear of crime. It has also shown that lie scales and instructional set manipulations can be used to detect deceptive responding and determine its impact on the results of fear of crime surveys.

Nonetheless, the studies by Sutton and his colleagues assume that gendered deceptive responding is driven by a stereotype that women are more fearful than men. The logic is that men downplay fears because they intuitively, and perhaps unconsciously, fear the social 'backlash' that often accompanies violations of gender stereotypes. Women are assumed to exaggerate their fears for the same reason. However, there is no empirical evidence that people really do believe that women are more fearful than men, and therefore think that their responses might conform to or deviate from gender type. So, an important question about the antecedent conditions of this form of deceptive responding remains unanswered.

Also remaining unanswered is an important question about the consequences of men's reluctance to disclose fear, versus women's willingness, or even eagerness, to do so. Theoretically, this gender difference in the communication of fear is not confined to the context of surveys: it reflects basic principles of gender roles, enshrined in pervasive cultural practices (for example, Goodey 1997). Therefore, men are likely to impression manage in everyday settings by minimising their fears, whereas women are not (Sutton and Farrall 2005). Indeed, when women do engage in deceptive responding, it appears that they may exaggerate rather than minimise their fear (Sutton *et al*. 2007). Just as deceptive responding in surveys leads to a misrepresentation of the extent to which fear is gendered, impression management in everyday life may lead lay people, who attribute emotions to others based on what they see them do and hear them say, to infer that gender differences in fear are larger than they really are. In short, if the deceptive responding we have seen operating in surveys reflects a broader pattern of impression management in everyday life, we would expect to see that respondents subscribe to exaggerated stereotypes of gender differences.

These untested hypotheses suggest the possibility of a positive feedback loop (see also Giddens 1984 on the double hermeneutic). Based on a stereotype that men are fearless and women fearful, males are reluctant to display or disclose their fears, whereas women are encouraged to do so. This gendered form of impression management reinforces the popular stereotype, because men are essentially acting fearless and women fearful. In the next section, we report initial tests of these hypotheses that we have conducted with a small community sample.

Empirically investigating gender stereotypes in the fear of crime

The respondents recruited were 50 men and 43 women customers of a high street café in Canterbury, England, with an average age of 40.36 years (SD = 13.79). Their participation was solicited by a female employee of the café.[2] Respondents were handed a questionnaire to complete at their tables, and did so anonymously. In this questionnaire, as in the survey by Sutton *et al.* (2007), respondents were asked 10 questions about their own fear of crime: how much they think about, and how afraid they are of, robbery, assault, sexual assault, vandalism, and burglary. They responded on much the same five-point scale as used in previous investigations (1 = not at all; 5 = all of the time: cf Sutton and Farrall 2005; Sutton *et al.* 2007). Respondents were asked to answer the same questions as if they were 'the average male', and as if they were 'the average female'. They therefore answered 30 questions in total. We took the mean of each block of 10 responses and subjected it to statistical analysis. These means are presented in Table 7.1.

We conducted a mixed-design analysis of variance (ANOVA) to detect differences in the fear levels attributed to the self, men, and women by male and female participants. The two factors in this ANOVA were the gender of *respondents* (men, women), and the *target* to whom fear was attributed (self, average male, average female). The ANOVA revealed a large main effect of target: ignoring for a moment the gender of respondents, very different levels of fear were attributed to the self, to males generally, and to females generally, $F(2, 182) = 144.65, p < .001$. The effect size statistic, η^2, was .61, showing that this effect accounted for fully 61 per cent of the variance in attributed fear of crime. When we average across men and women, we see that respondents attributed much more fear to the average female than to the average male, $p < .001$. This provides strong and direct evidence of the existence of a stereotype that women experience more fear than men. Respondents, regardless of their own gender, also attributed more fear to the average female than to themselves, $p < .001$. In contrast, respondents attribute roughly as much fear to themselves as to the average male, $p = .10$.

The main effect of target was qualified by a significant interaction between the gender of respondents and target, $F(2, 182) = 12.52, p < .001$, $\eta^2 = .12$. We unpacked this interaction with a limited selection of planned comparisons. The first of these planned comparisons compared the personal levels of fear reported by men and women. This showed that men reported lower levels of personal fear than women did $p < .005$, replicating the widely observed gender difference. Crucially, a further pair of planned comparisons

Table 7.1 Fear of crime levels in men, women, and the self, according to respondents

	Target to whom fear levels are attributed		
	Self	Average male	Average female
Men	1.77	1.94	3.13
(n = 50)	(0.62)	(0.63)	(0.66)
Women	2.16	1.77	2.83
(n = 43)	(0.68)	(0.68)	(0.64)
Total	1.95	1.86	2.99
(n = 93)	(0.68)	(0.65)	(0.66)

verified that both men, $p < .001$, and women, $p < .001$, attributed higher levels of fear to the average female than to the average male. Therefore, the stereotype of female fearfulness appears to be endorsed by both genders.

We conducted a final set of planned comparisons to get a preliminary indication of whether respondents' beliefs about the gendered nature of fear of crime were accurate. These planned comparisons contrast the fear levels that respondents attribute to the average male and female with the fear levels reported by men and women respectively.

The first comparison showed that men attributed much greater fear levels to the average female than women in the survey reported experiencing personally, $p < .001$. On the other hand, men's estimates of the fear of crime experienced by the average male were not significantly different from the personal fear that they reported, $p = .083$. These results suggest that whereas men may overestimate the fear of crime among females, they have a fairly accurate understanding of the extent to which males fear crime. For their part, women appeared to share this exaggerated stereotype of female fear. Specifically, they attributed higher levels of fear to the average female than they reported experiencing themselves, $p < .001$. Women also seemed to share the apparently accurate perception of male fear, attributing the same level of fear to the average male that men reported experiencing, $p = .901$.

In sum, the present investigation confirms the tendency for men to report lower fear of crime than women. Further, it reveals that men and women share a consensus that females are much more fearful than males. This result provides the first evidence of the gender stereotype that has been assumed to underlie the tendency for men to minimise and women to, if anything, exaggerate their fears (Sutton and Farrall 2005; Sutton *et al.* 2007). Further, results suggest that the 'feminine fear' stereotype endorsed by our respondents exaggerates the reality. In particular, respondents attributed much greater levels of fear to the average female than women actually reported experiencing themselves. This result is consistent with our hypothesis that the gender bias in willingness to disclose fears creates an exaggerated popular impression that women are fearful and men fearless. Therefore, the results together suggest that the positive feedback loop we have postulated might operate, whereby gender stereotypes regarding the fear of crime effectively perpetuate themselves by influencing how men and women present their fears.

There are, of course, some interpretive caveats that must be attached to this study. First, it employed a small convenience sample and as a result there can be no guarantee that the levels of fear reported by respondents accurately reflect the level of fear in the wider population. Clearly, replication with larger, more representative samples is required before we can regard these findings as definitive. That said, the levels of fear reported by men and women in the present investigation, M(males) = 1.77, M(females) = 2.16 respectively, are broadly comparable to those in previous investigations using the same response scale. For example, in a Strathclyde sample, Sutton and Farrall (2005) reported $M = 2.30$ for men and $M = 2.53$ for women; in a sample of county council customers in the market town of Leek, Staffordshire, Sutton et al. (2007) observed Ms of 1.62 and 2.04 respectively. In contrast, the level of fear that our present respondents attributed to the average female, at 2.99, is considerably higher than the values that any sample of women has reported experiencing.

A second caveat is that our present study assumes, in practice, that the levels of fear which respondents report are accurate. Of course, we have strong theoretical and now empirical grounds to doubt the veracity of these reports. However, we do not think that this can fully account for key aspects of our findings. Women do not minimise their fears (Sutton and Farrall 2005); under some circumstances, they may even exaggerate them (Sutton et al. 2007). Therefore, it is highly unlikely that in the present study, women downplayed their own fears, and that such minimisation was responsible for respondents' attribution of higher levels of fear to the average female than women reported themselves.

Discussion: Adventures in deceptive responding

The fear of crime is a concept of too much social and theoretical significance for social scientists to ignore. Unfortunately however, empirical approaches to the concept are fraught with the kind of problems that are associated with the study of mental and emotional states – that is, of 'other minds' (cf Ryle 1949). One of the key problems is the unreliability of people's reports of these states. Our investigations thus far suggest that deceptive responding may be responsible for the appearance of an illusory, or at least exaggerated, gender difference in research on the fear of crime.

Deceptive responding therefore appears to be a serious problem for fear of crime scholars. However, it is, at least, a problem that we can detect and quantify. Researchers who suspect that the relationship between a given variable and fear crime may be an artefact of deceptive responding can confirm or disconfirm their suspicions by using lie scales or instructional set manipulations in the way that we have done with gender. Also, there are established procedures for reducing the impact of deceptive responding. For example, in the 'bogus pipeline' technique, respondents are led to believe that researchers have direct access to their 'real' attitudes, through for example a piece of biometric equipment or through carefully designed survey questions. Under these conditions, respondents are more willing to report socially unacceptable attitudes and behaviours (see Sutton and Farrall 2005: Appendix, for other suggestions). Even emphasising the importance of honesty and accuracy in responding to a greater extent than is usual, as in the 'be honest' instructions of Sutton *et al.* (2007), appears to alleviate the problem: under those instructions, the gender difference in fear of crime all but disappeared.

Also, deceptive responding is not *just* a problem. The study of this phenomenon promises to lead to a deeper understanding of the dynamic between the private *experience* of the fear of crime, overt *expressions* of fear of crime, the public *idea* of the fear of crime, and wider social and political processes. Thus far, for example, we have focused on how men and women provide gender-typified responses to fear of crime questions when setting out to create a positive impression of themselves (this being measured in Sutton and Farrall 2005, and manipulated in Sutton *et al.* 2007). However, trying to come across well is not the only motive underlying impression management (cf Goffman 1959). In the domain of fear of crime specifically, it is likely that there are a number of value-expressive, instrumental, and even political reasons for deceptive responding.

In this regard, consider the following thought experiment. There has been some public debate about whether to invest more resources in policing in your immediate area. You receive a knock on your door and are asked a number of fear of crime questions. Are you likely to understate or overstate your fears, with self-interest at stake? How reluctant are you going to be to talk about the occasions on which you have, in fact, felt concerned, apprehensive or intimidated? Imagine, however, some months later that you are selling your house, and talking to potential buyers who are new to the area. They ask you about how safe you have felt in the neighbourhood. Now how likely are you to overstate your fears?

In a study analogous to this thought experiment, Braginsky and Braginsky (1967) showed that institutionalised schizophrenics presented themselves as high-functioning when they believed they were being interviewed for a place in an open ward reserved for high-functioning patients. However, when they believed the purpose of an interview was to decide whether they were to be released into the community – generally an unattractive prospect for these chronically institutionalised people – they presented themselves as low-functioning. Notably, these patients, whose social skills we might reasonably expect to be impaired by their condition and by the conditions of their life, were largely successful in convincing a panel of psychiatrists.

This illustration shows that at least, in principle, respondents may have other reasons than the desire to look good to cast their fear of crime in a particular light. Individuals may report low or high levels of crime to pursue their economic and political self-interest, which in some circumstances might require that they boost the image of their neighbourhood, and in others that they acquire more policing resources for it. Further, because crime appears to function as a neo-Durkheimian symbol of social dysfunction (Jackson and Sunshine, 2007), people may be motivated to report high levels of fear as a form of protest against the prevailing social order: be it the condition of housing and public amenities in a local area, or the economic, penal, and immigration policies of national government. These kinds of political motivations are likely to be especially strong in an era of declining faith and participation in electoral democracy. In short, respondents may see fear of surveys as a rare opportunity to make themselves heard, not just on the topic of crime but on society as a whole. The role of these political motivations in deceptive responding may be experimentally examined, by presenting the social or political function of a survey in different ways to different respondents. In light of the logic above, for example, we would expect to see higher levels of fear reported in a survey with the ostensible title 'Local Policing and Crime', than, say, 'Estate Agents' Neighbourhood Desirability Survey'.

Of course, the fear of crime, and in particular, the public representation of fear of crime, is politically loaded in other ways (Lee 2007). In radio interview on 25 November 2004, David Blunkett, who was at the time the UK's Home Secretary, defended his criminal justice policies from the charge that they were eroding civil liberties by arguing that they were designed to secure 'freedom from fear' for the public (Blunkett 2004). In this way, authoritarian social policies often seem to be justified by the claim that they lighten the burden of fear – fear of crime, fear of terrorism – on the populace. It seems that not just people's reports of their own fears, but the fears they attribute to others, are of tremendous political importance. Individuals who support authoritarian politics are more likely therefore to attribute fear of crime to the public in general, including social groups to which they may or may not belong themselves. We see here an exciting possibility to extend the line of research we initiated in this chapter, where respondents are asked to indicate not just their own fears but those of women and men (for an example in a related area of research, see Sutton *et al*, 2008). Do authoritarians – especially in surveys they believe to be 'public' or otherwise to have some impact on social policy – attribute high levels of fear to others? Do liberals ascribe low levels of fear? Theoretically, the notion of deceptive responding, and more generally of impression management, suggests that people may 'spin' their own and others' fears for political purposes. This biased 'fear talk' may affect the public's understanding of the levels of fear experienced overall and by certain demographics in particular. Public perceptions of high (or low) fear levels may create pressure to tighten or relax crime policies.

On this note, it is worth taking some time to refine our concept of deceptive responding in light of Jackson and his colleagues' related concept of 'expressive' fear (Jackson 2004; Jackson and Sunshine 2007; Farrall *et al.* 2006). Expressive fear refers to expressions of fear that, rather than being directly related to individuals' emotional experience, constitute an outlet for concerns with threat to underlying values, such as social cohesion. Such expressions might be seen as a variety of deceptive responding, because they constitute a case in which respondents are motivated to report high levels of fear independently of the levels of fear that they experience. However, the concept of expressive fear seems to us to have theoretical corollaries that we have not explored here in relation to deceptive responding. For example, whereas we have characterised deceptive responding as an essentially communicative process, designed consciously or unconsciously to influence others, expressive fear may also serve an important intrapsychic function, independently of whom respondents think will have access to their answers. So, expressive fear may be a cathartic outlet for emotions that are not driven by anxiety about crime *per se* but about the overall condition of society. Further, expressive fear may allow respondents to reaffirm their values and identities, regardless of the consequences for how others view them. Theoretically, we believe there is much potential in working towards further explication, and perhaps eventually, integration of these concepts, both of which refer to systematic variations in reported fear from experienced fear. Empirically, a fruitful line of investigation might be to investigate how reports of fear vary when the motives to express and affirm one's values, versus create an impression in others, vary orthogonally (for example, where antecedents of value-expressive and impression-management oriented deceptive responding are measured or manipulated independently).

Before we conclude, we would like to tease out an implication of our work thus far for social processes that extend beyond the fear of crime. In particular, the concept of deceptive responding, and the methods we have demonstrated to detect it, appear to demonstrate that it is possible to catch respondents in the act of 'doing gender' (West and Zimmerman 1983). In its most general form, our hypothesis suggests that men and women will tend to enact gender-typed behaviour when they are conscious of being evaluated and keen to make a good impression. This entails that under the right conditions, gendered impression management, and therefore deceptive responding, may occur with respect to other gender-typed traits such as aggression, emotionality, assertiveness, achievement orientation, and nurturance (see Prentice and Carranza 2002, for an inventory of such traits).

Going further, we have already suggested one mechanism by which gender differences in deceptive responding may perpetuate gender stereotypes regarding the fear of crime in a kind of positive feedback loop. Specifically, in response to a stereotype that males are less fearful, males are more reluctant than women to overtly express fear, which reinforces the gender stereotype, and so on. There is another important psychological mechanism by which deceptive responding may result in a positive feedback loop. A number of experiments have shown that individuals tend to internalise representations of themselves that initially were purely strategic 'acts', put on with impression management goals in mind. For example, after being instructed in experiments to temporarily act in an extroverted, depressed, or self-confident manner, people tend to see themselves in those terms, and even continue to behave in that fashion well after the instructions have relapsed (for example, Jones *et al.* 1981; Schlenker and Trudeau 1990; Tice 1992).

Over time, therefore, the distinction between the authentic private self and the strategic public façade may therefore dissolve. In the case of fear of crime, this raises an intriguing chicken-and-egg problem that is not easily resolved empirically, and which urges interpretive caution about apparent gender differences. Imagine, for example, that research in the coming years shows definitively that some of the gender difference in reported fear of crime reflects a difference in the intensity of fear that is genuinely experienced. Even in this case, we could not exclude the possibility that men and women's fears may have become different because, throughout their lives, and through the generations, they have been doing gender when talking about and enacting their fears.

In this chapter, we have introduced the concept of deceptive responding and have explored its relevance to the socially and scientifically important topic of fear of crime. Deceptive responding presents a profound challenge to researchers, but also presents a number of exciting opportunities to examine the social forces which affect how the fear of crime is strategically represented, and in turn, the social ramifications of these representations. In short, we believe that it is well worth 'untangling the web', or perhaps more accurately the webs, spun by respondents who engage in deceptive responding.

Notes

1 We use the word 'motivate' herein not to refer to consciously driven goals or desires, but to unconscious drives as well – see our discussion below.
2 We thank Amy Molineux for her assistance in collecting these data.

References

Bargh, JA, and Chartrand, TL (1999) 'The unbearable automaticity of being', *American Psychologist*, 54: 462–79.

Barrett, PT, and Eysenck, SB (1992) 'Predicting EPQR full scale scores from the short form version', *Personality and Individual Differences*, 13: 851–3.

Belson, WA (1986) *Validity in Survey Research*, Aldershot: Gower Publishing.

Bem, SL (1981) 'Gender schema theory: A cognitive account of sex typing', *Psychological Review*, 88: 354–64.

Blunkett, D (2004) 'Today', BBC Radio 4, 25 November, available at www.bbc.co.uk/radio4/today/listenagain/zthursday_20041125.shtml (accessed 28 August 2007).

Braginsky, BM and Braginsky, DD (1967) 'Schizophrenic patients in the psychiatric interview: An experimental study of the manipulative tactics of mental patients', *Journal of Consulting Psychology*, 31: 543–7.

Brownmiller, S (1975) *Against Our Will: Men, Women, and Rape*, London: Secker and Warburg.

Chomsky, N (1967) 'A review of BF Skinner's *Verbal Behavior*', in LA Jakobovits and MS Miron (eds), *Readings in the Psychology of Language*, New York: Prentice Hall, pp 142–3.

Deaux, K and Lafrance, M (1998) 'Gender', in ST Fiske, DT Gilbert and G Lindzey (eds), *The Handbook of Social Psychology*, vol 1, 4th edn, New York: McGraw-Hill, pp 788–827.

Descartes, R (1637/1960) *Discourse On Method and Other Writings*, London: Penguin.

Dodd, T, Nicholas, S, Povey, D, and Walker, A (2004) *Crime in England and Wales 2003/2004*, Home Office Statistical Bulletin, 10/04. London.

Farrall, S (2004) 'Revisiting crime surveys: Emotional responses without emotions', *International Journal of Social Research Methodology*, 7(2): 157–71.

Farrall, S, and Gadd, D (2004) 'Research note: The frequency of the fear of crime', *British Journal of Criminology*, 44: 127–32.

Farrall, S, Bannister, J, Ditton, J, and Gilchrist, E (1997) 'Questioning the measurement of the "fear of crime": Findings from a major methodological study', *British Journal of Criminology*, 37(4): 658–79.

Farrall, S, Gray, E. and Jackson, J (2007) *Combining the New and Old Measures of the Fear of Crime: Exploring the 'Worried Well'*, Working Paper No. 4, ESRC Grant RES 000 23 1108.

Farrall, S, Jackson, J. and Gray, E (2006) *Everyday Emotion and the Fear of Crime: Preliminary Findings from 'Experience and Expression'*, Working Paper No. 1, ESRC Grant RES 000 23 1108.

Forgas, JP, Williams, KD, and Laham, SM (eds) (2005) *Social Motivation: Conscious and Unconscious Processes*, New York: Cambridge University Press.

Förster, J, Liberman, N, and Friedman, RS (2007) 'Seven principles of goal activation: A systematic approach to distinguishing goal priming from priming of non-goal constructs', *Personality and Social Psychology Review*, 11: 211–33.

Giddens, A (1984) *The Constitution of Society*, London: Polity Press.

Goffman, I (1959) *The Presentation of Self in Everyday Life*, Garden City, NY: Doubleday.

Goodey, J (1997) '"Boys don't cry": Masculinities, fear of crime and fearlessness', *British Journal of Criminology*, 37(3): 401–18.

Hale, C (1996) 'Fear of crime: A review of the literature', *International Review of Victimology*, 4: 79–150.

Harris, R (1969) *The Fear of Crime*, New York: Praeger.

Heider, F (1958) *The Psychology of Interpersonal Relations*. New York: Wiley.

Jackson, J (2004) 'Experience and expression: Social and cultural signficance in the fear of crime', *British Journal of Criminology*, 44: 946–66.

Jackson, J and Sunshine, J (2007) 'Public confidence in policing: A neo-Durkheimian perspective', *British Journal of Criminology*, 47: 214–33.

Jones, EE, Rhodewalt, F, Berglas, S and Skelton, JA (1981) 'Effects of strategic self presentation on subsequent self-esteem', *Journal of Personality and Social Psychology*, 41: 407–21.

Leary, MR and Baumeister, RF (2000) 'The nature and function of self-esteem: Sociometer theory', in MP Zanna (ed), *Advances in Experimental Social Psychology*, vol 32, San Diego, CA: Academic Press, pp 1–62.

Lee, M (2007) *Inventing Fear of Crime*, Collompton: Willan Publishing.

Loo, D and Grimes, R-E (2004) 'Polls, politics and crime: the "law and order" issue of the 1960s', *Western Criminology Review*, 5(1): 50–67.

McCrae, RR and Costa, PT (1983) 'Social desirability scales: More substance than style', *Journal of Consulting and Clinical Psychology*, 51: 882–8.

Martin, BA, Bowen, CC and Hunt, ST (2002) 'How effective are people at faking on personality questionnaires?', *Personality and Individual Differences*, 30: 247–56.

Page, B, Wake, R and Ames, A (2004) *Public Confidence in the Criminal Justice System: Home Office Findings*, Home Office Statistical Bulletin, 221, London.

Paulhus, D (1991) 'Measurement and control of response bias', in JP Robinson, PR Shaver and LS Wrightsman (eds), *Measures of Personality and Social Psychological Attitudes*, San Diego, CA: Academic Press, pp 17–59.

Prentice, DA and Carranza, E (2002) 'What women should be, shouldn't be, are allowed to be, and don't have to be: The contents of prescriptive gender stereotypes', *Psychology of Women Quarterly*, 26: 269–81.

Rudman, LA and Fairchild, K (2004) 'Reactions to counterstereotypic behavior: The role of backlash in cultural stereotype maintenance', *Journal of Personality and Social Psychology*, 87: 157–76.

Ryle, G (1949) *The Concept of Mind*, Harmondsworth: Penguin.

Sanchez, DT and Crocker, J (2005) 'Why investment in gender ideals affects well-being: The role of external contingencies of self-worth', *Psychology of Women Quarterly*, 29: 63–77.

Scandell, DJ and Wlazelek, B (1999) 'The relationship between self-perceived personality and impression management on the NEO-FFI', *Personality and Individual Differences*, 27: 147–54.

Schlenker, BR and Trudeau, JV (1990) 'Impact of self-presentations on private self-beliefs: Effects of prior self-beliefs and misattribution', *Journal of Personality and Social Psychology*, 58: 22–32.

Schwarz, N, Groves, RM and Schuman, H (1998) 'Survey methods', in DT Gilbert, ST Fiske and L Gardner (eds), *The handbook of social psychology*, vol 1, 4th edn, New York: McGraw Hill, pp 143–79.

Skinner, BF (1965) *Science and Human Behavior*, New York: Free Press.

Smith, WR and Torstensson, M (1997) 'Gender differences in risk perception and neutralizing fear of crime: Toward resolving the paradoxes', *British Journal of Criminology*, 37(4): 608–29.

Snedker, KA (2006) 'Altruistic and vicarious fear of crime: Fear for others and gendered social roles', *Sociological Forum*, 21: 163–95.

Stanko, EA and Hobdell, K (1993) 'Assault on men: Masculinity and male victimization', *British Journal of Criminology*, 33(3): 400–15.

Sutton, RM and Farrall, SD (2005) 'Gender, socially desirable responding and the fear of crime: Are women really more anxious about crime?', *British Journal of Criminology*, 45: 212–24.

Sutton, RM and McClure, J (2001) 'Covariational influences on goal-based explanation: An integrative model', *Journal of Personality and Social Psychology*, 80: 222–36.

Sutton, RM, Douglas, KM, Wilkin, K, Elder, TJ and Cole, JM (2008) 'Justice for whom, exactly? Beliefs in justice for the self and various others', *Personality and Social Psychology Bulletin*, 38: 528–41.

Sutton, RM, Robinson, B and Farrall, SD (2007) 'How men and women 'fake good' on fear of crime surveys: An experimental investigation', manuscript submitted for publication.

Tice, DM (1992) 'Self-concept change and self-presentation: The looking glass self is also a magnifying glass', *Journal of Personality and Social Psychology*, 63: 435–51.

Tourangeau, R, Rips, L and Rasinski, K (2000) *The psychology of survey response*, Cambridge: Cambridge University Press.

Warr, M and Stafford, MC (1983) 'Fear of victimization: A look at the proximate causes', *Social Forces*, 61: 1033–43.

West, C and Zimmerman, DH (1983) 'Doing gender', *Gender and Society*, 1: 125–51.

Wilson, TD, Lindsey, S and Schooler, TY (2000) 'A model of dual attitudes', *Psychological Review*, 107: 101–26.

Woldoff, RA (2006) 'Emphasizing fear of crime in models of neighborhood social disorganization', *Crime Prevention and Community Safety*, 8: 228–47.

Yin, P (1982) 'Fear of crime as a problem for the elderly', *Social Problems*, 30(2): 240–5.

Zickar, MJ and Robie, C (1999) 'Modeling faking good on personality items: An item-level analysis', *Journal of Applied Psychology*, 84(4): 551–63.

Chapter 8

Anxiety, defensiveness and the fear of crime

David Gadd and Tony Jefferson

How scared are we?

(*Guardian2* headline, 13 February 2003)

It's a panic for sure. But it's a calm panic
Since the [US] government issued its guidelines for families to prepare a 'disaster supply kit' in case of chemical, biological or nuclear attack ... the nation's DIY shops have become the epicentre for a wave of subdued but nonetheless palpable panic ... 'We've had three times the amount of business we normally have in a day', said Bill Hart, at a hardware store in Bethesda, Maryland.

(*The Guardian*, 14 February 2003)

Public blind to fall in crime
The crime rate in England and Wales is falling again but most people do not believe it, according to the latest Home Office figures. The results of the British Crime Survey, published yesterday, suggested that crime fell by 9% during 2002 ... The BCS ... shows that the risk of becoming a victim of crime fell slightly, from 28% in 2001 to 26% in 2002 ... Nevertheless, the results show a sharp rise in the number who believe crime is getting worse in England and Wales: the proportion rose from 56% in 2001 to 71% last year.

(*The Guardian*, 5 April 2003)

Open any daily newspaper on almost any day and the chances are you will find an article related to the 'fear of crime'. In the wake of September 11, such articles are probably on the increase. Some, like the first *Guardian* article quoted above will try to assess, in the words of its headline, 'How scared are we?'. Others, like the second quotation, seem to recognise the issue of overreaction. Still others, like the final quotation, draw attention to the disjunction between fear and risk – in this case to the fact that despite the falling crime rate in England and Wales increasing numbers of people 'believe crime is getting worse'. What these and other similar articles reveal, if nothing else, is that the issue of the fear of crime is more complex than might appear at first sight. Our intention is to show how and why our present knowledge of the topic is so muddled, and what is necessary to clarify matters. The latter point involves showing how the adoption of a psychosocial approach to the topic manages to do this.

The articles featured above could be said to be operating at either the level of the individual – asking how scared we are or exploring the disjunction between an individual's risk and an individual's fear – or at the level of the social, that is, as contributions to public discourses about fear of crime. With this distinction in mind, we aim to approach the topic both in terms of what is known about the *fearful individual*, and of what is known about the *social meanings of the fear of crime*. Although this may look like a consideration of the matter moving from psychology to sociology, both sorts of approach have been sociological rather than psychological. This is because there has been little interest in the psychology of the fear of crime; only in the social demographic characteristics associated with the fearful individual. The real difference between the two sorts of approach then resides in whether fear is seen as arising from within individuals, albeit individuals who are only of interest as group members: young/old; male/female; black/white, etc., or is seen as a consequence of the way politicians or the media sensationalise particular problems.

Our concern will be to show how neither approach is adequate to the task of understanding fear of crime *fully*, that is, both its socially constructed meanings *and* how particular individuals relate to such meanings. To do so requires transcending this fearful individual/constructed discourse dichotomy psychosocially. This entails both a theoretical and a methodological shift: from fearing individuals as constellations of demographic characteristics to defended subjects; and from decontextualised survey-based information to biographical interviewing designed to illuminate the connections between defended subjectivity and investments in the fearful subject position within fear of crime discourses. We end with case study material designed to exemplify our argument. In this instance, we examine the case of one highly fearful elderly man, showing how the threat of criminal victimisation had become a repository for other anxieties pertaining to his life, and how the positioning of the interviewer functioned, intersubjectively, to inhibit this elderly man's capacity to surmount, however temporarily, his identification with the position of the crime-fearing subject.

What do we know about the fearful individual?

Although there has been a great deal of research into fear of crime – Hale (1996) refers to the presence of over 200 reports, and a recent online search dredged up 837 entries – surprisingly little can be said conclusively about fear of crime.

(Ditton and Farrall 2000: xxi)

Ditton (2000) also suggests that the field is riddled with contradictory findings. Threading through this morass of inconclusive contradictions is what has been called the 'fear-risk paradox' (Hollway and Jefferson, 2000: 12), namely, the tendency for fear and risk (of criminal victimisation) to be inversely related. The most at risk group, young men, tend to be least fearful; whilst women, especially older women, tend to be more fearful than men but less at risk. From the first British Crime Survey (Hough and Mayhew 1983) onwards, this finding has been 'discovered with monotonous regularity' (Gilchrist *et al.* 1998), thus contributing to, if not actually creating, the common stereotype of the old woman too fearful to go out after dark. Given these findings, to the extent that we can conclude anything at all about who is most likely to be fearful of crime, the answer is that the most fearful individuals are those least at risk of becoming victims of crime. How can we explain this paradoxical, apparently irrational, finding?

A start can be made by looking at the way in which this knowledge was produced, namely, by aggregating the answers given by survey respondents to a single, standard question: 'how safe do you or would you feel being out alone in your neighbourhood at night' (Ditton and Farrall 2000: xix), with potential responses confined to 'very safe', 'fairly safe', 'a bit unsafe' or 'very unsafe'. Rather than start with a theoretically informed definition of what fear of crime might be before proceeding to measure it, in producing this standard question crime survey researchers clearly assumed this was unproblematic. As a result, what exactly was being measured is anybody's guess, as various critics have implicitly recognised. Ditton and Farrall (2000: xix), for example, have this to say about the question:

> Kenneth Ferraro and Randy LaGrange [1987]... criticize it (rightly in our opinion) for failing to mention the word 'crime', for relying upon a vague geographical reference, for asking about something they may do very rarely, and for mixing the hypothetical with the real. In addition, we would add that the use of the word 'how' at the start of the question is leading in the extreme.

Hollway and Jefferson (2000: 8–9) are similarly scathing about the question, suggesting that this scenario probably means different things to different people, assumes a consistency to feelings of fear and, in conjuring up a generalised threat not specific fears, may 'be eliciting more about general anxiety than the "fear of crime"'.

In order to demonstrate more generally the symbiotic relationship between survey questions and the knowledge produced, some researchers have tried asking different questions, changing the question order, or even asking the same question more than once in the interview. Each change has produced different results. For example:

One well-known piece of American research showed that if you ask people *which* of these is the most important problem facing this country at present?' and then show them a short list which includes 'crime' as a possibility, 35% will pick crime as the most important problem. But if you ask them, as they did, the open question, *'what* do you think is the most important problem facing this country at present?', and *don't* give them a list to choose from, only 15% will suggest crime. So, 60% of the apparent 'importance' of crime as a problem is created by the way the question is asked.

(Ditton 2000)

The underlying problem clearly rests with the nature of survey research interviews and their Likert scale responses. As a methodology for studying something as complex as fear of crime, it is simply inadequate to the task. Basically, this is because respondents' answers are thoroughly decontextualised: their meanings in relation to either the interview itself or the life world of the interviewee are unsought; their subsequent coding renders them even more abstract. With no knowledge of the situated meanings of the responses being coded and with the coding process adding a new layer of artificiality, the aggregated data, suitably broken down by age, sex, race, area, etc, is then presented as a real world picture of who is and who is not fearful of crime. Small wonder that the results of such research are so inconclusive, contradictory and paradoxical. As Josselson (1995: 32) neatly put it: 'when we aggregate people, treating diversity as error variable, in search of what is common to all, we often learn about what is true of no one in particular'.

If survey-based methodology is responsible for the extraordinary muddled findings about the fear of crime, perhaps a better starting point would be an attempt to define 'fear of crime' *theoretically?* In attempting to do so, we come up against Ditton's (2000) provocative statement that 'fear of crime doesn't exist'. This is not intended to mean that nobody is worried about crime; rather, it is a short hand way of saying that the *meaning* of fear of crime 'doesn't exist' at the individual level. Because meaning is established at the *social* not the *individual* level, we must attend first to the *social* origins of the term. So, if we wish to understand what fear of crime is, we shall need to shift to what is known about the topic at the social level: the social construction of discourses relating to fear of crime.

What do we know about the social construction of the fear of crime?

The fear of crime debate within criminology is dominated by the attempt to produce more accurate measurements of the numbers of fearful individuals. The literature on the social construction of fear is broader, less focussed exclusively on crime and criminal victimisation. Law and order is an issue, but as part of broader processes of politics and change. Examples of such approaches can be found across a wide spectrum of sociological work. We focus on three distinct but related such approaches: Zygmunt Bauman's thesis on the insecurities of postmodernity, the work on moral panics; and Murray Lee's exploration of the discursive origins of the current debate about fear of crime.

Bauman on the insecurities of postmodernity

Bauman argues, broadly, that today individual freedom is evaluated more highly than collective economic security and this produces widespread fear and anxiety:

> [W]hether or not Sigmund Freud was right in suggesting that the trading off of a considerable part of personal liberty for some measure of collectively guaranteed security was the main cause of psychical afflictions and sufferings, unease and anxiety in the 'classic' period of modern civilization – today, in the late or postmodern stage of modernity, it is the opposite tendency, the inclination to trade off a lot of security in exchange for removing more and more constraints cramping the exercise of free choice, which generates the sentiments which seek their outlet (or are being channelled) in the concerns with law and order.
>
> (Bauman 2000: 213)

Bauman's argument is that the trade off between economic security and the desire for free choice, in terms of employment and cultures of consumption, has given rise to pervasive fears and anxieties that find sanctuary in the authoritative interpretation of social ills, most notably, the demand for greater law and order. Bauman goes on to argue that for many of us the sanctuary of our homes – conceived as a kind of 'body-safe extension ... has become the passkey to all doors which must be locked up and sealed' as we find ourselves bereft of safety, security and certainty (Bauman 2000).

Work on moral panics

Stan Cohen (1972) famously started his classic book *Folk Devils and Moral Panics* with a definition of a moral panic. The idea of societies undergoing profound changes being prone, periodically, to overreact to 'old' threats as if they were new and unprecedented, to scapegoat a few to protect threatened ways of life and to call for firm measures, has become, now, a core sociological concept. Hall *et al.* (1978) went on to develop the idea in their book, *Policing the Crisis*, by suggesting that moral panics were part of the political scene when governments were suffering a 'crisis of hegemony' (unable to rule through the routine production of consent). Later, Pearson

(1983) was to use the notion in his book, *Hooligan: A History of Respectable Fears*, to show how moral panics about the 'hooligan' were a regular feature of the social landscape because of the way nostalgia for the 'good old days' vitiated past wrongs and relocated them in certain kinds of contemporary youth.

In each of these examples – and countless other works too numerous to mention – there is a notion of overreaction to an imagined threat of some kind, and a sense that the threat (or 'folk devil') being responded to is being used as a scapegoat for some other issue. Some level of social flux plus the existence of relatively powerless groups who are available for scapegoating, and threatened groups who have sufficient power successfully to label others are all pre-requisites. From this baseline, fear of crime can be understood as a specific variant of this prototype moral panic.

Lee on the discursive origins of fear of crime

Lee's (2001) discursive understanding of the origins of fear of crime is an attempt to trace, specifically, 'the genesis of "fear of crime"'. In a cogently argued piece, Lee concludes that fear of crime, or what he calls, 'a self-sustaining *"fear of crime" feedback loop'*, is a product of the politics of law and order in the US since the 1960s:

> [T]he constitutive discursive elements of fear of crime's genealogy could be listed as – although not exclusive to – the following: the increasing sophistication of statistical inquiry; criminological concern with new forms of crime statistics; the emergence of victim surveys; rising rates of recorded crime in the USA and new attempts to govern this; racialized concerns about 'black rioting'; a particular form of populist political discourse; and a historical moment where the conditions of possibility were such that these seemingly diffuse discourses could converge – the debating and passing of *The Omnibus Crime Control and Safe Streets Act 1968*. All the sites of power/knowledge and the discursive arrangements required to set in train a self-sustaining *'fear of crime' feedback loop* fell into place in the USA at this point in its history, and 'fear of crime' emerged as a legitimate governmental and disciplinary object of calculation, inquiry and regulation.
>
> (Lee 2001: 480; emphases in original)

Lee goes on to say what he means by the term *"fear of crime" feedback loop'*:

> By *'fear of crime' feedback loop*, I mean, inter alia, that the constituent elements I have listed above operate symbiotically to produce and intensify crime fear and the research related to it; that research into

victims produces and maintains the criminological concept of 'fear of crime' quantitatively and discursively; that this information operates to identify fear as a legitimate object of governance or governmental regulation; that the techniques of regulation imagine particular types of citizens – *fearing subjects*; that these attempts to govern 'fear of crime' actually inform the citizenry that they are indeed fearful; that this sensitises the citizenry to 'fear of crime'; that the law and order lobby and populist politicians use this supposed fearing population to justify a tougher approach on crime, a point on which they grandstand, and in doing so sensitize citizens to fear once again; and that this spurs more research into 'fear of crime' and so on.

(Lee 2001: 480–1; emphases in original)

More brusquely, Ditton and Farrall (2000: xv) suggest that 'what we now rather blandly refer to as fear of crime began life as the 'fear of blacks'' and, slightly more extensively, that:

'[P]ublic alarm' about crime emerged, via the manipulation of the Nixonian silent majority, from right-wing concern about the extension of rights to the poor and the black. Indeed... one of the very first academic essays on the subject – Frank Furstenberg [1971] comments, 'fear of crime is the symptom of the silent majority's lashing back'..

(Ditton and Farrall 2000: xvi)

Lee, and Ditton and Farrall acknowledge the importance to their work of a book by Harris (1969) that details the 'senatorial shenanigans' (Harris 1969: xv) preceding the passage of the *Omnibus Crime Control and Safe Streets Act*. Ditton and Farrall (2000: xvi) end their overview of work on the topic by linking the social and the individual levels. It is also a fitting endpoint for us:

In sum, gradually over that 30-year period, general – if bigoted – societal concern about crime has been transmuted into a personal problem of individual vulnerability.

If we want to understand fear of crime, the sociological work briefly glossed here offers important pointers to its social and political dimensions. It is in and around issues such as these that offer the essential social starting point for criminological work on fear of crime. But what this work fails to do is to discuss which particular individuals are vulnerable to the new insecurities consequent upon the transformations of post- or late modernity, are susceptible to the blandishments of a moral panic, or are likely to become invested in the predominant discourse about fear of crime. The discourse of fear of crime may produce or make possible 'fearing subjects' as Lee suggests, but he cannot explain why some people become 'fearing subjects' – at least some of the time – and others do not; why it is, for example, as Ditton *et al.* (1999) argue elsewhere, many people are more angry about crime than afraid?; and why it is that the conventional social discriminators of age, class, and risk of victimisation largely fail to predict which kinds of emotional reactions people are likely to express?

Approaching fear of crime psychosocially

We need, then, to bring the feeling individual back in, but without losing sight of this understanding of fear of crime's social origins. In other words, we need to understand the relationship between individuals, with their unique biographies, and what Lee calls the '"fear of crime" feedback loop'. How might this new knowledge be produced? We have already established the inadequacies of the survey-based methodology to do so. What are the alternatives? Broadly speaking, those wishing to explore the meanings people attach to their experiences in a properly contextualised fashion, have turned to qualitative research. Here, the in-depth or semi-structured face-to-face interview is usually the method of choice. For example, feminist critics of early work on fear of crime, who thought women's experiences of sexual harassment or rape were not properly taken into account (Stanko 1990; Junger 1987; Riger *et al.* 1978), often used such interviews to ask women (and men in some cases) about their fears (Stanko 1990; Gilchrist *et al.* 1998).

However, despite a lot of work trying to produce an interview instrument adequate to the task of capturing people's experiences and the meanings these held for them (Maynard and Purvis 1994; Mishler 1986), the qualitative research interview remained deficient in several respects. It continued to assume that the interviewer's questions meant the same thing to the interviewee as they did to the interviewer asking them, and *vice versa*, that is, that both shared a common understanding of the words used. It also assumed that interviewees knew themselves well enough to be the faithful chroniclers of their own experiences and that interviewers knew themselves well enough to understand what was being said. In other words, qualitative researchers tended to operate with the same assumptions about subjectivity as survey researchers. Subjects were rational-unitary beings, transparent to themselves and able to be transparent to another when given a chance to tell their stories.

Conversely, our position is that subjects are not rational unitary beings with full self-knowledge, but psychosocial subjects with a split consciousness, constantly unconsciously defending themselves against anxiety. This unconscious defensive activity affects what and how anything is remembered, with painful or threatening events being either forgotten or recalled in a safely modified fashion; it also affects how such memories are communicated to any interviewer, given that the context of the interview may be more or less threatening. At both stages, the act of remembering and the act of communication, meaning is rarely straightforward – and never wholly transparent. The interviewer too is a defended subject, and so the same applies: the meanings – of the questions asked and how answers are understood – will also be affected by the interviewer's dynamic unconscious with its own 'logic' of defensive investments. What are the implications of this version of subjectivity for the research interview? Two things seem central: the importance of trying to understand something of a person's whole biography in order better to understand how any remembered part might best be made sense of; the importance of the psychoanalytic idea of free associations as a way of trying to glimpse what might lie behind communicated meanings.

The biographical–interpretative method and the importance of gestalt

The biographical–interpretative method was first developed by German sociologists producing accounts of the lives of holocaust survivors and Nazi soldiers (Rosenthal 1993; Rosenthal and Bar-On 1992; Schutze 1992). It is a disarmingly simple method. It starts with a simple invitation to respondents: 'please, tell me your life story' (Rosenthal 1990). This open invitation allows the respondent to start where they wish and to fashion their story (or stories, since lives usually consist of multiple accounts) as they wish. The importance of this attempt to elicit stories is that life stories refer to things that have actually happened to people. While these are rarely the whole story, the way that people tell their stories – remembering particular details, drawing particular conclusions, etc. – will be revealing (more so than the teller realises), once we know how to 'read' them. Once the initial story has been told, the interviewer, who has listened attentively and taken notes, follows up the emergent themes – in their narrated order – using the respondent's own words and phrases. This invitation to elaborate on themes is effectively an invitation to tell further stories. No attempt is made to evaluate or judge the material, nor to get respondents to explain themselves. Thus 'why' questions, often the staple of semi-structured interviews, are eschewed. This has the advantage of ensuring people stick to their revealing stories and avoids the premature closure, and intellectualisations, which explanations tend to promote.

This, in essence, is the way the biographical–interpretative method produces the data that, when analysed and written up, becomes someone's life story. This is not the place to appraise the analytic procedure of 'objective hermeneutics' preferred by the German biographers, except to refer the reader to other sources (Oevermann *et al.* 1987; Flick 1998; Wengraf 2001) and say that the whole process is guided by the theoretical idea that people's lives, however apparently disjointed and contradictory, have a 'gestalt': a whole that is greater than the sum of its parts. Wertheimer, the founder of gestalt psychology, thought that it was impossible to 'achieve an understanding of structured totals by starting with the ingredient parts which enter into them' and that 'parts are defined by their relation to the system as a whole in which they are functioning' (cited in Murphy and Kovach,1972: 258). Following this gestalt principle, and assuming the interviewer has managed to elicit appropriate stories and not destroyed them by clumsy intrusions, the analytical task is to reveal the whole that enables sense to be made of the various parts. It is this principle of the importance of the whole that makes decontextualised data – from the Lickert scale tick box response to the coded themes abstracted from their texts of origin – so problematic for us. Whole lives, whole texts, have to be the starting point, not abstracted parts.

Interpreting the gestalt: the importance of free associations

The German biographical–interpretative tradition remained agnostic about the value of psychoanalytic concepts, despite the fact that their material, not surprisingly, contained examples of 'defended' story telling (Gadd 2004). Schutze, for example, revealed that elicited accounts such as those of Nazi soldiers would be highly defensive ones, given the difficult and painful subject-matter. This needed a methodological strategy to uncover 'faded-out memories and delayed recollections of emotionally or morally disturbing war experiences' (Schutze 1992: 347). As we have seen, this strategy was guided by the principle of gestalt. Given our understanding of the role of unconscious defences against anxiety in people's lives, and hence in the stories they tell, we needed to give the gestalt principle a central role in producing and analysing data.

One of the methods Freud used to understand unconscious defensive activity was 'free association'. This involved him allowing the patient to 'choose the subject of the day's work' in order that he could 'start out from whatever surface [the patient's] unconscious happens to be presenting to his notice at the moment' (quoted in Kerr 1994: 98). This starting point is remarkably similar to the gestalt-inspired invitation to 'please, tell me your life story'. The difference is that by asking the patient to say whatever comes to mind, the psychoanalyst assumes that the narrative thus elicited is structured by unconscious dynamics; that is the 'logic' is emotionally motivated rather than rationally intended like the logic guiding consciousness. Once this unconscious activity is better understood, and its relationship to the conscious self and behaviour, one can begin to make sense of the 'whole' person in all of their contradictoriness: how what we say is so often at odds with what we do; how our rational self co-exists with a self capable of all kinds of apparently irrational behaviour.

So, the key to a person's gestalt if one assumes a defended subject is to be found in expressions of anxiety and the unconscious defences and identity investments these give rise to. And the free associations made in interviewees' narratives provide the key to accessing these expressions of anxiety. This route to a person's gestalt has the added advantage that it is alert to a story's incoherences (for example, its contradictions, elisions, avoidances), in a way that many more conventional approaches are not.

Hollway and Jefferson (2000) used just such a method, the biographical–interpretative method modified by free association narrative interviewing, in a research project investigating the fear of crime of men and women, young, middle-aged and old, on two estates in a northern city. The initial invitation to respondents to tell their life story was modified to reflect the core theoretical concerns of the project; so respondents were invited to tell the interviewer about their experiences of crime, risk, safety and anxiety with follow up invitations shadowing the associations they had made. Hollway and Jefferson's argument, broadly, is that the already anxious are most likely to become the highly fearful subjects of fear of crime discourse (thus helping to explain the fear-risk paradox). In a paper attempting to explain why fear of crime was such a powerful vehicle in the contemporary period, Hollway and Jefferson (1997: 260) argued that because the fear of crime discourse produces risks that are (potentially) knowable, actionable and controllable, this makes it a 'powerful modernist tool in the quest for order, in contrast to Beck's unknowable risks of late modernity'. They went on to show, how, at the level of the anxious individual, crime, and the potential for victimisation associated with it, 'could actually serve unconsciously as a relatively reassuring site for displaced anxieties which otherwise would be too threatening to cope with' (Hollway and Jefferson 1997: 264). This, then, was a psychosocial account of fear of crime: what fear of crime meant as a socio-political discourse of late modernity; for whom it might provide a suitable identity investment. To render all this more concrete, we end with a case study from Hollway and Jefferson's project, together with some reflections on how both the interviewee's biographically-laden anxieties and the interviewer's inability to identify wholly with them, colluded to produce an unshakeably fearful subject.

Anxiety and fear of crime: A psychosocial case study of Hassan

Hassan was a 68-year-old man who lived alone. An immigrant to Britain in the 1940s, he remained single until his forties, had a marriage arranged with a much younger woman who joined him in England, with whom he raised five children in quick succession. These were happy years; everything was 'smashing'. Hassan was fulfilled as husband, father and provider – and unafraid. Then his wife listened to her communist brother and challenged

Hassan's authority, eventually leaving, taking the children. Later Hassan was persuaded to sign over his half of the house to his wife and children, leaving him with nothing. Soon after, Hassan's health gave out. He was forced to retire early from his job as a nursing assistant and 'now' spends his days in considerable pain.

'Now' – which seemed to refer generally to his years as a divorced, retired man, living on the estate – everything was 'terrible'. Hassan felt frightened to go out at all, especially after dark – and rarely did except to pray during Ramadan:

> I mean I don't go out at night at all. I'm frightened if I go out, if somebody pinch me, or hit me, or – and I don't open the door to nobody. I'm frightened to death. I wish the government do something about it.

Even at home, where he claimed to feel safest, Hassan jumped when the fridge made a noise and found watching television scary, especially because of the stories of old people getting killed (unable to read English he was spared lurid press accounts of crime). Yet despite his repetitive talk of all this 'pinching and killing' frightening him and all the elderly 'to death' Hassan had few experiences of criminal victimisation. The examples he could recount included: an experience of racially abusive behaviour (two men calling him a 'black bastard' from their car window and throwing eggs and bottles at him when he was returning from the mosque one evening) and the mischief making of local children (ill-behaved kids ringing his doorbell and running away, and on one occasion, throwing a stone at his window and cracking it). Now Hassan is reluctant to go on holiday through fear of being burgled and often feels fearful for his life – 'I don't like somebody to kill me if they hate me' – even though, since the racial harassment, his nephew and a friend drive him to the mosque.

Judged against either his present experience of life in a fairly protected corner of the estate in purpose-built accommodation for the elderly, or his 'smashing' past experience as a happy family man and worker, Hassan's present fears could, from a rationalistic, risk-based perspective, be construed as excessive. Coupled with his appraisal that the crime situation was getting 'worse' and merited immediate government intervention, his fears are perhaps better conceived as quite heavily invested, the 'upset' of the racial harassment notwithstanding. Clues as to why this might be so could be found both in Hassan's account of his marriage breaking down and the fact that his vehement tirade against crime was part of a general tirade against the ills of modernity, including sexual permissiveness and drugs. He sometimes interjected that life was better in Saudi Arabia, where people did not steal from each other because they were afraid of having their hands cut off. A traditional, conservative, religious man, Hassan's marriage broke down when his wife challenged his traditional patriarchal right to order her life. A younger woman who picked up the language quicker than him, she chose modern independence over traditional religious and patriarchal authority – as did their children – to the extent that they were in a position to choose freely – in going with her. The loss of all he ever worked for (his years as a single man seem to have been spent largely saving and preparing for his future marriage and family: he bought and fully furnished a house, 'everything new', to the wide-eyed bemusement of his young wife) left him disappointed, with only a painful old age ahead. His family – now all living in London – like many of those living in his community, were too busy to make much time for him: 'nobody bother … nobody wants to know you'. Hassan's devout and fatalistic religious Muslim beliefs had helped him come to terms with some of these worries. Yet, there was ample evidence in his account that his underlying anxieties had not been eradicated. The more Hassan insisted otherwise the more it became clear that he could not 'forget' the emotional pain of his separation from his family:

> I left the house, I left the wife, I left the kids. That make me a bit worried at first, you know. But I forgot about it. Tell you true. I forgot about – it's no good to kill myself about that, you know. It happened, it happened, it finished … And from that – I forgot about everything, you know what I mean? The kids ring me up, the girls are talking to me and that's it. And I forgot about everything …

The strength of Hassan's investment in the position of the fearful subject is indicative, we suggest, of how deep was his loss and how unbearable it felt: unbearable enough to bring to mind the notion that it might have killed him, and dominant enough to need to be consciously driven from memory (witness the constant reminder that he 'forgot about' it all). Unsurprisingly, then, the memories refused to go away. As Hassan surmised, late on in his second interview, he would sometimes find himself talking to himself about the very things he wanted to forget:

> Sometime[s] I – I forgot the things that past, you know, but sometime it there … I used to talk to myself sometime[s]. I say, 'Well I've been 49 years, and I bought the house … and I lost everything … [and am] now lonely and things like that' … Always I want to forgot things like that, you know? [TJ: Mmm] But sometime[s] you can't help it, you know what I mean? Is a bit hard for me, you know what I mean? It's a bit hard. When I'm lonely now or … when my health is not really well, you know?

Might Hassan's fear of someone killing him because of hate, which had become consciously associated with racially motivated harassment, also be unconsciously connected to the inevitable turmoil of being spurned by a loved one and all the hate, self-hate, denial and regret that can entail? Likewise, Hassan's repetitive 'you know' that punctuates the passage above, can perhaps be read as an implicit request for some recognition of the many difficulties that made up his life: his losses; his loneliness, his poor health. His plaintive 'is a bit hard', also repeated, seemed to ask for an acknowledgement that was not forthcoming from the interviewer. One important reason for the interviewer's (TJ) reticence had to do with the prescriptions of the Free Association Narrative Interview method: to be non-intrusive in the interests of eliciting the respondent's story in their own words. However, there was probably more to it than that, given that, in any interview situation, the interviewer with his or her own pre-existing prejudices, concerns, anxieties and investments is also positioning the interviewee, consciously and unconsciously, as well as being positioned by him or her.

In Hassan's case, my (TJ) first conscious impressions were of a rather anxious man (needing to check me out from an upstairs window before letting me in), in poor health (he walked with a stick). Inside, his house was full of stereotypically feminine touches: it was neat and tidy; he served me tea in dainty teacups; evidence of his sewing was strewn around. As the interview progressed, it was hard not to feel sorry for this lonely, ageing man in poor health, often in physical pain and with a storehouse of painful emotional memories, growing old far from home and without even the solace of the written word, for the most part. On the other hand, he was quite a difficult interviewee whose repetitive complaints had a slightly self-pitying tone. This, combined with an apparently inordinate fear of everyday occurrences like untoward household noises and badly behaved kids, made him seem, at times, stereotypically weak and effeminate, notwithstanding the fact that he was an ageing man whose physical powers were, indeed, weakening.

In addition, Hassan's experiences of racist abuse were completely beyond my direct personal experience, even though as an academic who had spent a long time researching and writing about racism I had had a lot of indirect experience of it. It may have been the case, therefore, that although, consciously, I identified with him and his very difficult life, I may have been less well-equipped, unconsciously, to fully identify with what he was feeling. What for him, from a culture with long experience of racial victimisation, must have felt generally frightening – having eggs and bottles thrown at him, for example – perhaps sounded to my less identified unconscious like a nasty but fairly isolated example (in his case) of racial violence and thus an inadequate basis for his general fearfulness of crime. Similarly, although I am consciously aware of the importance of cultural differences in story-telling, and the role these may have played in the production of what I saw then as his self-pitying tone, I may well have been less attuned at an unconscious level. In other words, although it is possible, in general, consciously, to identify across very different positionings in discourses of gender and race, particular situations and circumstances may well trigger defensively motivated unconscious responses. With my own conscious investments in a strong and stoical masculinity, for example, it may well have been the case that the manner of Hassan's story-telling made it difficult – at that time – to fully identify with Hassan's fearfulness and his weak, somewhat self-pitying effeminacy. Moreover, this unconscious failure to fully identify with Hassan had considerable discursive support. Where Afro-Caribbean males have to contend with a discursive stereotype of themselves as tough, macho and sexy, the discursive construct of the Asian male (at least until comparatively recently) was almost the reverse (plus a notion of deviousness). To the extent that Hassan's behaviour chimed with discursive stereotypes and, perhaps, with my lingering unconscious identification with them, it becomes possible to read Hassan's apparently excessive identification with the fearful subject of the fear of crime discourse as a contingent co-production of both interviewer and interviewee.

Conclusion

In essence then, what we are arguing is that subject positions are negotiated in relation to the individual's biography and attendant anxieties, the discursive fields available to the individual (often constrained by their class, ethnicity and gender), and intersubjectively through the responses of others. Whether someone invests in the position of the fearful subject preoccupied with the ever-growing threat of victimisation depends in part, as Ditton's research (2000) has shown, on how available that position is to him or her. This availability is partly a consequence of how social researchers pose and follow up questions as well as how the individual feels about crime. Of course, sometimes people's feelings about crime – or other matters – are so strong or entrenched that it matters little how they are asked about them. Hence, some people, probably a minority, will say they feel fearful about crime no matter how the question is posed or who is doing the asking. That said, most people are not completely fixed into the subject positions they occupy and thus can be enabled to occupy other positions if their anxieties can be sufficiently contained through identification with and recognition by another person. This, it appears, was not something the interviewer managed to do for Hassan, partly because of the injunctions of the FANI method and partly because of the interviewer's own positionings at that time. This reduced the possibilities for Hassan to step outside the position of the crime-fearing subject and thus, perhaps, become more conscious of his ulterior motives for being so afraid.

Our approach is consistent with Lee's and Ditton and Farrall's arguments that the fear of crime has only become an issue since there has been a widely available public (or social) discourse about fear of crime; an argument that is not the same as suggesting that people are not fearful of crime. What we add to this approach is the recommendation that criminologists should re-include the individual, but without simply returning to the traditional individualist approach underpinning most of the research on this topic. This means not seeking out the fearful individual but attending to the question of why some individuals and not others come to be heavily invested in the fear of crime discourse. Risk levels are not able to account for this differential investment, but theoretically attuned case analyses, like the one we have presented above, can. Through the case of Hassan we have shown how anxiety is crucial to understanding the appeal of the fear of crime, albeit mixed in its psychological benefits. That is to say, for the highly anxious, fear of crime is one discourse (amongst many) which can provide a ready vehicle for feelings that are difficult to face up to simply because within this discourse crime is depicted as knowable, actionable and controllable. This helps us explain why it is that, law and order, as Bauman highlights, has become one of the primary outlets through which postmodern insecurities are worked through – and hence why talking tough about crime currently appears to politicians so critical to their electability. It also – to continue the theoretical engagement with Bauman – helps explain why the home, the place in which we invest so much of ourselves, can often be imagined as a kind of 'body-safe extension', the infiltration of which by strangers, irrespective of whether they take anything of value, seems so threatening to our sense of bodily integrity. This is why Leach and Kearon – in an analysis informed by the work of the psychoanalyst Winnicott – liken burglary to an 'invasion of the "body snatchers"':

> [T]he significance of the invasion is problematized by the embodied nature of the relationship to home and things: by their very nature, familiar objects are conceived of and lived as extensions of the body ... things that are so close to the body ... that they feel amputated by burglary... The loss of objects, crucially, is much more than the loss of part of a cognitive, discursive identity ... Objects are valuable because they are rich with sensory and memory-laden experience, as well as representing identity ... Thus the experience of loss is often experienced retrospectively in burglary (people do not always know what something means until it is gone) and this loss can be of apparently unsentimental items.
>
> (Kearon and Leach 2000: 466–7)

Thinking again about Hassan, this may be one further reason why he was so afraid of crime. Having lost the family home in which he invested so much, not just financially but also emotionally in terms of his dreams and expectations, for him 'pinching and killing' had become synonymous: invoking a potential loss of self, the psychical amputation of the few remaining remnants of all he had ever hoped and striven for.

References

Bauman, Z (2000) 'Social issues of law and order', *British Journal of Criminology*, 40(2): 205–21.

Cohen, S (1972) *Folk Devils and Moral Panics*, London: MacGibbon & Kee.

Ditton, J (2000) 'Inaugural Lecture', presented 16 February 2000, Sheffield University (unpublished manuscript).

Ditton, J and Farrall, S (2000) 'Introduction', in J Ditton and S Farrall (eds), *The Fear of Crime*, Aldershot: Ashgate, pp xv–xxiii.

Ditton, J, Bannister, J, Gilchrist, E and Farrall, S (1999) 'Afraid or angry? Recalibrating the "fear" of crime', *International Review of Victimology*, 6(2): 83–99.

Ferraro, KF and LaGrange, R (1987) 'The measurement of fear of crime', *Sociological Inquiry*, 57(1): 70–101.

Flick, U (1998) *An Introduction to Qualitative Research*, London: Sage.

Furstenberg Jr, FF (1971) 'Public reaction to crime in the streets', *The American Scholar*, 40(4): 601–10.

Gadd, D (2004) 'Making sense of interviewee-interviewer dynamics in narratives about violence in intimate relationships', *International Journal of Social Research Methodology*, 7(5): 383–401.

Gilchrist, E, Bannister, J, Ditton, J and Farrall, S (1998) 'Women and the "fear of crime"', *British Journal of Criminology*, 38(2): 283–98.

Hale, C (1996) 'Fear of crime: a review of the literature', *International Review of Victimology*, 4(2): 79–150.

Hall, S, Critcher, C, Jefferson, T, Clarke, J and Roberts, B (1978) *Policing the Crisis*, London: Macmillan.

Harris, R (1969) *The Fear of Crime*, New York: Praeger.

Hollway, W and Jefferson, T (1997) 'The risk society in an age of anxiety: situating fear of crime', *British Journal of Sociology*, 48(2): 255–66.

——(2000) *Doing Qualitative Research Differently*, London: Sage.

Hough, M and Mayhew, P (1983) *The British Crime Survey: First Report*, London: HMSO.

Josselson, R (1995) 'Imagining the real: empathy, narrative and the dialogic self', in R Josselson and A Lieblich (eds), *The Narrative Study of Lives Volume 3*, London: Sage, pp 27–44.

Junger, M (1987) 'Women's experience of sexual harassment', *British Journal of Criminology*, 27(4): 358–83.

Kearon, T and Leach, R (2000) 'Invasion of the "body snatchers": burglary reconsidered', *Theoretical Criminology*, 4(4): 451–72.

Kerr, J (1994) *A Most Dangerous Method*, London: Sinclair-Stevenson.

Lee, M (2001) 'The genesis of "fear of crime"', *Theoretical Criminology*, 5(4): 467–85.

Maynard, M and Purvis, J (eds) (1994) *Researching Women's Lives from a Feminist Perspective*, London: Taylor & Francis.

Mishler, EG (1986) *Research Interviewing*, Cambridge, MA: Harvard University Press.

Murphy, G and Kovach, JK (1972) *Historical Introduction to Modern Psychology*, 6th edn, London: Routledge and Kegan Paul.

Oevermann, U, Allert, T, Konau, E and Krambeck, J (1987) 'Structures of meaning and objective hermeneutics', in V Meja (ed), *Modern German sociology*, New York: Columbia Press, pp 436–48.

Pearson, G (1983) *Hooligan: A History of Respectable Fears*, London: Macmillan.

Riger, S, Gordon, M and Bailley, R (1978) 'Women's fear of crime', *Victimology*, 3: 274–84.

Rosenthal, G (1990) 'The structure and "gestalt" of autobiographies and its methodological consequences', unpublished paper presented to the 12th World Congress of Sociology, Madrid.

—— (1993) 'Reconstruction of life stories', in R Josselson and A Lieblich (eds), *The Narrative Study of Lives Volume 1*, London: Sage, pp 59–91.

Rosenthal, G and Bar-On, D (1992) 'A biographical case study of a victimizer's daughter's strategy: pseudo-identification with victims of the Holocaust', *Journal of Narrative and Life History*, 2(2): 105–27.

Schutze, F (1992) 'Pressure and guilt: the experience of a young German soldier in World War Two and its biographical consequences', *International Sociology*, 7(2): 187–208; (3): 347–67.

Stanko, EA (1990) *Everyday Violence*, London: Pandora.

Wengraf, T (2001) *Qualitative Research Interviewing*, London: Sage.

Chapter 9

Bridging the social and the psychological in the fear of crime

Jonathan Jackson

What explains the gap between the fear of crime and the reality of crime? How important to public anxieties are perceptions of the likelihood and consequence of victimisation? What about feelings of control and the personal vividness of risk? How significant is past experience of crime, or hearing from family and friends about danger and threat, or consuming mass media reports of criminals, victims, eroding norms, and loosening moral standards? What about perceptions of our social and physical environment – the people we encounter, our feelings of community trust and social cohesion, the state and ownership of public space and social decay?

More questions arise. Do anxieties about crime distil a broader set of concerns about neighbourhood breakdown, diversity, moral consensus? Does the fear of crime fuel stereotypes, dramatise what is wrong with our culture, and define and redefine moral boundaries in society? Do panics about crime reflect a cynically manipulated culture of fear? Might political discourse, the mass media, and social scientific research be implicated in the creation and feedback of fear?

These are some of the queries that scholars have in the back of their mind – or perhaps in the front of their mind – when they question the theoretical base of much fear of crime research. That such questions have so far gone (to some) degree unanswered reminds us that this literature has been rather more successful at providing information on who reports what (in standardised interviews) than at producing descriptions of how worry manifests in people's everyday lives, or indeed explaining why they feel anxious in the first place (Hale 1996; Farrall *et al*, 1997; Girling *et al.* 2000; Farrall and Gadd 2004; Jackson *et al.* 2008; Gray *et al.* 2008). As Vanderveen (2006: 7) notes, '... many studies are concerned what might be called the prevalence of "fear of crime" in socio-demographic categories ... less is known about the variety in the nature, meaning, relevance and experience of "fear of crime" in people's personal lives'. A literature dominated by survey research might be aptly described, in the words of C Wright Mills, as *abstracted empiricism* (Mills 1953), where the sophistication of large-scale surveys and statistical procedures are not matched by impoverished theory:

Overall, reading the literature on fear of crime produces a sense that the field is trapped within an overly restrictive methodological and theoretical framework ... What is needed is a strategy which begins by unpacking the concept of fear of crime. So doing will open up a rich area for debate.

(Hale 1996: 141)

The questions posed at the very beginning of this chapter might be divided into those of a predominantly psychological nature and those of a predominantly sociological nature. The processes that link risk perception to emotion fall in the first group. The social and cultural significance of crime, deviance and social stability are more sociological issues. In this chapter I argue that a comprehensive account of the fear of crime needs to bridge these two levels of analysis. I present a tentative and briefly sketched out theoretical treatise that tries to do just that. In order to integrate and develop disparate insights I draw upon an area of interdisciplinary research that has so far gone untapped within criminology: risk perception. Working within what Thompson and Dean (1996) call a contextualistic formulation of risk, the framework considers the psychology of risk; how risk is constructed and information circulated; the institutional processes and interests at play in amplification and attenuation; and the social meaning of crime that infuses and inflects public perceptions of risk.

Overall, the framework states that the public thinks about risk in terms of likelihood, control, consequence, vividness and moral judgement. People generate representations of risk which include imagery of the criminal event and its consequences, a sense of who might be responsible and where it might take place, and a sense of outrage – the 'how dare they' factor. Moreover, information about crime and images of risk circulate around society, creating what Sunstein (2005) calls 'availability cascades.' Certain actors amplify risk for their own institutional ends. Finally, normative and cultural dispositions influence which risk individuals pay attention to. People worry about crime not just for themselves (and loved ones) but also because crime damages the social fabric of the whole community. Indeed, because of the nature of crime, I argue that lay concerns reveal a kind of lay seismograph of social disorganisation and anomie (see Jackson 2004, 2006). Rather than fear of crime being solely about crime, it encompasses and expresses a whole set of public perceptions of symbols of crime. And these symbols reveal neo-Durkheimian evaluations of moral and ideological boundaries: people identify things in their community that are hostile to social order; they designate these as representative of criminal threat; and they identify individuals, behaviours and communities as somehow lacking – on the wrong side of acceptability.

Towards an integrative framework

Thompson and Dean (1996) distinguish between two conceptions of risk. One formulation, they write, is probabilist. From this standpoint, risk is purely a matter of the probability of an event or its consequences. Broadly mapping onto the scientific/quantitative approach and on the dominant mode of governmental rationality, the hazard that gives rise to the possibility of this possible event is real, independent of our perception of it. Any particular risk will be laden with other characteristics, for example, genetically modified food may engender fears about infection and illness, nuclear power risks may invite horror of environmental catastrophe. However, just as the colour of an eye plays no part in deciding whether something is or is not an eye, these 'accidental' attributes of a risk do not provide criteria in themselves for deciding whether something is, or is not, a risk.

On the other hand is a contextualist formulation of risk. This opens the door to a wide range of other questions that colour public understanding and response, including control, the cultural resonance of a risk and its consequences, and aspects of trust and blame. As such, risk has no single determining criterion. A risk will always be associated with a number of characteristics such as whether it is voluntarily undertaken, whether it is familiar or unfamiliar, or whether it involves societal or personal danger. Probability, in this view, is simply one among a number of risk attributes, none of which is singularly a necessary condition for something to be classified as a risk.

According to Thompson and Dean (1996) the distinction between these poles is most apparent in informal discussion. When a probabilist talks of the 'risk of an earthquake' occurring, s/he really speaks of the probability of the event occurring. By contrast, a contextualist would speak of the risk of an earthquake according to the particular danger relevant from a given perspective. For example, the risk would be different for someone who had no choice but to live in the hazardous area compared to the risk as seen by a geologist who chose to move to the area in order to study it. The implication of the strong contextualist position is that probability estimation may be irrelevant to determining the existence of a risk, much less for understanding it or communicating related information to others.

The practical result of these competing conceptions of risk is that misunderstandings and disputes occur that are difficult to resolve. Within a more contextualist understanding of risk, it is apparent that people who raise questions about particular risks – for instance violent crime – may be using risk language to articulate all kinds of legitimate claims dependent on the context in which these claims are made. For the probabilist, such claims will likely as not make little sense because probability is the single essential component of any discussion about risk: that is, how probable is it that one will become a victim of such crime? Furthermore, it is generally experts that incline towards the probabilist pole. The communication of quantified probability estimates as input to public deliberations on such risks may sometimes, as a result, be simply irrelevant.

In a paper, Thompson (1999) suggests that the language of risk has been adopted by scientists doing risk assessment and is, in general functionally equivalent to the language of probability. The practical use for such language is in the field of decision-making. Risk analysis utilises mathematical and scientific techniques to arrive at the best estimate of likely costs and benefits to any course of action. This process is highly deliberative, in the sense that people are engaged explicitly in evaluating and weighing the options.

But much human behaviour and cognition is not deliberative. It is habitual, even unconscious that any particular course of action is being adopted. Risk in lay or 'everyday' usage, Thompson argues, 'functions as a cognitive gatekeeper between the deliberative and the non-deliberative dimensions of practice ... in this respect, the concept of risk functions as a category for organising or prioritising the expenditure of deliberative resources' (Thompson 1999: 499). In this account, in the practice of risk assessment, once something is categorised as being a risk, the deliberative process of determining probabilities and weighing costs and benefits begins. Where risk or risk language enters lay discourse, it can be dysfunctional in the sense that once something is categorised as risky, the lay person no longer acts as if there is zero or negligible risk, but often neither has the resources, nor the information to arrive at a more 'rational' judgement.

A contextualistic conception of risk opens up the definition of risk perception beyond just lay judgements about the chances of falling victim. Decades of psychometric research have shown the primacy of control and consequence in public perceptions. A sense of efficacy over the possibility of victimisation speaks to the differential sense of vulnerability in the general population. A differential sensitivity to the impact and effects of crime explains why one person worries more than another. Thus, people may develop an image of risk which includes a sense of its likelihood, a sense of one's control over it happening, and a sense of the event and its aftermath – the resonance and impact of the event from a material, physical, emotional and psychological perspective. Moreover, 'crime' is not some abstract category; it is attached, by the observer, to individuals and contexts. Social influence plays a key role and issues of morality and blame come quickly to the fore (Sparks, 1992).

It is the goal of the rest of the chapter to sketch out such images or narratives of risk in more detail.

Emotion and risk perception in the fear of crime

Vulnerability and the fear of crime

Perceived vulnerability to victimisation is a key theme in fear of crime research (Hale 1996). Killias (1990: 98) identifies three dimensions: exposure to risk; the anticipation of serious consequences; and the loss of control ('that is, lack of effective defence, protective measures and/or possibilities of escape'). All of these are necessary to produce fear according to Killias, and each is associated with physical, social and situational aspects of vulnerability. For example, more serious consequences are expected to occur amongst women, the elderly and people in bad health (physical factors), amongst victims without networks of social support (social factors), and in deserted areas where no help is available (situational factors).[1]

Anticipated vulnerability to victimisation can explain differences in levels of anxiety between certain social groups. Examining the puzzle that females are typically at less risk of personal crime (for example, mugging or physical attack rather than burglary or car crime) than males[2] yet worry more frequently, Jackson (2008a) found that the gender difference in the frequency of worry either disappeared or was attenuated once one controlled for any single of the following self-assessments:

- Ability to fend off attack;
- Assessment of the personal consequence of victimisation;
- Judgements of control over the risk;
- Perceptions of the likelihood of victimisation; and,
- Beliefs about the relative-risk levels.

The gender difference in worry was thus partly explained by females (compared to males) typically feeling less able to fend off attack, judging themselves to be less able to control risk than males, and judging the consequences of the event to be more serious.

Warr (1987) has a phrase for this: 'differential sensitivity to risk'. His study found that individuals were more 'sensitive' to a given level of perceived risk when they viewed the consequences of victimisation to be especially serious. In other words, a certain level of perceived likelihood resulted in higher levels of fear when a crime was generally judged to be especially serious. Extending this model, Jackson (2008b) showed that subjective probabilities strongly predicted the frequency of worry but also that control and consequence each: (a) shaped the judgement of likelihood; and (b) moderated the impact of likelihood on worry. Both judgements of consequence *and* control operated as differential sensitivity to the risk of criminal victimisation: when individuals judged crime to be especially serious in its personal impact, and when individuals judged that they have little control over the event, a lower level of perceived likelihood was needed to raise the frequency of worry.

These studies, in sum, support the argument that: '... circumstances or events that appear innocuous or comparatively minor to males or younger persons are apt to be viewed as more dangerous to females and the elderly because of the offences they imply or portend' (Warr 1994: 19). The heterogeneity of different types of crime regarding 'relevance, explanation and consequences' (Gabriel and Greve 2003: 6) means that the same crime has different anticipated resonance or impact from one individual to the next. For example, one person may associate burglary with the risk of physical or sexual assault; another person may associate burglary with the loss of material goods and a great deal of inconvenience. Indeed, Ferraro (1995: 87) argues that sexual harassment: 'may shadow other types of victimisation among women. Rape may operate like any other master offence among women, especially younger women who have the highest rate of rape, heightening fear reactions for other forms of crime'.

Representations of risk: lessons from psychology

A large body of empirical evidence from risk perception research suggests that the public think about crime risk in terms of likelihood, consequence and control (see Jackson 2006). Examining the psychological mechanisms which underpin lay perception of terrorism-risk in Turkey and Israel, Shiloh *et al.* (2007) differentiate between (a) cognitive representations of risk; and (b) emotional representations of risk. An initial qualitative study explored individual's thoughts and feelings about terrorist attacks and the findings fed into the development of a questionnaire. Subsequent survey data showed one theme of 'negative affect' and four cognitive themes: cost (perceived consequence of terrorist attack); vulnerability (perceived likelihood of terrorist attack); control (perceived self-efficacy over becoming a victim in a terrorist attack); and trust in authorities (assessment of the ability of government and security forces to prevent terrorist attacks). Negative affect was measured using semantic differential scales where individuals reported their feelings about terrorist attacks on a seven-point scale (1 = 'I do not feel' and 7 = 'I strongly feel') for each of fear, helplessness, hopelessness, anger, intolerance, pain, loneliness, insecurity, sadness and anxiety. Of the four cognitive themes, perceived consequence was the most powerful predictor of negative affect. Indeed, while perceptions of likelihood and feelings of control were associated with affect at the bivariate level, there was a strong correlation between affect and consequence.

The *availability heuristic* (Tversky and Kahneman 1973) predicts that the size of a class tends to be judged by the ease with which instances of it can be retrieved from memory. This offers one explanation why people tend to over-estimate the probability of victimisation: individuals substitute a relatively difficult question (how likely is it that I will become a victim of crime?) with a relatively easy question (how easy can I imagine becoming a victim of crime?). In other words, people overestimate the frequency of very rare, spectacular events, and underestimate the incidence of more frequent, less spectacular events (Lichtenstein *et al.* 1978). When individuals hold a particularly resonant and vivid image of the risk event – which may involve mental imagery of victimisation with especially serious consequences – they judge the likelihood of victimisation to be especially high. As Loewenstein *et al.* (2001: 279) suggest:

> To the extent that anticipatory emotions are generated in response to mental imagery about the experience of decision outcomes [including judgements of risk], factors that influence the occurrence or vividness of mental images are likely to be important determinants of anticipatory emotions.

Emotion and cognition may also show independence. Feelings may arise without cognitive mediation. Thoughts may arise without emotional mediation. Cognitive evaluations may tend to be composed of assessments of likelihood and cost; emotional reactions may involve the vividness with which consequences can be imagined, mood and prior experience with the event (Loewenstein *et al.* 2001). And two modes of information processing may be important. On the one hand, is a formal, logical and numeric style of reasoning, a style more applicable to conscious cognitive assessments of risk. On the other hand, is a type of thinking that Epstein (1994: 710) calls 'intuitive, automatic, natural, non-verbal, narrative, and experiential'. For Slovic *et al.* (2004), the 'experiential' system is affect-laden rather than formally logical like the 'analytic system'. It involves rapid processing and the encoding of reality in images and metaphors rather than abstract symbols and numbers. Sloman (1996) suggests that such associative processing operates by using more rapid pathways based on context and similarity rather than the conscious use of logic and evidence.

Consistent with this, Sunstein (2003) argues that when strong emotions are involved, individuals focus more on consequence than likelihood (cf Rottenstreich and Hsee 2001):

> The resulting 'probability neglect' helps to explain excessive reactions to low-probability risks of catastrophe ... As a result of probability neglect, people often are far more concerned about the risks of terrorism than about statistically larger risks that they confront in ordinary life.
>
> (Sunstein 2003).

Thus, once people become anxious about crime, they might be unlikely to think about the low probability of victimisation, and more likely to think about the many unpleasant consequences of victimisation. This idea has parallels with Warr's (1987) model of risk sensitivity, which predicts a relatively low level of perceived likelihood will tend to result in relatively high levels of fear when anticipated consequences are especially high.

Applying such findings promises to stimulate criminological research into the fear of crime (cf Chadee *et al.* 2007). Individuals may develop over time a set of cognitive and affective representations of the risk of various forms of victimisation. Representations or narratives of risk may originate in mass media and interpersonal communication, but get picked up and translated by individuals into personal concerns. These representations of risk may involve, from one individual to the next, different weightings of consequences, likelihood, control and affect to the potential of particular forms of criminal victimisation. One individual may imagine that being burgled would involve serious material, physical and psychological effects; another may feel that the consequences would be comparatively manageable. For the first person, the risk may be weighted by consequence more than likelihood; for the second person, it may be most important in their composition of perceived risk. What is important, therefore, is the vividness and composition of risk. Another example: the risk of rape may be appraised through the affective route because of its severe consequences, constituted by a sense of the resonance of the consequences, the vividness of the event, and the ease with which one can summon up a frightening image. By contrast, another crime, such as car crime, may be appraised through the cognitive route, with the perceived likelihood of it happening more important than any resonant image of the impact of the event.

Once one is emotionally animated by the possibility of an event, a knock-on effect may be that one's judgements about that event and surrounding issues are then influenced. Someone already emotionally animated by risk builds over time a more extensive and vivid image of the risk event, fleshing out effects, protagonists and relevant causes and circumstances, making the risk more substantial, structured and relevant to that individual. Emotions can create and shape beliefs, amplifying or altering them and making them resistant to change (Frijda *et al.* 2000), providing information and guiding attention. Beliefs backed up by emotion additionally direct attention towards belief-relevant information (Clore and Gasper 2000). For example, those who worry may interpret ambiguous environmental cues or situations as threatening. In a heightened emotional state one might more quickly see risk in ambiguity; one might more readily associate people, situations and environments with criminal intention and threat. Preoccupied with negative information and future unpleasant outcomes, worriers scan the environment for salient material relating to threat (Mathews 1990), making ambiguous events more threatening (Butler and Mathews 1983, 1987; Russell and Davey 1993). Indeed, those who worry frequently are likely to think about the consequences, mull over the effects, and thus make the possibility more salient and more available.

Emotion and the effects of the 'fear' of crime

The focus thus far has been on the psychology of risk and emotion. But what does the fear of crime mean as a 'daily' experience? The answer to this straightforward question may be more complicated than one might at first imagine. For a series of studies have questioned whether fear of crime necessarily manifests as an 'everyday' experience which damages wellbeing and reduces quality of life.

Farrall *et al.* (1997) found that allowing individuals to talk about their perceptions and feelings in some depth (through a qualitative interview) revealed that anxieties were rather rare. By comparison, standard quantitative measurement tools led to a rather inflated sense of the impact of anxieties on people's quality of life. Turning to data from an omnibus survey of England, Wales and Scotland, Farrall and Gadd (2004) subsequently showed that the frequency of 'fear of crime' was relatively infrequent. One more study drew on data from the 2003/2004 British Crime Survey for confirmation: 35 per cent of respondents reported worry about mugging, yet only 16 per cent had worried once in the past year (Gray *et al.* 2008); a full 60 per cent of those who were 'very worried' had not experienced a single event of emotion in that period (Jackson *et al.* 2008).

These studies suggest that there is, on the one hand, the everyday experience of worry about crime. On the other hand, there is something more akin to diffuse anxiety (see Hough 2004; and Farrall 2004). In fact, those who reported being worried about crime but did not actually worry (that is, the anxious) tended to live in lower crime areas, have fewer victimisation experiences, and know fewer victims (Jackson *et al.* 2008). This suggests that the fear of crime manifests in the everyday when individuals are typically at the 'sharp end of life' – perhaps they find themselves in threatening situations more frequently than those who lead more protected lives, who if they have some kind of 'fear' are more likely to be 'anxious'.

An account of the fear of crime may consequently need to consider two 'types' of emotion: everyday worry which manifests as concrete moments; and a more diffuse but emotionally-tinged attitude towards risk (more akin to ambient insecurity). Both involve emotional representations of risk but everyday worry also involves specific moments of emotion (perhaps stimulated by environmental cues).

Moreover, there is some evidence for the existence of *functional fear.* Jackson and Gray (2008) found that around one-quarter of those who said they are worried about crime when probed also stated that they took precautions, that their quality of life was not affected (by worry or by the precautions they took), and that their precautionary activities only served to make them feel safer and less at risk. In such instances, worry is arguably something adaptational and malign (at least compared to those individuals who worry, who take precautions, and whose quality of life is affected in significant ways). Indeed, clinical psychologists have long been clear about the functional or problem-solving characteristic of worry. According to Mathews (1990): 'In the same way that fear has been described as a biological alarm system preparing the organism for escape ... so worry can be seen as a special state of the cognitive system, adapted to anticipate future dangers'. As Warr (2000) asks: if we could turn a magic dial to control or regulate the fear of crime, would we want to? Would it not reduce people's natural defences to crime?

Bridging the social and the psychological in the fear of crime

Adding 'flesh and blood' to public representations of risk

So far, this chapter has painted a rather solipsistic picture of the fear of crime. The focus has been on the psychology of risk and how people's emotions about the threat of crime manifest in their everyday lives. Perceptions of risk have been presented as complex and multi-faceted. Cognitive and emotional representations of risk interact and develop over time. Yet it is as if the social world has been bracketed out. 'Crime' is not something that drops from the sky (Sparks 1992). It is a deeply symbolic issue. Attached by the observer to individuals and contexts (Girling *et al.* 2000), crime speaks to our sense of community cohesion and social decay (Jackson 2004). Issues of morality and blame and battles over world-views come to the fore (Douglas 1992; Sparks 1992).

Elsewhere, I have begun to sketch out the hypothesis that individuals infuse their representation of risk with *flesh and blood* (Jackson 2006; Jackson *et al.* 2006). The remainder of this chapter looks to develop this speculative framework.

Circulating representations of crime and danger

One of the earliest approaches to explaining the fear of crime focused on estimates of the risk of crime and on actual victimisation experience. According to this perspective, the more *actual* victimisation experiences (experienced directly), or the more *likely* victimisation is, the more fearful an individual will be (see *inter alia* Balkin 1979; Liska *et al.* 1988; Skogan 1987). Yet such a simple model lacks empirical support. To be sure, there is some evidence (for example, Garofalo 1979; Skogan 1987; Stafford and Galle 1984; Liska *et al.* 1988; Covington and Taylor 1991; Hough 1995; McCoy *et al.* 1996; Kury and Ferdinand 1998; Rountree 1998) that direct victimisation experience is related to worry about certain types of crime. But such experience seems but a small part of any explanation of the fear of crime (Hale 1996). Weak correlations between fear and the risk of crime have given rise to the risk–fear paradox: more people worry about crime than are likely to fall victim and the wrong people seem to be worrying (Conklin 1975; DuBow *et al.* 1979; Hale 1996).

It therefore seems unlikely that people's representations of risk stem from their own personal, first-hand experience of criminal incidents. By contrast, a good deal of research suggests that *hearing* about events (via the mass media or interpersonal communication) and *knowing* victims play stronger roles in raising public perceptions of risk (Skogan and Maxfield 1981; Tyler 1980, 1984; Covington and Taylor 1991; LaGrange *et al.* 1992; Ferraro 1995; Hough 1995; Chirico *et al.* 1997). Taylor and Hale (1986: 152–3) describe this as a 'crime "multiplier:" processes operating in the residential environment that would "spread" the impacts of criminal events'. Such evidence exists that hearing of friends' or neighbours' victimisation increases anxiety that Hale (1996) concludes that indirect experiences of crime may play a stronger role in anxieties about victimisation than direct experience. However, Skogan (1986: 211) offers a cautionary note: '… many residents of a neighbourhood only know of [crime] indirectly via channels that may inflate, deflate, or garble the picture'.

The mass media and interpersonal communication are obvious sources of second-hand information about crime. Stories are told, narratives outlined – perpetrators, victims and motives named and discussed. Surveying crime victims, Tyler and Rasinski (1984; see also Tyler 1980) found that perceptions of risk and worry about future victimisation were associated with both what individuals learnt from their particular experience of crime (how much the experience told them about the likelihood of victimisation occurring again in the future, how much they learnt from the crime, and how much they learnt about how to protect themselves in the future) and the emotional reactions they had to the experience (whether they were upset, stunned, outraged, frightened, and shocked). In the last of three studies, Tyler and Rasinski (1984) also found the same processes at play when individuals read a report of a particular crime, thus suggesting that informativeness and affect are important mediators of the impact of first-hand *and* second-hand experience on fear of crime. Also important is the notion of 'stimulus similarity,' which describes how the reader of a newspaper (for example) might identify with the described victim or feel that their own neighbourhood bears resemblance to the one described (Winkel and Vrij 1990). Stapel *et al.* (1994) found subjects who received car crash information and who shared social identity with the victims provided elevates estimates of risk compared to those who had no basis for assumed similarity.

Sunstein (2005) argues that hearing about events has an impact on public perceptions of risk through an interaction between availability and social mechanisms which generate so-called 'availability cascades':

[these are] social cascades, or simply cascades, through which expressed perceptions trigger chains of individual responses that make these perceptions appear increasingly plausible through their rising availability in public discourse. Availability cascades may be accompanied by counter-mechanisms that keep perceptions consistent with the relevant facts. Under certain circumstances, however, they generate persistent social *availability errors*—widespread mistaken beliefs grounded in interactions between the availability heuristic and the social mechanisms we describe.

(Kuran and Sunstein 1999: 685) (original emphasis)

Thus, 'fear-inducing accounts' of events – such as the incident in 2002 in Virginia when two snipers killed 10 people – are likely to be highly publicised, noticed and repeated, leading to cascade effects as the event becomes available to an increasing number of people. Sunstein (2005: 93) also speculates that existing predispositions may determine in large part what individuals pay attention to. One example he gives relates to genetic modification of food. Those who are predisposed to be fearful of this issue are more likely to seek out information about genetic modification. Furthermore, 'group polarisation' describes how, when individuals discuss with each other certain events and risks, they typically end up with a more extreme view (Sunstein 2005: 98).

People may, therefore, develop personalised images of risk as a result of hearing about specific events of crime that are brought home to them in a very vivid way – 'as if it could happen to me'. High levels of coverage make the events available. Personal images of risk develop. And through their focus on the sensational and dramatic, crime reports may end up stressing certain attributes to the criminal event which only increase the fearfulness. Crimes that are especially serious in their consequence or morally reprehensible in their character get the most attention (from both media outlets and readers), as do those which show a lack of control and predictability. Thus, in addition to increasing cognitive availability, the consumer of media reports may give most attention to representations of events which have high levels of consequence and low levels of control for the victim. This, as outlined earlier in this chapter, may then have an especially strong influence on observers through probability insensitivity and consequent emotional response.

Risk entrepreneurs, and the cynical amplification of risk

More should be said about the diffusion and circulation of reports of crime in society. And here we might turn to the loose but inclusive set of concepts organised by the Social Amplification of Risk Framework (SARF, see Pidgeon *et al.* 2003). According to this framework, risk signals are received, interpreted and passed on at a series of 'amplifier' stations and diffused through different channels in society. Kasperson *et al.* (2003: 15) state that: ' ... as a key part of [the] communication process, risk, risks events, and the characteristics of both become portrayed through various risk signals (images, signs, and symbols), which in turn interact with a wide range of psychological, social, institutional, or cultural processes in ways that intensify or attenuate perceptions of risk and its manageability'. While the media are primary amplifiers, stations can also include individuals, groups and organisations such as activist groups of government agencies, driven by their interests and functions. The results are signals that can be increased or decreased in intensity, as well as transformed in their cultural content.

There are some parallels here with the concept of the *moral panic*. While this is not the place for a detailed discussion, it is worth mentioning some equivalencies:

- The stereotyping, sensitising and sensationalising of certain behaviours (for example, 'hoodies' and 'feral' gangs of 'listless' youths);
- An element of disproportionately between media coverage and the reality *on the ground*;
- An affront to the moral order and the identification of 'folk devils; and,
- A call for moral regulation and the neo-Durkheimian re-establishment of order through punishment and government action.

The SARF framework shifts our focus on those who amplify risk for their own ends. These might be insurance and real estate industries, whose interests lie in capitalising on anxiety to stimulate demand for gated communities, CCTVs and the like. Or they might be political parties, who use the rhetoric of danger and anarchy to further agendas and manipulate public opinion, whether inflating (to gain right-wing ground on crime and to justify hard-line solutions) or derogating fear of crime (to claim credit for reducing crime the public do not feel safer). Lee (1999, 2001, 2007) has argued for a kind of 'fear of crime industry' which includes politicians, corporate interests, and even academic researchers. According to his view, studies 'discover' anxieties about crime, then reify the phenomenon, and present to the public and to officials a 'legitimate' social problem. When politicians then try to govern fear, they only serve to sensitise citizens to crime. Moreover certain politicians push more right-wing approaches to criminal justice, which only heighten levels of public anxiety. The term 'fear of crime' has been used to justify various crime control policies which some on the libertarian-left have found hard to accept. When introducing more punitive sentences, restrictions on the rights of the accused, or more intensive forms of supervision and surveillance, politicians have sought to justify the proposed measures in terms of reducing the fear of crime (Fattah 1993: 61).

An interlude

In the first part of this chapter I speculated that people develop particular representations of risk. These include judgements of likelihood, control, consequence and vividness, as well as emotional responses to these risks. I also discussed one way of bringing the social back into the picture, Namely, we might address how individuals learn about risk through the circulation of reports of crime in society. Under certain circumstances these circulating representations can be picked up by individuals and develop into specific personal risk perceptions. Moreover, social and political actors influence the ways in which crime is talked about and risk is amplified.

Yet crime is a risk with a specific social character. In the public mind, 'crime' might be inseparable from: (a) conditions conducive to crime; and (b) signs of hostility to established group values. People may link crime with certain groups, with symptoms of social decay (the low-level disturbance that has come to be called antisocial behaviour), and with certain community conditions (low social trust, cohesion, collective efficacy, and moral consensus). Fear of crime may thus be as much about judgements of actual criminal threat as it is about judgements of a range of things seen as threatening to social order.

Moreover, criminal victimisation has a social aspect in a more direct sense: it is typically a harmful act committed by one individual on another individual, and its commission erodes valued social norms and conditions. Indeed, the very act of designating a certain group as a threat and representational of crime may lead to a neo-Durkheimian call for censure to re-establish that social order: people look to formal social controls to re-affirm group values when threats are identified (Jackson and Sunshine 2007).

Let us consider in a little more detail some aspects of the social character of crime-risk.

Morality and outrage

Crimes stimulate outrage and moral judgement in the observer. Crime is typically intentional: someone is seeking to deprive someone else of something – to damage them physically, psychologically or emotionally. The 'how dare they' factor may thus add a certain inflection to the risk of crime, an extra layer of significance and importance, raising the salience and inflecting the meaning of crime and crime-risk.

Take a rather straightforward example. Terrorism expresses a disdain for human life and the desire to damage a way of life. We may be outraged by terrorist acts partly because of what these acts express (consider how less outraged we are by car accidents that result in a comparable number of fatalities). First, our outrage may give it a charge and a resonance: the very idea that it is possible strikes at our sense of justice. Second, our identification of terrorism as a salient risk may be partly a defence of what it seeks to destroy: we give the risk of terrorism special significance because of the value we place on what terrorists seek to threaten.

Crime may be similar. There may be something about the intentionality of crime that moves people, making it a more salient and symbolically charged risk. Victimisation may strike at our deep-seated sense of fairness and co-operation, the value we place on the sanctity of property and liberty, our desire to censure those who defect. We value a sense of safety and security of our home and neighbourhood. We value healthy and predictable norms of social conduct. Crime damages the community. Transgression of the shared moral values of society challenges the authority and appropriateness of a moral and social structure, harming social cohesion, moral consensus and informal social controls. If transgression goes unpunished it further erodes social order, tainting group identity. Thus, the desire to punish and censure defectors reflects our desire to protect order, stability and organisation.

Symptoms of social decay

There is another element to the social nature of crime-risk. Much criminological research has demonstrated that fear of crime is as much a response to day-to-day encounters with 'symbols associated with crime' as it is about specific beliefs about crime (Hale 1996). Perceptions of the likelihood of victimisation are shaped by these individual evaluations of the social and physical environment (Ferraro 1995; Innes 2004; Jackson 2004), including judgements about: (a) social cohesion, trust and informal social control; (b) incivilities or 'broken windows'; and (c) the values, norms and morals of the people who make up the community (Skogan and Maxfield 1981; Wilson and Kelling 1982; Taylor *et al.* 1985; Smith 1986; Lewis and Salem 1986; Taylor and Hale 1986; Box *et al.* 1988; Skogan 1990; Covington and Taylor 1991; LaGrange *et al.* 1992; Ferraro 1995; Perkins and Taylor 1996; Rountree and Land 1996a, 1996b; Taylor 1999; Innes 2004; Robinson, *et al.* 2003; Jackson 2004; Jackson and Sunshine 2007).[3] Furedi argues that:

> The fear of crime is a distinctive feature of a society where the influence of informal relations and taken-for-granted norms has diminished in influence. It is anxieties about the uncertainties of day-to-day existence that people echo in discussions about the subject of crime. Insecurity towards expected forms of behaviour and suspicion about the motives of others provide a fertile terrain where perceptions of threats can flourish. These perceptions are intensified in circumstances where social isolation has become pervasive.
>
> (Furedi 2006: 5)

The risk of crime therefore seems to be projected into a given environment and elaborated with a face (the potential criminal) and a context (the place it might take place); it is rooted and situated. A key process in fear of crime may thus be the evaluative activity that links crime with individuals or groups who are judged by the observer to be: (a) hostile to the local social order; (b) untrustworthy; and (c) representative of some sort of social breakdown. Perceptions of risk may therefore express this evaluative activity. In other words, perceptions of the risk of crime may disclose a host of subtle evaluations of and responses to the social world – a way of responding to variable levels of social order and control, a sense of unease in an unpredictable environment, the association of particular individuals or conditions with deviance and hostile intent – just as much as they comprise specific appraisals of being attacked in the street, being burgled, or having someone stolen one's car.

If it is true that perceptions of crime risk reveal processes of designation (where certain groups, behaviours or community conditions are labelled as potentially criminal and dangerous) then another aspect moves into view on a contextualistic definition of risk. Crime may be used as a way of articulating evaluations of people, community conditions and social control, a lens through which people understand social order, low-level deviance and diversity.[4] The identification of dangerous individuals may operate to establish 'moral communities' by locating 'immoral communities' (cf Douglas 1990: 4–5). Stereotypes of particular groups may operate as distancing strategies for placing others, perpetuating normative boundaries of social conduct, roles and judgements, strengthening one's own social identity. They may reinforce and identity the boundaries of a given community by identifying what that community is against: for example, certain troublesome individuals, or particular groups defined by their social class or their ethnicity. Social psychology shows that the identification of an out-group operates the strength solidarity within the in-group. Scapegoating may also arise, where one group comes to embody a particular social problem. Such evaluative activity, if this analysis is correct, reveals how people define social order and what they think is hostile to social order. It also means that risk is culturally conditioned: what one defines as dangerous depends on where one stands.

Clashing worldviews

In a review of Sunstein's (2005) work, Kahan *et al.* (2006) argued that cultural values play a greater role in risk perception than his account suggests. The idea is simple: individuals hold attitudes toward risk which reflect and strengthen their values, commitment to particular ways of life, and preferred visions of society (see, for example, Douglas and Wildavsky 1982; Rayner 1992):

The priority of culture to fact is the organizing premise of the 'cultural theory of risk.' Associated most famously with the work of anthropologist Mary Douglas and political scientist Aaron Wildavsky, the cultural theory of risk links disputes over environmental and technological risks to clusters of values that form competing cultural worldviews – egalitarian, individualistic, and hierarchical. Egalitarians, on this account, are naturally sensitive to environmental hazards, the abatement of which justifies regulating commercial activities that produce social inequality. Individuals, in contrast, predictably dismiss claims of environmental risk as specious, in line with their commitment to the autonomy of markets and other private orderings. Hierarchists are similarly sceptical because they perceive warnings of imminent environmental catastrophe as threatening the competence of social and governmental elites.

According to Mark Douglas, people's conception of what constitutes danger, or a risk, vary according to the way their social relations are organised. People select risks as being important or trivial because this reinforces established social relations within their culture, although they may revise their thinking over time. Moreover, beliefs about purity, danger and taboo are essentially arbitrary. Once they become fixed, they serve to organise and reinforce social relations according to hierarchies of power.

Kahan *et al.* (2006) go on to outline why risk regulation politics are so often conflictual and value-based. Referencing Gusfield's (1986) work on status politics and symbolic conflicts, they argue that the battlefield is often about values and opposing cultural positions about the 'ideal society'. So hierarchists will be especially attuned to the threat of crime, since crime threatens social cohesion and moral consensus, and quickly gets linked to individuals and behaviours that are seen to be hostile to social order. People may attend to information about crime risk from the mass media and interpersonal communication because crime speaks to and dramatises their concerns about social cohesion, relations and change. Crime may get into such a symbolic tangle with issues of cohesion because the act of crime communicates hostility to the social order of a community and damages its moral fabric. The prevalence of crime may thus signal the community to be suffering from deteriorating standards of behaviour, diminishing power of informal social control, increasing diversification of norms and values, and decreasing levels of trust, reciprocity and respect.[5]

Risks may quickly become battles over competing values and definitions of social order. Different groups select and dramatise dangers to make their points and maintain the solidarity of their group. As Tansey (2004: 24–5) suggests: '... groups with marginal political or economic power can only exert their influence by appealing to the populace through accusations that those in power are responsible for exposing them to danger'. He continues:

Risk becomes politicized not simply because it is a threat to life but because it is a threat to ways of life. Rather than ask how a risk comes to be magnified or how risk perceptions are influenced by heuristics, irrationality or pure emotion, this approach asks indirect questions: At whom is the finger of blame being pointed? Who is being held accountable? What is being rejected and what is being defended in a particular collective social action? This implies that for issues such as genetically modified organisms, research that seeks to demonstrate the safety of the technology will not dissipate political opposition since protest is in defence of a moral boundary.

(Tansey 2004: 29)

All this raises doubts on whether, as Sparks explains:

risk can be domesticated, kept strictly within the bounds of probability calculations ... one consequence is that moments of intense controversy or recrimination (such as those engendered in debates about criminal sentencing or prison escapes or the release of convicted sex offenders) crystallize social anxieties and expose lines of division about the competence, trustworthiness and legitimacy of authorities. But this is also why, in Douglas's view, the vocabulary and associations of risk are always semantically denser, more culturally embedded, more episodic in their appearance and more open to politicization than attempts by specialists to numericize and rationalize them can admit. Risk does not 'unload its ancient moral freight'.

(Sparks 2001: 168–9)

Concluding remarks

This chapter has sketched out some early thoughts on ways to integrate the social and the psychological in fear of crime research. The task has been integrative (bringing together research from a number of disciplines) and speculative (developing ideas that may be useful in future empirical work). Culture does not hover over individuals. A cultural analysis of risk perception needs to account for the psychology of an individual: a sociological account needs to encompass individual thoughts and feelings about uncertainty and danger. And individuals do not operate in a vacuum. A psychological analysis of risk perception needs to account for the culturally embedded meaning of risk: psychology has tended to ignore why people select one risk and not another. I have argued that a contextualistic formulation of risk that bridges both levels of analysis offers a promising way forward. Much is brief. Much is speculative. More research is needed. But I hope the reader is convinced that research into the fear of crime needs to be more ambitious in its theory and more interdisciplinary in its approach.

Notes

1 To explore one aspect of this model, Killias and Clerici (2000) drew upon data from a sample survey of Swiss nationals to show that respondent assessments of their physical ability to defend themselves was an important predictor of anticipated feelings of safety in a number of situations.

2 At least according to mainstream statistics – for critiques and alternative perspectives see: Stanko 1985, 1987, 1990, 1997; Pain 1993, 1997; Madriz 1997; Gardner 1995; and Hollander 2001, 2002.

3 This body of empirical research has implications for the everyday experience of the fear of crime. Feelings of control may extend beyond control of concrete risks (that is, explicit events of victimisation) to control over the social and physical environment. This is a good deal of evidence that the fear of crime is an emotional response to symbols of crime as well as concrete expectations of victimisation. Fear of crime may thus be a visceral response to the symbols associated with crime even in the absence of specific inferences about the threat of crime – a diffuse sense of unease and lack of control within an unpredictable and disorderly environment. An environment judged as unpredictable, unfamiliar and beyond the control of oneself or one's community may generate a sense of disquiet and an instinctive need to scan the environment for signs of trouble, and a sense that 'anything could happen'. As Goffman (1971) describes: '… the minor incivilities of everyday life can function as an early warning system; conventional courtesies are seen as mere convention, but non-performance can cause alarm'. Threat can be signalled by the presence of certain persons who act counter to the 'minor civilities of every day life', who behave in ways that are 'improper or appear out of place'. Such people or behaviours may signal an 'absent, weakened or fragile local social order' (Innes 2004). Other signs of the violation of norms of behaviour and symbols of the lack of informal social controls – such as graffiti, and vandalism – may generate the sense that the social order is in flux (Ferraro 1995; Innes 2004), through a loss of authority over space. People may feel they lack a sense of control over what may or may not happen – being unsure how to read a situation – leading to a lack of trust that screens out negative interpretations in the people around them.

4 Fear of crime may express a broader sense of trust in strangers. In an examination of trust as a moral value, Uslaner (2002: I) argues that: 'Trusting strangers mean accepting them into our "moral community." Strangers may look different from us, they may have different ideologies or religions. But we believe that there is an underling commonality of values'. The fear of crime may consequently articulate individual's sense of common underlying values in their neighbourhood and their society more generally.

5 Sunstein's (2006) response to Kahan et al. (2006) was to defend his version of bounded rationality in risk perception. He questions whether the United States can best be divided into specific cultures. Instead, people have different normative positions, and these positions in his view bias their judgements in questions of fact. Moreover, he questions the evidence base for the notion that 'culture produces different *factual* judgements about the magnitude of social risks' (Sunstein 2006: 6, original emphasis). He accepts that moral commitments, rather than factual judgements, can lead people to give special attention to certain risk. For a response to this response, see Kahan and Slovic (2006).

References

Balkin, S (1979) 'Victimization rates, safety and fear of crime', *Social Problems*, 26(3): 343–58.

Box, S, Hale, C and Andrews, G (1988) 'Explaining Fear of Crime', *British Journal of Criminology*, 28: 340–56.

Butler, G and Mathews, A (1983) 'Cognitive processes in anxiety', *Advances in Behaviour Research and Therapy*, 25: 51–62.

—— (1987) 'Anticipatory anxiety and risk perception', *Cognitive Therapy and Research*, 11: 551–65.

Chadee, D, Austen, L and Ditton, J (2007) 'The relationship between likelihood and fear of criminal victimization: Evaluating risk sensitivity as a mediating concept', *British Journal of Criminology*, 47: 133–53.

Chiricos, T, Hogan, M and Gertz, M (1997) 'Racial composition of neighborhood and fear of crime' *Criminology*, 35(1): 107–29.

Clore, Gerald L and Gasper, K (2000) 'Feeling is believing: Some affective influences on belief', in NH Frijda, ASR Manstead and S Bem (eds), *Emotions and Beliefs: How Feelings Influence Thoughts*, Cambridge: Cambridge University Press, pp 10–44.

Conklin, JE (1975) *The Impact of Crime*, New York: Macmillan.

Covington, J and Taylor, RB (1991) 'Fear of crime in urban residential neighbourhoods: implications of between- and within- neighborhood sources for current models' *The Sociological Quarterly*, 32(2): 231–49.

Douglas, M (1966) *Purity and Danger: Concepts of Pollution and Taboo*, London: Routledge and Kegan Paul.

—— (1990) 'Risk as a forensic resource', *Daedalus*, 119: 1–16.

—— (1992) *Risk and Blame: Essays in Cultural Theory*, London: Routledge.

Douglas, M and Wildavsky, A (1982) *Risk and Culture: An Essay on the Selection of Technical and Environmental Dangers*, Berkeley, CA: University of California Press.

DuBow, F, McCabe, E and Kaplan, G (1979) *Reactions to Crime: A Critical Review of the Literature*, Washington, DC: National Institute of Law Enforcement and Criminal Justice, US Government Printing Office.

Epstein, S (1994) 'Integration of the cognitive and psychodynamic unconscious', *American Psychologist*, 49: 709–24.

Farrall, S (2004) '*Can* we believe our eyes?: A response to Mike Hough', *International Journal of Social Research Methodology*, 7: 177–9.

Farrall, S and Gadd, D (2004) 'The frequency of the fear of crime', *British Journal of Criminology*, 44: 127–32.

Farrall, S, Bannister, J, Ditton, J and Gilchrist, E (1997) 'Questioning the measurement of the fear of crime: Findings from a major methodological study', *British Journal of Criminology*, 37(4): 657–78.

Fattah, EA (1993) 'Research on fear of crime: Some common conceptual and measurement problems', in W Bilsky, C Pfeiffer and P Wetzels (eds), *Fear of Crime and Criminal Victimisation*, Stuttgart: Ferdinand Enke Verlag.

Ferraro, KF (1995) *Fear of Crime: Interpreting Victimization Risk*, New York: SUNY Press.

Frijda, NH, Manstead, ASR and Bem, S (2000) 'The influence of emotions on beliefs', in NH Frijda, ASR Manstead and S Bem (eds), *Emotions and Beliefs: How Feelings Influence Thoughts*, Cambridge: Cambridge University Press, pp 144–70.

Furedi, F (2006). *The Politics of Fear; Beyond Left and Right*, London: Continuum Press.

Gabriel, U and Greve, W (2003) 'The psychology of fear of crime: Conceptual and methodological perspectives', *British Journal of Criminology*, 43: 600–14.

Gardner, CB (1995) *Passing by: Gender and Public Harassment*, Berkeley, CA: University of California Press.

Garofalo, J (1979) 'Victimisation and the fear of crime', *Journal of Research in Crime and Delinquency*, 16: 80–97.

Girling, E, Loader, I and Sparks, R (2000) *Crime and Social Control in Middle England: Questions of Order in an English Town*, London: Routledge.

Goffman, E (1971) *Relations in Public*, New York: Basic Books.

Gray, E, Jackson, J and Farrall, S (2008) 'Reassessing the fear of crime', *European Journal of Criminology*.

Gusfield, JR (1986) *Symbolic Crusade*, 2nd edn, Champaign, IL: The University of Illinois Press.

Hale, C (1996) 'Fear of crime: a review of the literature', *International Review of Victimology*, 4: 79–150.

Hollander, JA (2001) 'Vulnerability and dangerousness: the construction of gender through conversation about violence', *Gender and Society*, 15: 83–109.

—— (2002) 'Resisting vulnerability: the social reconstruction of gender in interaction', *Social Problems*, 49: 474–96.

Hough, M (1995) *Anxiety about Crime: Findings from the 1994 British Crime Survey*, Home Office Research Study No. 147, London: Home Office.

—— (2004) 'Worry about crime: mental events or mental states?', *International Journal of Social Research Methodology*, 7(2): 173–6.

Innes, M (2004) 'Signal crimes and signal disorders: notes on deviance as communicative action', *British Journal of Sociology*, 55(3): 335–55.

Jackson, J (2004) 'Experience and expression: social and cultural significance in the fear of crime', *British Journal of Criminology*, 44(6): 946–66.

—— (2006) 'Introducing fear of crime to risk research', *Risk Analysis*, 26(1): 253–64.

—— (2008a) 'A psychological perspective on vulnerability in the fear of crime', under review.

—— (2008b) 'Sensitivity to risk in the fear of crime: control, consequence and the psychology of worry', under review.

Jackson, J and Gray, E (2008) *Functional Fear: Adaptational Features of Worry about Crime*, Working Paper, London: LSE.

Jackson, J and Sunshine, J (2007) 'Public confidence in policing: a neo-Durkheimian perspective', *British Journal of Criminology*, 47: 214–33.

Jackson, J, Allum, N and Gaskell, G (2006). 'Bridging levels of analysis in risk perception research: the case of the fear of crime' *Forum Qualitative Sozialforschung / Forum: Qualitative Social Research* [On-line Journal], T7T(1), Art. 20. Available at: http://www.qualitative-research.net/fqs-texte/1-06/06-1-20-e.htm (accessed 26 February 2008).

Jackson, J, Farrall, S, Gray, E and Kuha, J (2008) *A New Way of Measuring the Fear of Crime*, Working paper, London: LSE.

Kahan, D and Slovic, P (2006) *Cultural Evaluations of Risk: "Values" or "Blunders"?*, 14 March 2006, Yale Law School, Public Law Working Paper No. 111, available at http://ssrn.com/abstract=890800 (accessed 26 February 2008).

Kahan, D, Slovic, P, Braman, D and Gastil, J (2006) 'Fear of democracy: a cultural evaluation of Sunstein on risk', *Harvard Law Review* 119: 1071.

Kasperson, JX, Kasperson, RE, Pidgeon, N and Slovic, P (2003) 'The social amplification of risk: assessing fifteen years of research and theory', in Pidgeon, N, Kasperson, Roger E and Slovic, P (eds), *The Social Amplification of Risk*, Cambridge: Cambridge University Press, pp 13–46.

Killias, M (1990) 'Vulnerability: towards a better understanding of a key variable in the genesis of fear of crime', *Violence and Victims*, 5(2): 97–108.

Killias, M, and Clerici, C (2000) 'Different measures of vulnerability in their relations to different dimensions of fear of crime', *British Journal of Criminology*, 40(3): 437–50.

Kuran, T and Sunstein, C (1999), 'Availability cascades and risk regulation', *Stanford Law Review*, 51: 683–768.

Kury, H and Ferdinand, T (1998) 'The victim's experience and fear of crime', *International Review of Victimology*, 5: 93–140.

LaGrange, R,L, Ferraro, KF and Supancic, M (1992) 'Perceived risk and fear of crime: The role of social and physical incivilities', *Journal of Research in Crime and Delinquency*, 29: 311–34.

Lee, M (1999) 'The fear of crime and self-governance: Towards a genealogy', *The Australian and New Zealand Journal of Criminology*, 32(3): 227–46.

—— (2001) 'The genesis of "fear of crime"', *Theoretical Criminology*, 5(4): 467–85.

—— (2007) *Inventing Fear of Crime: Criminology and the Politics of Anxiety*, Cullompton: Willan Publishing.

Lewis, DA and Salem, G (1986) *Fear of Crime: Incivility and the Production of a Social Problem*, New Brunswick: Transaction Books.

Lichtenstein, S, Slovic, P, Fischhoff, B, and Combs, B (1978) 'Judged frequency of lethal events', *Journal of Experimental Psychology: Human Learning and Memory*, 4: 551–78.

Liska, AE, Sanchirico, A and Reed, MA (1988) 'Fear of crime and constrained behaviour: specifying and estimating a reciprocal effects model', *Social Forces*, 66: 760–70.

Loewenstein, GF, Weber, EU, Hsee, CK and Welch, N (2001) 'Risk as feelings', *Psychological Bulletin*, 127: 267–86.

Madriz, E (1997) *Nothing Bad Happens to Good Girls: Fear of Crime in Women's Lives*, Berkeley, CA: University of California Press.

Mathews, Andrew (1990) 'Why worry? The cognitive function of anxiety', *Behaviour Research and Therapy*, 28: 455–68.

McCoy, HV, Woolredge, JD, Cullen, FT, Dubeck, PJ and Browning, SL (1996) 'Lifestyles of the old and not so fearful: life situation and older persons' fear of crime', *Journal of Criminal Justice*, 24(3): 191–205.

Mills, CW (1953) 'Two styles of social science research', in *Power, Politics, and People: The Collected Essays of C. Wright Mills*, New York: Ballantine Books, pp 553–67.

Pain, R (1993) 'Women's fear of sexual violence: explaining the spatial paradox', in H. Jones (ed), *Crime and The Urban Environment*, Aldershot: Avebury.

—— (1997), 'Whither women's fear? Perceptions of sexual violence in public and private space', *International Review of Victimology*, 4: 297–312.

Perkins, D and Taylor, R (1996) 'Ecological assessments of community disorder: their relationship to fear of crime and theoretical implications', *American Journal of Community Psychology*, 24: 63–107.

Pidgeon, N, Kasperson, RE and Slovic, P (2003) *The Social Amplification of Risk*, Cambridge: Cambridge University Press.

Rayner, Steve (1992) 'Cultural theory and risk analysis', in S Krimsky and D Golding (eds), *Social Theories of Risk*, Westport: Praeger, pp 83–116.

Robinson, JB, Lawton, BA, Taylor, RB and Perkins, DD (2003) 'Multilevel longitudinal impacts of incivilities: fear of crime, expected safety, and block satisfaction', *Journal of Quantitative Criminology*, 19(3): 237–74.

Rottenstreich, Y and Hsee, CK (2001) 'Money, kisses and electric shocks: on the affective psychology of risk', *Psychological Science*, 12(3): 185–90.

Rountree, PW (1998) 'A reexamination of the crime-fear linkage', *Journal of Research in Crime and Delinquency*, 35(3): 341–72.

Rountree, PW and Land, KC (1996a) 'Perceived risk versus fear of crime: Empirical evidence of conceptually distinct reactions in survey data', *Social Forces*, 74: 1353–76.

—— (1996b) 'Perceived risk versus fear of crime', *Journal of Research in Crime and Delinquency*, 33: 147–80.

Russell, M and Davey, GCL (1993) 'The relationship between life event measures and anxiety and its cognitive correlates', *Personality and Individual Differences*, 14: 317–22.

Shiloh, S, Guvenc, G and Dilek, O (2007) 'Cognitive and emotional representations of terror attacks: a cross-cultural exploration', *Risk Analysis*, 27(2): 397–409.

Skogan, W (1986) 'Fear of crime and neighborhood change', *Crime and Justice*, 8: 203–29.

Skogan, W (1990) *Disorder and Decline: Crime and the Spiral of Decay in American Neighborhoods*, New York: The Free Press.

Skogan, W and Maxfield, M (1981) *Coping with Crime*, Beverly Hills, CA: Sage.

Skogan, WG (1987) 'The impact of victimisation on fear', *Crime and Delinquency*, 33(1): 135–54.

Sloman, SA (1996) 'The empirical case for two systems of reasoning', *Psychological Bulletin*, 119: 3–22.

Slovic, P (2000) *The Perception of Risk*, London: Earthscan.

Slovic, Paul, Finucane, M, Peters, E and MacGregor, DG (2004) 'Risk as analysis and risk as feelings: Some thoughts about affect, reason, risk, and rationality', *Risk Analysis*, 24(2): 311–22.

Smith, SJ (1986) *Crime, Space and Society*, Cambridge: Cambridge University Press.

Sparks, R (1992) 'Reason and unreason in left realism: some problems in the constitution of the fear of crime', in Matthews, R and Young, J (eds), *Issues in Realist Criminology*, London: Sage.

Sparks, Richard (2001) 'Degrees of estrangement: The cultural theory of risk and comparative penology', *Theoretical Criminology*, 5: 159–76.

Stafford, MC and Omer R Galle (1984) 'Victimization Rates, Exposure to Risk, and Fear of Crime', *Criminology*, 22: 173–85.

Stanko, E (1985) *Intimate Intrusions: Women's Experience of Male Violence*, London: Routledge and Kegan Paul.

Stanko, EA (1987) 'Typical violence, normal precaution: men, women and interpersonal violence in England, Wales, Scotland and the USA', in J Hanmer and M Maynard (eds), *Women, Violence and Social Control*, London: Macmillan.

—— (1990) 'When precaution is normal: a feminist critique of crime prevention', in L Gelsthorpe and A Morris (eds), *Feminist Perspectives in Criminology*, Milton Keynes: Open University Press.

—— (1997) 'Safety talk: conceptualising women's risk assessment as a "technology of the soul"', *Theoretical Criminology*, 1(4): 479–99.

Stapel, DA, Reicher, SD and Spears, R (1994) 'Social identity, availability and the perception of risk', *Social Cognition*, 12(1): 1–17.

Sunstein, C (2002) 'The law of fear', *Harvard Law Journal*, 115(4): 1111–68.

—— (2003) 'Terrorism and probability neglect', *Journal of Risk and Uncertainty*, 26: 121–36.

—— (2005) *The Laws of Fear: Beyond the Precautionary Principle*, Cambridge: Cambridge University Press.

—— (2006) 'Misfearing: A reply', *Harvard Law Review*, 119: 121.

Tansey, James (2004) 'Risk as politics, culture as power', *Journal of Risk Research*, 7(1): 17–32.

Taylor, RB (1999) 'The incivilities thesis', in R Langworthy (ed), *Measuring What Matters*, Washington, DC: National Institute of Justice.

Taylor, RB and Hale, M (1986) 'Testing alternative models of fear of crime', *The Journal of Criminal Law and Criminology*, 77(1): 151–89.

Taylor. RB, Shumaker, SA and Gottfredson, SD (1985) 'Neighborhood-level links between physical features and local sentiments: Deterioration, fear of crime, and confidence', *Journal of Architectural and Planning Research*, 2: 261–75.

Thompson, P (1999) 'The ethics of truth-telling and the problem of risk', *Science and Engineering. Ethics*, 5(4): 489–510.

Thompson, P and Dean, W (1996) 'Competing conceptions of risk', available at www.piercelaw.edu/risk/vol7/fall/thompson.htm (accessed 26 February 2008).

Tversky, A and Kahneman, D (1973) 'Availability: A heuristic for judging frequency and probability', *Cognitive Psychology*, 5: 207–32.

Tyler, T and Rasinski, K (1984) 'Comparing psychological images of the social perceiver: Role of perceived informativeness, memorability, and affect in mediating the impact of crime victimisation', *Journal of Personality and Social Psychology*, 46(2): 308–29.

Tyler, TR (1980) 'Impact of directly and indirectly experienced events: the origin of crime-related judgements and behaviours', *Journal of Personality and Social Psychology*, 39: 13–28.

Tyler, TR (1984) 'Assessing the risk of crime victimization: The integration of personal victimization experience and socially transmitted information', *Journal of Social Issues*, 40: 27–38.

Uslaner, EM (2002) *The Moral Foundations of Trust*, New York: Cambridge University Press.

Vanderveen, G (2006) *Interpreting Fear, Crime, Risk and Unsafety*, Cullompton: Willan Publishing.

Warr, M (1987) 'Fear of victimisation and sensitivity to risk', *Journal of Quantitative Criminology*, 3(1): 29–46.

—— (1994) 'Public perceptions and reactions to violent offending and victimization' in Albert J Reiss, Jr and Jeffrey A Roth (eds), *Consequences and Control*, vol 4 of *Understanding and Preventing Violence*, Washington, DC: National Academy Press.

—— (2000) 'Fear of crime in the United States: Avenues for research and policy', *Criminal Justice*, 4: 451–89.

Wilson, JQ and Kelling, GL (1982) 'Broken windows', *Atlantic Monthly*, March: 29–38.

Winkel, FW and Vrij, A (1990) 'Fear of crime and mass media crime reports: Testing similarity hypotheses', *International Review of Victimology*, 1: 251–65.

Chapter 10

State-trait anxiety and fear of crime

A social psychological perspective

Derek A Chadee, Nikiesha J Virgil and Jason Ditton

State-trait anxiety and fear of crime

This chapter assesses the relationship between types of anxiety and levels of fear of crime. In short, we attempt to discover how much *reported* fear of crime has more to do with anxiety than it has to do with crime. Data are from a random sample survey of Trinidadian respondents ($n = 636$) undertaken in 2000. This study utilised Ferraro's (1995) fear of crime scale as a measure of fear and Spielberger's (1983) State-Trait Anxiety Inventory to measure respondents' levels of anxiety. Findings suggest that state and trait anxiety exert an influence on fear of victimisation.

Anxiety is an intrinsic, necessary, uninhibited, and natural part of being human. It is not just a theoretical concept but also a profound and pervasive phenomenon that confronts humans in the course of their daily lives. Anxiety can be considered as a construct and as a system of constructs. It is a complex reaction characterised by subjective feelings of tension, apprehension, nervousness, worry, and dread (Levitt 1980; Spielberger 1972a), as well as the activation of the autonomic nervous system and increased physiological arousal (Spielberger 1983). Anxiety can also be manifested in shame, embarrassment, guilt, and distress (Averill 1976; Epstein,1972; Finney 1985; Izard 1991).

If allowed to persist, anxiety can cause disruptions to the normal daily functioning of individuals and too much can be debilitating (Finney 1985). It can become a condition that is unremitting or obsessive (Sluckin 1979) and can lead to anxiety disorders such as agoraphobia, generalised anxiety disorder, or post-traumatic stress disorder.

Despite its unpleasant effects, an average amount of anxiety is beneficial in that it can invigorate and motivate an individual to perform, and result in an increased ability to concentrate on important tasks (McLellan *et al.* 1986). Anxiety 'helps an individual to anticipate and avoid danger' (Williams *et al.* 2002: 314). In fact, anxiety is vital to the continued existence of organisms because it is a mechanism that protects the living being by signalling the flight or fight response.

Anxiety

Anxiety has been a subject of inquiry in many areas including psychology, sociology, and psychiatry. It has also been explored in literature, philosophy, education, politics and theology (May 1950). The concept of anxiety originated in the Hellenistic era of the Classic Greek period (McReynolds 1985). According to May, Freud was the first to see the fundamental significance of the problem that anxiety poses. Although much of Freud's writings and research on anxiety has been debated, his work has provided considerable insight into appreciating the nature of anxiety. He was the pioneer in exploring the relationship between anxiety and psychological disorders. He (Freud 1959 [1926]: 111) saw this state as being experienced by the total personality leading him to believe that anxiety was a 'fundamental phenomenon' experienced by individuals, and 'the central problem of neurosis'. Prior to the 1950s the area of anxiety was under-researched mainly because of the 'complexity of anxiety phenomenon, the ambiguity and vagueness in theoretical conceptions of anxiety, the lack of appropriate measuring instrumental and ethical problems associated with inducing anxiety in laboratory settings' (Spielberger 1983: 4).

State-trait anxiety

In the literature on anxiety a historical distinction is often made between anxiety as a mood or frame of mind and anxiety as a characteristic or quality. Although Hanfmann (1950) was the first to hint at this difference, it was Cattell (1966; Cattell and Scheier 1961, 1963) who coined the phrases 'state anxiety' and 'trait anxiety'. These terms were then made popular by Lazarus (1966), Spielberger (1966, 1972a, 1975) and Levitt (1980). Several other researchers (Cattell 1966; Endler *et al.* 1991; Spielberger 1983) have also distinguished between state and trait anxiety.

In examining the characteristics of state anxiety and trait anxiety, Levitt (1980) asserted that the former is an immediate and probably ephemeral state, whereas the latter type of anxiety is a constant condition without a time limitation. In a similar manner, Spielberger (1983: 5) maintained, 'although personality states are often transitory, they can recur when evoked by appropriate stimuli; and they may endure over time when evoking conditions persist'.

Spielberger *et al.* (1970) shared this view of state anxiety. They believed anxiety to be a transitory emotional state or condition existing in an individual at a specific point in time. This description of state anxiety points to its critical defining characteristic – state anxiety is a momentary condition, unpleasant and can fluctuate over time and occasion varying in intensity. Spielberger (1972b: 39), offered this distinction: 'State anxiety (A-State) is characterised by subjective, consciously perceived feelings of apprehension and tension, accompanied by or associated with activation or arousal of the autonomic nervous system'. He added that 'Personality traits can be conceptualised as relatively enduring differences among people in specifiable tendencies to perceive the world in a certain way and in dispositions to react to behave in a specified manner with predictable regularity'. On the other hand, Spielberger (1983) suggested that:

> Trait anxiety (T-Anxiety) refers to relatively stable individual differences in anxiety proneness, that is, to differences in between people in the tendency to perceive stressful situations as dangerous or threatening, and to respond to such situations with elevations in the intensity of their state anxiety (S-Anxiety) reactions.
>
> (Spielberger 1983: 5)

The implication of trait anxiety, then, is that there exists among individuals, differences in their character in terms of their ability to act in response to demanding situations with varying amounts of state anxiety (Spielberger 1983). However, someone who is high in trait anxiety, or is 'anxiety prone', would experience greater than average anxiety in any situation (Benet *et al.* 1993).

It seems, therefore, reasonable to assume, that with regards to the expression of trait anxiety, the condition in which the behaviour occurs is just as important as the individual's character. Moreover, there seems to be a proportional relationship between state and trait anxiety, where the stronger the trait anxiety, the more chances there are that: (1) the individual will experience the equivalent emotional state (state anxiety); and (2) the more frequently and intensely these emotional states and associated behaviours will be manifested (Kokotsaki and Davidson 2003).

State anxiety and trait anxiety are intricately related. Spielberger (1983) explained that because persons with high trait anxiety tend to interpret a wider range of situations as dangerous or threatening, these persons will exhibit high state anxiety more frequently than persons with low trait anxiety. Furthermore, persons with high trait anxiety have a greater inclination to display more intense levels of state anxiety in situations that threaten their self esteem or involve their interpersonal relationships. On the other hand, when confronted with physical danger the responses of persons high in trait anxiety and low in trait anxiety are similar.

Research on state-trait anxiety

There have been limited inquiries into understanding and recognising the phenomenon of anxiety as experienced by non-clinical populations (Harrigan *et al.* 1992; Harrigan *et al.* 1994; Harrigan *et al.* 1996; Jurich and Jurich 1974). In fact, inquiry into the nature of trait anxiety has largely been with clinical populations (Hoehn-Saric *et al.* 1995; Turner *et al.* 1986) whereas state anxiety has been measured in areas such as competition in sports and athletic performance (Martens 1971; Eysenck 1992; Raglin and Turner 1993; Turner and Raglin 1996); task difficulty when solving statistical problems by hand (Farbey and Roberts 1981); and musical performance (Kokotsaki and Davidson 2003).

Research outside sport and exercise psychology has indicated that individuals with high trait anxiety who are state anxious attend to threat related information, while individuals with low trait anxiety who are state anxious will attend away from threat related information (MacLeod 1990). Prior research has also shown that even though 'high and low trait persons do not appear to differ in their reactions to threats posed by physical dangers' (Spielberger 1975: 137), trait anxiety is on average higher among lower social class individuals than among middle class individuals (Lewis 1996; Lenzi *et al.* 1993; Zeidner 1988).

With respect to the relationship between state anxiety and age, as well as strait anxiety and gender, there seems to be conflicting results. In a study conducted by All and Fried (1996) on HIV/AIDS rehabilitation workers, it was stated that previous measurements obtained utilising Spielberger's State/Trait Anxiety Inventory showed that the age and the amount of previous contact with persons with HIV/AIDS or homosexuals were the only factors that influenced state anxiety levels of the rehabilitation workers. In contrast, Wetherell *et al.* (2002) reported that age showed no significant correlations with state anxiety. When looking at the effect of gender on state anxiety however, Abel and Larkin (1990) found that females had significantly greater state anxiety than males. However, Kokotsaki and Davidson (2003) found no differential effects of trait anxiety on gender.

Spielberger (1983) also conceived that an individual's perception of a situation could mediate the relationship between state anxiety and trait anxiety, in that:

> Whether or not people who differ in T-Anxiety will show corresponding differences in S-Anxiety depends on the extent to which each of them perceives a specific situation as psychologically dangerous or threatening and this is greatly influenced by each individual's past experience. It therefore seems likely that individuals who have had been previous victims of crime are likely to show high state anxiety and correspondingly high levels of trait anxiety.
>
> (Spielberger 1983: 5)

The relationship between anxiety and fear

There has been extensive debate about the relationship between anxiety and fear (Frijda 1993; Ohman 1993; Power and Dalgleish 1997). The terms anxiety and fear are often used synonymously in the English language. This could be attributed to the similarities between the two constructs. Like anxiety, fear is an unpleasant, complex emotional state that is common to most human beings and involves physiological arousal, the function of which, Williams *et al.* (2000) stated, is to avoid danger.

Freud (1920), however, provided one of the most widely known distinctions between anxiety and fear. His discrimination of the terms is based on the location and specificity of the evoking stimulus (Kreitler 2004). For Freud, fear is based on whether the object is realistic and one is aware of the source of threat or danger, while anxiety is imagined and one is unaware of the source of threat or danger. Freud (1959 [1926]) also maintains that the catalyst for fear is external and specific while that of anxiety is internal and non-specific. He goes on to say that anxiety refers to the condition of the individual that is part of the self-preservation instinct.

Another early writer, May (1950), recognised that fear and anxiety were intrinsically bound together. However, he also admits that the reactions in fear and those in anxiety are quite different and represent threats to different levels in the personality. May further states that anxiety is the organism's capacity to react to threats to its existence and values while fear is the differentiated reaction to specific dangers. Contemporary writers have also pondered on the dynamics between fear and anxiety. Izard (1972, 1977) believed that there is a link between anxiety and fear in that anxiety is a complex emotion comprised of fear and two or more other emotional states.

Levitt (1980) used three criteria to distinguish between 'anxiety' and 'fear'. These include: (1) the basis of the stimulus for the reaction; (2) the specificity of the reaction; and (3) the proportionality of the reaction. Bowlby (1973) focused on the individual's reaction to natural dangers (fear) and threat to attachment (anxiety). Michels *et al.* (1985) adopted a psycho-dynamic approach to understanding the difference between fear and anxiety. For these authors, fear is evoked under conditions of threat to one's physical existence whereas anxiety is evoked under conditions of threat to psychological existence, which may be endangered by the activation of drives, primarily the sexual and aggressive ones. Rachman (1990: 3) asserted that 'fear describes feelings of apprehension about tangible and predominately realistic dangers' while 'anxiety refers to feelings of apprehension that are difficult to relate to tangible sources of stimulation'. Lazarus (1991) made the distinctions based upon whether there is physical imminent harm (fear) or existential threat (anxiety) to the individual. Gray and McNaughton (2000) highlighted the function of the behaviour that the phenomenon produces – active avoidance, as in the case of fear or passive avoidance, as in the case of anxiety.

Warr (2000) contended that the term 'fear' as used by psychologists refers to reactions to immediate threats while 'anxiety' is a reaction to future or past events. He further maintained that in research on fear of crime there is no clarity in the distinction between anxiety and fear but rather the measures of fear that are used in fear of crime research are actually designed to capture anxiety rather than fear of victimisation. This updates an original distinction made by Croake and Hinkle (1976: 197) of fear when the object that threatens is clearly in focus, and anxiety when it is not. The comment, sourly, that '[m]any studies that report fears may actually have investigated anxiety, and many reporting the results of anxiety studies may have been researching fears'. Despite the various ways of looking at the association between fear and anxiety, one thing is certain – 'the understanding of fear hinges upon the understanding of ... anxiety' (May 1950: 205).

Fear of crime

Crime can be considered as one of many fear-evoking stimuli. Fear of crime is perceived as chronic and menacing social problem that can affect people in more ways than the actual occurrence of crime itself – or so we are led to believe. According to Pain (2001), a clear definition of fear of crime has been the subject of much discussion and debate in recent years. She defined fear of crime as the emotional and practical responses to crime and disorder that are made by individuals. The focus here is on the effect of crime on the individual's everyday life and fear of crime could be aroused by an immediate danger, or by the anticipation of threat, by environmental cues that imply danger (Warr 2000). It is a multidimensional concept and, therefore, the complexity of fear of crime cannot be tapped into with a single variable measure (Ferraro and LaGrange 1987a; Roundtree 1998). According to Warr the intensity, prevalence and duration among individuals and within social units are characteristic properties of fear of crime. The fear related to crime that humans experience usually occurs in brief episodes.

Over the last three decades, the relationship between age, sex, perceived risk of victimisation and prior victimisation and fear of crime has been widely researched (Clemente and Kleiman 1977; Baumer 1978; Garofalo 1979). Living arrangements also appear to be associated with *fear of crime in that* those who live alone express greater *fear* (for example, Donnelly 1989). It has generally been believed that levels of fear of crime are higher in the elderly, yet the findings are inconsistent (Chadee and Ditton 2003; Clarke and Lewis 1982; Clemente and Kleinman 1977; Ferraro and LaGrange 1992; Stafford and Galle 1984), females (*Liska et al.* 1988; Warr 1984), with those with higher perceived risks of victimisation (Ferraro 1996) and those persons who have been previous victims of crime (Liska *et al.* 1988; Skogan and Maxfield 1981) being more fearful. Dull and Wint (1997) further show that victims have a greater fear of property crime, but lower fear of personal crime than non-victims. As stated by Ferraro and LaGrange (1987b), a common assumption in our culture is that victimisation fear, which would imply anxiety proneness, is pervasive among the elderly. However, the results of the LaGrange and Ferraro study do not support this assumption.

Numerous explanations have been offered with respect to these findings. Ferraro and LaGrange (1987a) posit that women are more likely to perceive certain situations as dangerous, therefore their levels of fear of crime are higher than that of men. Rohe and Burby (1988) suggest that because women and the elderly view themselves as physically vulnerable, they feel less capable of resisting physical attacks. Smith and Uchida (1988) and Warr (1987) offer that women have an inordinate fear of sexual assault, especially rape, and this fear pervades all aspects of their lives, causing them to express greater overall fear levels. Ferraro (1995) and Warr (1984) argue that fear of sexual victimisation is the single greatest cause of the deferential levels of fear of crime among women. It is noteworthy that some researchers have found conflicting results, which have brought the general findings into question. Particularly, Gilchrist *et al.* (1998) found that men do fear crime just like women but they are less likely to express this fear because of cultural expectations. More recently, Sutton and Farrall (2004) have demonstrated that men under-report fear levels (see also Sutton and Farrall, Chapter 7, in this book).

In the last two decades, a number of researchers have examined the relationship between fear of crime and actual crime victimisation (Ferraro 1995; Ferraro and LaGrange 1987b; Forde 1993; LaGrange *et al.* 1992; Lupton 2000; Roundtree 1998; Smith and Torstensson 1997; Warr 1984, 2000; Warr and Stafford, 1983; Williams *et al.* 2000). In a review of the literature, Hale (1996) reports that there is some evidence that there is a positive relationship between victimisation and fear of crime while other evidence points to a weak or non-existent one. Hale attributes the inconsistent results to a number of factors including: (1) the failure of researchers to control for previous victimisation experience when examining specific fear of crime; (2) the failure to distinguish the type of victimisation experience when examining the effect of victimisation experience on fear of crime; and (3) the use of global instead of specific measures of fear of criminal victimisation. However, research by Vitelli and Endler (1993) has shown that anxiety predicts fear of crime and fear of victimisation.

What makes fear of crime and state/trait anxiety such an important area of investigation is their profound impact not only on the quality of the daily lives of individuals but also on the economics and politics of entire societies (see both Lee, Chapter 3, and Loo, Chapter 2, in this book). Investigators have identified many behaviours that are related to fear of crime. These include protective behaviours such as getting a guard dog or purchasing knives and guns for protection, and avoidance behaviours such as avoiding unsafe areas. These behaviours can unnecessarily constrain behaviour, restrict freedom and personal opportunity, and threaten the foundation of communities (Warr 2000). Fear of crime can also have other pervasive effects. Kilpatrick *et al.* (1987) identified victims of various crimes such as assault, robbery and burglary, and 15 years later these victims showed a high prevalence of post-traumatic stress disorder. The exploration of the relationship between anxiety and fear of crime is therefore a worthwhile endeavour as it can provide deeper insight into the motivations, reactions and behaviour of individuals. Hence it is important for researchers to explore the effects in anxiety on the experiences of individuals.

As Gabriel and Greve (2003) explained, there are individual differences in fear of crime. They applied Spielberger's (1966) conceptual analysis of state and trait anxiety to an understanding of fear of crime. As Gabriel and Greve put it:

> I may be afraid of becoming a victim of crime in situations ... here, fear of crime is a transitory state that will generally pass quickly. In the long term, however, such emotional occurrences (Frijda, 1993) may contribute ... to my general disposition of being afraid of becoming a victim of crime. In contrast, fear of crime as a disposition (trait) describes my tendency to experience fear of crime in certain situations; it is comparatively stable within subjects, but varies between subjects. Such an individual disposition is characterised by experiencing more situations as being relevant to fear, being more likely to experience fear in a given situation and possibly, experiencing fear more intensely.
>
> (Gabriel and Greve 2003: 601)

They described the first type of fear of crime as 'situational fear of crime', and the latter as 'dispositional fear of crime'. In the same way as Spielberger (1983) asserted in his notion of state and trait anxiety, Gabriel and Greve (2003) maintained that there is a relationship between situational and dispositional fear of crime. An increase in dispositional fear of crime increases the probability that a particular situation will evoke situational fear of crime. The application of Spielberger's state and trait anxiety to fear of crime by Gabriel and Greve certainly hints at the dynamics of the relationship between state and trait anxiety and fear of crime.

There is a marked relationship between fear of crime and anxiety. According to Steven (1992):

> Fear manifests itself in various ways depending on the person involved and the basis for their anxiety. Some individuals fear walking on the streets in their neighborhood while others fear physical attack within their home ... regardless of the source of this fear, it is real for those individuals who perceive these threat.
>
> (Steven 1992: 8)

One may carry this idea further to say that fear of crime would also be manifested in various ways depending on whether the individuals' basis for anxiety is situational (state anxiety) or dispositional (trait anxiety).

Method

Sample and procedures

This study adopted Ferraro's definition of fear of crime. This definition is: 'Fear of crime is an emotional response of dread or anxiety to crime or symbols that a person associates with crime' (Ferraro 1995: 24). The survey was conducted in Trinidad, West Indies during September 2000. Using a list of enumeration districts from the Central Statistical Office, 62 enumeration districts were randomly selected from low and high crime areas with 12 households subsequently and randomly selected from each district. Given the dispersion of the population this method allowed for randomness in a disperse population. The sample size was 636 and data collection involved face-to-face interviews with the head of the household (where possible) or the next most responsible adult. Contacts were limited to one call-back. In cases where a respondent was not available in the pre-selected household, the adjacent house was then selected for interview. This technique was used in some of the booster samples in the British Crime Survey prior to 2002, where it is referred to as 'focused enumeration'. The resulting Trinidadian sample consisted of 42 per cent males and 58 per cent females.

Measures

Fear of crime

Adopting the scale used by Ferraro (1995), respondents were asked the following question with these fixed choice responses (and in this order): 'very afraid = 4', 'afraid = 3', 'unafraid = 2' and 'very unafraid = 1'. How much are you afraid of each of the following 10 things:

- Being cheated, conned, or swindled out of your money
- Having someone break into your home while you are away
- Having someone break into your home while you are there
- Being raped or sexually assaulted
- Being murdered
- Being attacked by someone with a weapon
- Having your car stolen
- Being robbed or mugged on the street
- Having your property damaged by vandals
- Being kidnapped.

The measure for fear of having your car stolen was dropped because it depressed the Cronbach Alpha score (probably because about 48 per cent of respondents indicated that they did not have a car). Responses to the remaining items were combined to form a fear of crime scale ranging from 9 to 36 with a Cronbach Alpha of .89. Two sub-scales were created from the additive fear index – fear of crime against person and fear of crime against property scales. The fear of crime against property scale consisted of the following items: being cheated, conned, or swindled out of your money; having someone break into your home while you are away; having your property damaged by vandals. The fear of crime against person scale consisted of the following items: having someone break into your home while you are there; being raped or sexually assaulted; being murdered; being attacked by someone with a weapon; being robbed or mugged on the street; having your property damaged by vandals; being kidnapped. Both scales had Cronbach Alpha scores above .80. Variables were coded as follows: SEX, VICTIM and AREA were dummy coded with 'male' = 0 and 'female' = 1; 'non-victim' = 0 and 'victim' = 1; and 'low' = 0 and 'high' = 1. AGE was coded into the following categories: '18–24' = 1; '25–34' = 2; '35–44' = 3; '45–54' = 4; '55–64' = 5; '65–74' = 6; '75 and over' = 7.

State-trait anxiety

Spielberger's (1983) State-Trait Anxiety Inventory was used to measure respondents' levels of anxiety. The scale has 40 items with 20 items measuring state anxiety and 20 items measuring trait anxiety. Individuals are asked to respond to each item on a four-point Likert scale, on how he/she feels: (1) when he/she anticipates unforeseen events; (2) when he/she compares himself to others; and (3) in response to personal experiences. High scores on the S-Anxiety scale indicate more state anxiety and low scores indicate less state anxiety. Likewise for the T-Anxiety scale, high scores signify more trait anxiety and low scores point to less trait anxiety. The following responses were offered to respondents on the Likert scale for state anxiety items: 'not at all' = 1, 'somewhat' = 2, 'moderately so' = 3, 'very much so' = 4. The following responses were offered to respondents on the Likert scale for trait anxiety items 'almost never' = 1, 'sometimes'= 2, = 'often'= 3, 'almost always'= 4.

Results

An analysis of variance (ANOVA) showed that there was a significant difference between persons with respect to general fear of crime ($F (2, 603)$ = 13.22, $p<.001$). Persons with low state and low trait anxiety exhibited the lowest level of fear of crime ($M = 25.90$) while persons high in state anxiety and trait anxiety exhibited the highest levels of fear of crime ($M = 28.42$).

The ANOVA also revealed that persons who were high in state anxiety but low in trait anxiety exhibited slightly lower levels of fear of crime ($M =$ 27.41) than persons who were low in state anxiety but high in trait anxiety ($M = 28.02$).

Regarding fear of crime against the person, there was a significant outcome with the ANOVA (F (2, 603) $= 8.51$, $p<.001$). Those with low state and trait anxiety had the lowest level of fear of crime against the person ($M = 14.95$). In addition, persons high in trait anxiety were more likely to experience higher levels of fear of crime against the person than persons low in trait anxiety, irrespective of their level of state anxiety. This was indicated by the almost identical levels of fear of crime against person high in trait anxiety regardless of their state anxiety whether low ($M = 16.27$) or high ($M = 16.26$).

There was also a significant difference between the groups with respect to fear of property crime. (F (2, 603) $= 15.29$, $p<.001$). In particular, persons who were low in both state and trait anxiety had the lowest fear of property crime levels ($M = 10.96$) of any of the groups. Conversely, persons with high state and high trait anxiety had the highest levels of fear of property crime ($M = 12.14$). Since persons low in state anxiety but high in trait anxiety had higher levels of fear of property crime ($M = 11.80$) than persons high in state anxiety but low in trait anxiety ($M = 11.58$), one may infer that persons high in trait anxiety appear more likely to experience high levels of fear of property crime despite their level of state anxiety.

As shown in Table 10.1, respondents' overall recorded levels of fear of crime, fear of property crime and fear of personal crime were significantly and positively associated with state anxiety and trait anxiety, that is, high levels of fear of crime are related to correspondingly high levels of state anxiety ($r =.17$, $p<.05$), trait anxiety ($r =.19$, $p<.05$) and state- trait anxiety ($r =.20$, $p<.05$). This was also true for fear of property and fear of personal crimes.

A 2 (state anxiety) × 2 (area of respondents) ANOVA showed that there was a significant difference between persons with respect to fear of crime (F (2, 448) $= 9.76$, $p<.001$). Persons with low state anxiety living in low crime areas had the lowest level of fear of crime ($M = 25.17$) while persons low in

Table 10.1 Summary of correlations for anxiety, fear of crime, fear of property crime, and fear of personal crime

Anxiety	Fear of crime	Fear of property crime	Fear of personal crime
S-Anxiety	.17*	.17*	.13*
T-Anxiety	.19*	.20*	.15*
State-Trait Anxiety	.20*	.21*	.16*

* Correlation is significant at 0.01 level (2-tailed)

state anxiety living in high crime areas had the highest levels of fear of crime ($M = 28.51$). The ANOVA also revealed that persons who were high in state anxiety but living in a low crime area had lower levels of fear of crime ($M = 27.27$) than persons who were high in state anxiety living in high crime areas ($M = 28.21$).

Levels of fear of crime were also analysed using a 2×2 (trait anxiety $\times$ area of respondents) ANOVA. This analysis revealed that there was also a significant difference between the groups with respect to fear of crime (F (2, 447) $= 13.31, p<.001$). Persons who were low in trait anxiety living in low crime areas had the lowest fear of crime levels ($M = 24.74$) than any of the other groups. On the other hand, persons with high in trait anxiety living in high crime areas had the highest levels of fear of crime ($M = 28.88$). Overall, persons living in high crime areas had higher levels of fear of crime than persons living in low crime areas, however, of these persons, those low in trait anxiety had slightly lower levels of fear ($M = 28.16$) than persons with high trait anxiety ($M = 28.88$).

With respect to state-trait anxiety and area, the 2×2 ANOVA showed that there was a significant difference between the groups with respect to fear of crime (F (2, 446) $= 13.39, p<. 05$) where persons low in state-trait anxiety and living in low crime areas had the lowest levels of fear of crime ($M = 24.72$).On the other hand, persons with the highest level of fear of crime ($M = 28.81$) were residing in high crime areas and high in state-trait anxiety. Again, the level of fear of personal crime in low crime areas was lower than those living in high crime areas.

Table 10.2 displays results from a series of regression analysis. These analyses show that age, sex, area, state-trait anxiety and previous experience as a victim of crime predicted a significant proportion of variance in fear of crime ($R^2= .15, F$ (5, 437) $= 15.35, p < .001$). The analyses also shows sex, area, state-trait anxiety, and previous experience as a victim of crime predicted a significant proportion of variance in fear of property crime ($R^2 = .13, F$ (5, 445) $= 13.05, p < .001$) but age did not significantly predict fear of property crime. Furthermore, the analyses show that sex, area, and state-

Table 10.2 Regression of fear on age, sex, area, state-trait anxiety and victim

Variable	Fear of crime			Fear of propery crime			Fear of personal crime		
	B	SE B	β	B	SE B	β	B	SE D	β
Age	−.38	.19	−.09 *	−.15	.08	−.08	−.23	.13	−.08
Sex	3.05	.61	.23 ***	1.20	.27	.21 ***	1.88	.40	.22 ***
Area	2.60	.59	.20 ***	.81	.26	.14 **	1.73	.39	.20 ***
State-trait anxiety	.07	.02	.12 **	.03	.01	.14 **	.03	.02	.10 *
Victim	1.97	.86	.10 *	1.06	.38	.13 **	.91	.56	.07

$*p < .05. **p < .01. ***p < .001$

trait anxiety predicted a significant proportion of variance in fear of personal crime ($R^2 = .13$, F (5, 440) = 12.70, $p < .001$) but neither age nor previous victimisation experience had a significant impact of fear of personal crime.

The AMOS 4 program (Arbuckle 1994) was used to develop a structural equation model to test all proposed relations, the final version of which is shown in Figure 10.1. Standardised factor loadings ranged from -.070 to 0.486 on their respective constructs in the final model. Goodness-of-fit statistics suggested that this model provided a good fit to the data ($\chi^2(11)$ = 15.714, $p=.152$). Both the adjusted goodness of fit index (AGFI) and goodness of fit index (GFI) were well above the .900 threshold (.986 and .996 respectively).

Structural equation modeling indicated that age, sex, residence, state/ trait anxiety, risk, and previous victimisation explained 16 per cent of the variance in fear of crime. A fair amount of the variance in state anxiety was attributed to residence, sex, victim and trait anxiety ($R^2 = .25$). Overall, risk of victimisation, followed by trait anxiety, contributed the most in explaining levels of fear of crime.

The model also revealed that only residence, sex, and trait anxiety had a direct effect on risk. There was no relationship between state anxiety and risk, and previous victimisation experience and risk. The model also showed that state anxiety and previous victimisation experience did not have a direct effect on risk, however there was an indirect effect of sex and age on risk. Furthermore, the relationship between age and fear of crime was mediated by trait anxiety and risk. State anxiety was also a mediating factor in the

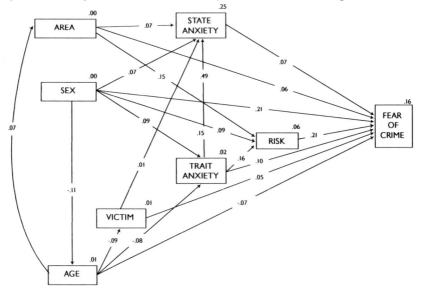

Figure 10.1 Structural equation model of the effect of area, sex, age, victim, state anxiety, trait anxiety and risk on fear of crime

relationship between residence and fear of crime. Likewise, risk mediated the relationship between sex and fear of crime.

Discussion

In low crime areas, respondents displayed low fear of crime levels regardless of level of anxiety (state, trait, and state-trait). This implies that crime area may have been an overriding factor in influencing fear of crime. However, persons living in high crime areas display a greater level of fear of crime when trait anxiety levels are high. This may be the result of the interaction of high crime area with high levels of trait anxiety. Similarly, persons living in high crime areas display a greater level of fear of crime when state-trait anxiety levels are high. Again, the interaction of high crime area with high levels of trait anxiety may have produced this outcome. Nevertheless, although state anxiety and trait anxiety 'performed' broadly as they were supposed to with attempts to relate them to other variables, neither (separately or together) showed much of a relationship to fear of crime. Indeed, state anxiety only correlated with fear at 0.17, trait anxiety at .19 and state-trait anxiety at .20. At most, then, our modelling suggest that only some 4 per cent of fear of crime is related to anxiety. The elusive nature of fear of crime thus remains so.

This chapter attempted to explore the relationship between anxiety and fear of crimes as articulated in the psychology literature. The literature on fear of crime has mostly dealt with this concept from a sociological/criminological perspective with no attempt to deconstruct the concept or even to reconstruct this very elusive construct. Many researchers accept as given the concept of fear of crime and the concomitant assumptions that go with the concept, which can be varied. The study on anxiety offers a further understanding and dimension to the appreciation of fear in the context of crime and by extension the development of definitions and measurements on fear of crime.

The findings here must be moderated by the fact that there is a neural bases for fear and anxiety. Theories of emotions assist in a further appreciation of the relationship between emotions (fear) and anxiety. For example, the James-Lange theory (Edwards 1999) states that emotions are the result of a person's perception of bodily changes and autonomic arousal. Levenson *et al.* (1990) found some support for the autonomic arousal argument made by the James-Lange theory. Their study demonstrated that there were some physiological differences among emotions (see Cannon 1927 for a critique of James-Lange theory). Anxiety, as well as fear, is an internal strategy of addressing threatening stimuli and is related to emotional responses. Dvorak-Bertsch *et al.* (2007) argued that anxiety moderates the interplay between the cognitive and affective processes.

Cognitive appraisal theory (Schachter and Singer 1962) also provides insights into the interpretation of physiological arousal and the emotion expressed and its intensity. The emotional labels (for example, fear, anger) are cognitively determined. Arousal fuelled by state or trait anxiety or both is but an intervening factor moderated by a host of other variables. From appraisal theory, therefore, fear is the outcome of a cognitive evaluation of a physiological arousal resulting from anxiety. In the case of fear of crime, anxiety (state) is created by cues related to crime. This view of fear is different from the convenient and easily operationalised definitions of fear as related to crime – fear of crime is an emotional response to crime or symbols associate with crime. Therefore, researchers must be cognisant of the elements that constitute fear in the development of a definition and measurement of fear. In so doing, issues of validity and reliability can easily be addressed. This study actually treated anxiety as an entity separated from fear of crime but attempted to assess the relationship.

Research has found that high anxiety is correlated with the appraisal of neutral situations as endangering. A self-focused attentional bias may lead anxious respondents to identify threatening cues more readily than non-anxious respondents. Calvo and Eysenck (2000) found a relationship between trait anxiety and a continued vigilance for danger processing. As noted, the relationship between anxiety and fear (of crime) is often moderated. For example, respondents who experience high anxiety may have a memory bias and attempt to decrease that anxiety by reducing their attention on danger and threatening stimuli (see Beck and Clarke 1997; MacLeod *et al.* 1986; Mogg *et al.* 1993). Further, respondents whose anxiety levels are exceedingly high may be hypervigilant and cognitively sensitivity towards threatening and danger cues (Beck and Clarke 1997). Future studies need to further investigate this area.

In summary, this study advances understanding of the relationship between fear of crime and anxiety. Further research needs to be undertaken to advance an understanding in this understudied area.

Acknowledgments

This study is partly funded by a Research and Publication Grant of the University of the West Indies.

References

Abel, J and Larkin, K (1990) 'Anticipation of performance among musicians: Physiological arousal, confidence, and state anxiety', *Psychology of Music*, 18: 171–82.

All, A and Fried, J (1996) 'Factors influencing anxiety concerning HIV/AIDS in rehabilitation workers', *Journal of Rehabilitation*, 62(4): 17–22.

Arbuckle JL (1994) *AMOS User's Guide: Version 3.6*, Chicago, IL: SmallWaters Corp.

Averill, J (1976) 'Emotion and anxiety: Sociocultural, biological, and psychological determinants', in M Zuckerman and C Spielberger (eds), *Emotions and anxiety*, Hillsdale, NJ: Erlbaum, pp 87–130.

Baumer, T (1978) 'Research on fear of crime in the United States', *Victimology: An International Journal*, 3(3/4): 254–64.

Beck, AT and Clarke, DA (1997) 'An information processing model of anxiety: Automatic and strategic processes', *Behaviour Research and Therapy*, 35: 49–58.

Benet, S, Pitts, R and LaTour, M (1993) 'The appropriateness of fear appeal use for health care marketing to the elderly: Is it OK to scare granny?', *Journal of Business Ethics*, 12(1): 45–56.

Bowlby, J (1973) *Attachment and Loss: Vol 2. Separation: Anxiety and Anger*, New York: Basic Books.

Calvo, MG and Eysenck, MW (2000) 'Early vigilance and late avoidance of threat processing: Repressive coping versus low/high anxiety', *Cognitive & Emotion*, 14: 763–87.

Cannon, WB (1927) 'The James-Lange theory of emotions: A critical examination and an alternative theory', *American Journal of Psychology*, 39: 106–24.

Cattell, R (1966) 'Patterns of change: Measurement in relation to state dimension, trait change, lability and process concepts', in R Cattell (ed), *Handbook of Multivariate Experimental Psychology*, Chicago, IL: Rand McNally & Co, pp 355–402.

Cattell, R and Scheier, I (1961) *The Meaning and Measurement of Neuroticism and Anxiety*, New York: Ronald Press.

—— (1963) *Handbook for the IPAT Anxiety Scale*, Champaign, IL: Institute for Personality and Ability Testing.

Chadee, D and Ditton, J (2003) 'Are older people most afraid of crime?: Revisiting Ferraro and LaGrange in Trinidad', *British Journal of Criminology*, 43: 417–33.

Clarke, A and Lewis, M (1982) 'Fear of crime among the elderly', *British Journal of Criminology*, 22: 49–62.

Clemente, F and Kleiman, M (1977) 'Fear of crime in the United States: A multivariate analysis', *Social Forces*, 56: 519–31.

Croake, J and Hinkle, D (1976) 'Methodological problems in the study of fears', *The Journal of Psychology*, 93: 197–202.

Donnelly, P (1989) 'Individual and neighborhood influences on fear of crime', *Sociological Focus*, 22: 69–84.

Dull, R and Wint, A (1997) 'Criminal victimization and its effect on fear of crime and justice attitudes', *Journal of Interpersonal Violence*, 12(5): 748–58.

Dvorak-Bertsch, JD, Curtin, JJ, Rubinstein, JB and Newman, P (2007) 'Anxiety moderates the interplay between cognitive and affective processing', *Psychological Sciences*, 18(8): 699–705.

Edwards, D (1999) *Motivation and Emotions: Evolutionary, Physiological, Social and Cognitive Influences*, Thousand Oaks, CA: Sage.

Endler, NS, Lobel, T, Parker, JDA and Schmitz, P (1991) 'Multidimensionality of state and trait anxiety: A cross-cultural study comparing American, Canadian, Israeli and German young adults', *Anxiety Research*, 3: 257–72.

Epstein, S (1972) 'The nature of anxiety with emphasis upon its relationship to expectancy', in C Spielberger (ed), *Anxiety: Current trends in theory and research*, New York: Academic Press, pp 291–337.

Eysenck, M (1992) *Anxiety: The Cognitive Perspective*. Hillsdale, NJ: Erlbaum.

Farbey, L and Roberts, D (1981) 'Effects of calculator usage and task difficulty on state anxiety in solving statistical problems', paper presented at the annual meeting of the American Educational Research Association, Los Angeles, CA.

Ferraro, K (1995) *Fear of Crime: Interpreting Victimization Risk*, Albany, NY: State University of New York Press.

—— (1996) 'Women's fear of victimization?', *Social Forces*, 75(2): 667–91.

Ferraro, K and LaGrange, R (1987a) 'The measurement of fear of crime', *Sociological Inquiry*, 57: 70–101.

—— (1987b) 'The elderly's fear of crime', *Research on Aging*, 9(3): 372–91.

—— (1992) 'Are older people most afraid of crime? Reconsidering age differences in fear of victimization', *Journal of Gerontology*, 45(5): 233–44.

Finney, J (1985) 'Anxiety: Its measurement by objective personality tests and self-report', in A Tuma and J Maser (eds), *Anxiety and the Anxiety Disorders*, Hillsdale, NJ: Erlbaum, pp 645–74.

Forde, D (1993) 'Perceived crime, fear of crime, and walking alone at night', *Psychological Reports*, 73: 403–7.

Frijda, N (1993) 'Moods, emotion episodes and emotions', in M Lewis (ed), *Handbook of Emotions*, New York: The Guildford Press, pp 381–404.

Freud, S (1920) *A General Introduction to Psychoanalysis*, New York: Boni & Liveright.

—— (1959) 'Inhibitions, symptoms and anxiety', in J Strachey (ed and trans), *The Standard Edition of the Complete Psychological Works of Sigmund Freud*, vol 20, London: Hogarth Press, pp 77–175 (original work published in 1926).

Gabriel, U and Greve, W (2003) 'The psychology of fear of crime: Conceptual and methodological perspectives', *British Journal of Criminology*, 43: 600–14.

Garofalo, J (1979) 'Victimization and the fear of crime', *Journal of Research in Crime and Delinquency*, 16: 80–97.

Gilchrist, E, Bannister, J, Ditton, J and Farrall, S (1998) 'Women and the "fear of crime": Challenging the accepted stereotype', *British Journal of Criminology*, 38(2): 283–98.

Gray, J and McNaughton, N (2000) *The Neuropsychology of Anxiety*, Oxford: Oxford University Press.

Hale, C (1996) 'Fear of crime: A review of the literature', *International Review of Victimology*, 4: 79–150.

Hanfmann, G (1950). 'Psychological approaches to the study of anxiety', in P H Hoch and J Zubin, (eds), *Anxiety*. New York: Grune and Stratton.

Hardy, L, Jones, G and Gould, D (1996) *Understanding Psychological Preparation for Sport: Theory and Practice of Elite Performers*, Chichester: J Wiley.

Harrigan, J, Harrigan, K, Sale, B and Rosenthal, R (1996) 'Detecting anxiety and defensiveness from visual and auditory cues', *Journal of Personality*, 64: 675–709.

Harrigan, J, Larson, M and Pflum, C (1994) 'The role of auditory cues in the detection of state anxiety', *Journal of Applied Social Psychology*, 24: 1965–83.

Harrigan, J, Lucic, K, Bailyn, L, Zarnowiecki, S and Rosenthal, R (1992) 'Judging others' anxiety', *Journal of Applied Social Psychology*, 22: 855–73.

Hoch, P and Zubin, J (1950) *Anxiety*, New York: Grune & Stratton.

Hoehn-Saric, R, McLeod, D and Hipsley, P (1995) 'Is hyperarousal essential to obsessive compulsive disorder?', *Archives of General Psychiatry*, 52: 688–693.

Izard, C (1972) *Patterns of Emotions*, New York: Academic Press.

—— (1977) *Human Emotions*, New York: Plenum Press.

—— (1991) *The Psychology of Emotions*, New York: Plenum Press.

Jurich, A and Jurich, J (1974) 'Correlations among nonverbal expressions of anxiety', *Psychological Reports*, 34: 199–204.

Kilpatrick, D, Saunders, B, Veronen, L, Best, C and Von, J (1987) 'Criminal victimization: Lifetime prevalence, reporting to police, and psychological impact', *Crime and Delinquency*, 33: 479–89.

Kokotsaki, D and Davidson, J (2003) 'Investigating musical performance anxiety among music college singing students: A quantitative analysis', *Music Education Research*, 5(1): 45–60.

Kreitler, S (2004) 'The dynamics of fear and anxiety', in P Gower (ed), *Psychology of Fear*, New York: Nova Science Publishers Inc, pp 1–17.

Lazarus, R (1966) *Psychological Stress and the Coping Process*, New York: McGraw Hill.

—— (1991) *Emotion and Adaptation*, New York: Oxford University Press.

LaGrange, R, Ferraro, K and Suspancic, M (1992) 'Perceived risk and fear of crime: Role of social and physical incivilities', *Journal of Research in Crime and Delinquency*, 29: 311–30.

Lenzi, A, Lazzerini, F, Marazziti. D, Raffaelli, S, Rossi, G and Cassano, G (1993) 'Social class and mood disorders: Clinical features', *Social Psychiatry and Psychiatric Epidemiology*, 28(2): 56–9.

Levenson, RW, Ekman, P and Friesen, WV (1990) 'Voluntary facial action generates emotion-specific nervous system activity', *Psychophysiology*, 27: 363–84.

Levitt, E (1980) *The Psychology of Anxiety*, Hillsdale, NJ: Erlbaum

Lewis, G (1996) 'Depression and public health', *International Review of Psychiatry*, 8(4): 289–94.

Liska, A, Sanchirico, A and Reed, M (1988) 'Fear of crime and constrained behaviour: Specifying and estimating a reciprocal effects model', *Social Forces,* 66: 827–37.

Lupton, D (2000) 'Part of living in the late 20th century: Notions of risk and fear in relation to crime', *Australian and New Zealand Journal of Criminology*, 33: 21–36.

MacLeod, C (1990) 'Mood disorders and cognition', in MW Eysenck (ed), *Cognitive Psychology: An International Review*, Chichester: John Wiley & Sons, pp 9–56.

MacLeod, C, Mathews, A and Tata, P (1986) 'Attentional bias in emotional disorders', *Journal of Abnormal Psychology*, 95: 15–20.

McLellan, T, Bragg, A and Cacciola, J (1986) *The Encyclopedia of Psychoactive Drugs: Escape From Anxiety And Stress*, New York: Chelsea House Publishers.

McReynolds, P (1985) 'Changing conceptions of anxiety: A historical review and proposed integration', *Issues Mental Health Nursing*, 7(1–4): 131–58.

Martens, R (1971) 'Internal-external control and social reinforcement effects on motor performance', *Research Quarterly,* 42: 107–13.

May, R (1950) *The Meaning of Anxiety*. New York: The Ronald Press Company.

Michels, R, Frances, A and Shear, K (1985) 'The psychodynamic models of anxiety', in A Hussain Tuma and J Maser (eds), *Anxiety and the Anxiety Disorders*, Hillsdale, NJ: Erlbaum, pp 595–618.

Mogg, K, Bradley, BP, Williams, R and Mathews, A (1993) 'Subliminal processing of emotional information information in anxiety and depression', *Journal of Abnormal Psychology*, 102: 304–11.

Ohman, A (1993) 'Fear and anxiety as emotional phenomena: Clinical phenomenology, evolutionary perspectives and information processing mechanisms', in M Lewis and J Haviland (eds), *Handbook of Emotions*, New York: The Guildford Press, pp 511–36.

Pain, R (2001) 'Gender, race, age and fear in the city', *Urban Studies*, 38(5/6): 899–913.

Power, M and Dalgleish, T (1997) *Cognition and Emotion: From Order to Disorder*, Hove: Psychology Press.

Rachman, S (1990) *Fear and Courage*, 2nd edn, New York: W. H. Freeman and Company.

Raglin, J and Turner, P (1993) 'Anxiety and performance in track and field athletes: A comparison of the inverted-U hypothesis with ZOF theory', *Personality and Individual Differences*, 14: 163–72.

Rohe, W and Burby, R (1988) 'Fear of crime in public housing', *Environment and Behavior*, 20(6): 700–20.

Roundtree, P (1998) 'A re-examination of the crime-fear linkage', *Journal of Research in Crime and Delinquency*, 35: 341–72.

Schachter, S and Singer, JE (1962) 'Cognitive, social and physiological determinants of emotional state', *Psychological Review*, 69: 379–99.

Skogan, W and Maxfield, M (1981) *Coping with Crime: Individual and Neighborhood Reactions*, Beverly Hills, CA: Sage Publications.

Sluckin, W (1979) *Fear in Animals and Man*, New York: Van Nostrand Reinhold.

Smith, W and Torstensson, M (1997) 'Gender differences in risk perception and neutralizing fear of crime', *British Journal of Criminology*, 37: 608–34.

Smith, D and Uchida, C (1988) 'The social organization of self-help: A study of defensive weapon ownership', *American Sociological Review*, 53: 94–102.

Spielberger, C (1975) Anxiety: State-trait process', in C. Spielberger and I. Sarason (eds) *Stress and Anxiety* (Vol. 1). Washington, DC: Hemisphere.

Spielberger, C (1966) *Anxiety and Behaviour*, New York: Academic Press.

—— (1972a) *Anxiety: Current Trends in Theory and Research*, vol 1, New York: Academic Press.

—— (1972b) 'Conceptual and methodological issues in anxiety research', in C Spielberger (ed), *Anxiety: Current Trends in Theory and Research*, vol 1, New York: Academic Press, pp 23–49.

Spielberger, C, Gorusch, R and Lushene, R (1970) *Manual for the State-Trait Anxiety Inventory (Self-Evaluation Questionnaire)*, Palo Alto, CA: Consulting Psychologists Press.

Spielberger, C, Gorusch, R, Lushene, R, Vagg, P and Jacobs, G (1983) *The State-Trait Anxiety Inventory for Adults: Sampler Set Manual, Test, and Scoring Key*, Palo Alto, CA: Consulting Psychologists Press.

Stafford, M and Galle, O (1984) 'Victimization rates, exposure to risk, and fear of crime', *Criminology*, 22: 173–85.

Steven P (1992) *Crime Prevention: Approaches, Practices and Evaluations*, 2nd edn, Cincinnati, OH: Anderson Publishing Co.

Sutton, R and Farrall, S (2004) 'Gender, socially desirable responding, and the fear of crime: Are women really more anxious about crime?', *British Journal of Criminology*, 45: 2112–224.

Turner, P and Raglin, J (1996) 'Variability in precompetition anxiety and performance in college track and field athletes', *Medicine and Science in Sports and Exercise*, 28: 378–85.

Turner, S, McCann, M, Beidel, D and Mezzich, J (1986) 'DSM-III classification of the anxiety disorders: A psychometric study', *Journal of Abnormal Psychology*, 95: 168–72.

Vitelli, R and Endler, N (1993) 'Psychological determinants of fear of crime: A comparison of general and situational prediction models', *Personality and Individual Differences*, 14: 77–85.

Warr, M (1984) 'Fear of victimization: Why are women and the elderly more afraid?', *Social Science Quarterly*, 65: 681–702.

—— (1987) 'Fear of victimization and sensitivity to risk', *Journal of Quantitative Criminology*, 3: 29–46.

—— (2000) 'Fear of crime in the United States: Avenues for research and policy', in Duffee (ed), *Measurement and Analysis of Crime and Justice, Criminal Justice 2000*, vol 4, Washington, DC: Department of Justice, pp 451–90.

Warr, M and Stafford, M (1983) 'Fear of victimization: A look at the proximate causes, *Social Forces*, 61: 1033–43.

Wetherell JL, Reynolds CA, Gatz M and Pedersen NL (2002) 'Anxiety, cognitive performance, and cognitive decline in normal aging', *The Journals of Gerontology Series B: Psychological Sciences and Social Sciences*, 57(3): 246–55.

Williams, F, McShane, M and Akers, R (2000) 'Worry about victimization: An alternative and reliable measure for the fear of crime', *Western Criminology Review*, 2(2): 1–31.

Williams, J, Watts, F, MacLeod, C and Mathews, A (2002) *Cognitive Psychology and Emotional Disorders*, New York: John Wiley & Sons.

Zeidner, M (1988) 'Health and demographic correlates of trait anxiety in Israeli adults', *Anxiety Research*, 1(2): 127–35.

Chapter 11

Revisiting fear of crime in Bondi and Marrickville

Sense of community and perceptions of safety

Mike Enders and Christine Jennett with Marian Tulloch

Introduction

In crime prevention it seems there are two dominant stories: removing motivated offenders and target hardening (Graycar *et al.* 2001). Fear of crime reduction on the other hand is a more complex issue made difficult because of the multitude of external factors that impact upon the levels of fear in a particular community. Offenders and crimes are somewhat concrete and able to be addressed directly. Fear of crime is an abstract concept that can vary from person to person and place to place. It seemingly exists independent of official crime statistics and levels of police presence (Tulloch and Enders 1998: 189). Indeed, some argue that fear of crime does not exist, at least in an objective form (Lee 2007: 202). It is therefore not surprising that most policing strategies aimed at reducing fear of crime focus on the people and things that are thought to create the fear, offenders and offences, and most local government strategies focus on the physical environment, improving safety by target hardening (NSWP 2006: 29; Enders 1998a; NSW Attorney General's Department 1998). While both these approaches can be effective at preventing or reducing crime they will not necessarily reduce fear of crime (Bennett 1991: 12). A plethora of research has indicated the subjective nature of fear of crime means that it is difficult to measure, let alone reduce (Hale 1996). Moreover, internal debates in the field of fear of crime studies have even had trouble agreeing on its rational or irrational basis and whether it is real or imagined (Sparks 1992; Young 1988). Recent studies also suggest that a distinction should be made between fear of crime and worry or anger about crime (for example, Ditton *et al.* 1999), another complication.

In this chapter the authors revisit two research projects in order to provide an insight to the construction of fear of crime and critically assess how the reduction of fear of crime has, and can, be pursued in communities. The first research project was a major national study which used a risk based approach to review existing fear of crime research and reduction strategies and carry out a number of studies, a main study on fear of crime and two smaller studies focusing on public transport and the media (Tulloch *et al.* 1998). The second research project was undertaken to explore a possible link between fear of crime and 'sense of community' in two local government areas (LGAs) within a large modern city: Marrickville, in the inner west of Sydney and Waverley (hereafter referred to as Bondi), in the East, which includes the beachside tourist destination of Bondi (Enders and Jennett, 2000).[1] This second project provides the empirical base for this chapter. In the concluding section we suggest a change in fear reduction strategies for local government and the police, consistent with the research. This would focus on specifically targeted fear of crime reduction strategies rather than crime prevention *per se* (with fear of crime reduction added as an expected collateral outcome).

The dynamics of fear of crime

In 1997 the authors were part of a team from the Centre for Cultural Risk Research at Charles Sturt University which undertook a national research project on behalf of the Australian Criminology Research Council, the National Campaign Against Violence and Crime (now National Crime Prevention) and the National Anti-Crime Strategy to carry out a comprehensive investigation of fear of crime. This study comprised an audit of the literature and existing fear reduction programmes, a fieldwork component including rural and metropolitan areas based around, then innovative, focus group sessions, and specific case studies on public transport and the role of the media in fear of crime. The results of this study were published as a two volume report accompanied by a 60-page summary volume (Tulloch *et al.* 1998). The studies key findings were consistent with a range of more recent critical and qualitative studies into fear of crime and included that:

- people's fear varies depending on their personal experience, location, time of day/night, and who else is around;
- public transport is a significant source of fear, particularly at night;
- young people are more fearful than previously recognised (principally they fear certain other categories of young people, but they still go out at night and use public transport);
- women, especially young women, are most afraid of sexual assault;
- older people are less fearful than previously thought;
- parents are particularly fearful for their children rather than themselves – altruistic fear;
- the media are not as influential regarding fear of crime as previously thought;
- most people have a general fear of 'unpredictable strangers';
- crime statistics do not reflect the constant low level incidents which contribute to people's fear – reducing reported crime rates does not necessarily reduce fear of crime; and
- people develop individual strategies to deal with their fear of crime.

These findings provided a basis for a new series of questions about fear of crime and what makes communities and individuals more, or less, fearful. It became apparent that levels of fear varied between apparently similar locations and suburbs and that levels of fear varied between individuals of apparently similar dispositions (Enders 1998b; cf Pain 2003).

The New South Wales Police Force (NSWPF) has fear of crime reduction as one of its key objectives at present (NSWP 2006: 22). However, its efforts to reduce fear of crime are wholly centred around two strategies: high visibility policing, particularly public order policing via 'Vikings' Operations',[2] and Police Accountability Community Team (PACT) meetings with community members. There does not appear to be any specific programme to monitor whether fear of crime is being lowered, though results are presented that show feelings of safety when 'walking/ jogging alone after dark' might be rising while confidence in the police is lower than the national average (NSWP 2006: 30). While a programme of (unpaid civilian) Volunteers in Policing (VIPs) visiting older members of the community to check on their welfare is also mentioned, it does not appear to have been evaluated (NSWP 2006: 30). This is a pity as similar programmes in the UK and Australia have proven to be effective in reducing anxiety and improving community cohesion (Burnett 2006: 134). It is questionable therefore whether the NSWPF's approach is resulting in any lowering of levels of fear of crime even though it might be preventing crime. This raises the question as to whether the NSWPF currently takes one of its key objectives seriously.

In light of the 1998 study by the Centre for Cultural Research into Risk (CCRR) (Tulloch *et al.* 1998), one must question the utility of basing the success or failure of a key objective on two questions of doubtful value (NSWP 2006: 30). Evidence suggests that people who are fearful do not walk or jog alone at night. For example, findings from the 1998 study (Lupton 1998: 18) show that only 19 per cent of those surveyed often walked alone at night and only a further 22 per cent sometimes walked alone at night. This could indicate that 59 per cent of people *might* be too fearful to go out at night. Likewise, the level of confidence in the police does not seem to provide information on fear of crime. The NSWPF approach to fear of crime seems based on the notion that fear is linked to crime and that the police are the solution. However, evidence suggests that in at least one case, Sydney teenagers (a group who experience a high level of crime victimisation compared to others), the police themselves are the source of much fear (Lupton 1998: 169; cf Renauer 2007: 55). Therefore, police may need to take a more pro-active stance regarding fear of crime reduction and actively pursue strategies specifically targeting fear of crime, particularly among younger people.

During their work on the major study (Lupton 1998), the authors of this chapter identified what appeared to be a social dimension to people's construction of fear of crime. Subsequently, they undertook a study of fear of crime in Marrickville and Bondi to investigate whether heightened levels of social cohesion and related feelings – sense of community – reduced levels of fear of crime. This was based in part on research conducted by Walklate (1997) in the UK which suggested that residents in high crime areas who were part of well developed social networks – part of a cohesive community – had lower levels of fear of crime than those who felt isolated. Because of the dearth of programmes which specifically aimed to reduce fear of crime, it was felt that if a relationship between fear and social isolation along the lines indicated by Walklate's research was found this could provide an incentive for government at all levels to help reduce fear of crime. This could be achieved through 'community building' without reverting to law enforcement based approaches, particularly since the CCRR's research suggested that fear of crime exists independently of crime rates and victimisation (Tulloch *et al.* 1998; Lewis and Salem 1981: 414).

If building a sense of community helps reduce people's fear of crime, then local government authorities, traditionally under budgetary pressure, can help justify expenditure on community activities, in terms of their fear of crime reduction role. Community activities should be valued for their fear of crime reduction role as well as their broader social functions. This brings us to a key difference identified between the two localities targeted by our second research project: Bondi specifically includes a focus on community building and increasing the use of public space within their crime prevention section as a fear reduction strategy (Waverley Council 2005: 35; Marrickville Council,2004). Marrickville does not.

Fear reduction and the case of Bondi and Marrickville

The contexts in which fear of crime is researched and discussed have changed significantly throughout the world since the September 11 terror attacks on the US in 2001, the 2002 Bali restaurant bombings, the 2004 Madrid train bombings and the 2005 London Underground bombings – in which John Tulloch, lead author of the CCRR's 1998 study, was seriously injured (see Smith and Pain, Chapter 4, and Weber and Lee, Chapter 5, in this book). Further, in the Australian context in December 2005 a series of riots occurred at Cronulla Beach, south of Bondi. These came as a result of a perception that South-West Sydney's Middle Eastern Australians were 'taking over' the beach. As a result widespread violence occurred between Anglo and Middle Eastern, predominantly Muslim, Australians.

In a sense these riots have increased the relevance of our Bondi–Marrickville study conducted in 1999–2000 with its focus on community and exclusion/cohesion. There are distinct similarities between the communities concerned: Cronulla, like Bondi is a beachside suburb (in fact, Bondi's sand comes from Cronulla), and Marrickville is regarded as part of the inner West area, an extension of the area that includes the Lakemba Mosque, where a significant proportion of Sydney's Muslim population live. The Cronulla riots also present something of a sociological paradox in the study of social cohesion: they demonstrate how close social cohesion of ethnic and racial groups can also operate against the social order and its policing, and, also illustrate the deep seated divisions with the broader community. On this second point Pain (2003) notes that this will also make the study of fear of crime more complex as 'society becomes more complex and more divided, with greater social exclusion and injustice for some'.

Yet, in an influential Australian study Carcach and Huntley (2002) use data from local government areas in the eastern states to show that:

> Crime rates are lower in local areas with high levels of participation in community-orientated activities; and a doubling in the rate of membership of community organisations has the potential to reduce violent crime by between one-fifth and one-third, and property crime by one-twentieth and one-tenth ... participation has the potential to overcome some of the negative impact that high population mobility has on local levels of crime.
>
> (Carcach and Huntley 2002: 1)

Importantly, they go on to argue that *social interaction* is central when analysing local crime and potentially feelings of safety. They suggest that:

> Social interactions affect the local stock of trust, cohesion and resources for collective action (social capital) in the community. Participation in community activities and local organisations is one of many ways residents contribute to the common good and the solution to local problems.
>
> (Carcach and Huntley 2002: 2)

They argue that *trust* must be present in a community for such participation to occur.

Revisiting our research on Bondi and Marrickville provides us with some information on how fear of crime impacts on and is constructed by residents in similar areas – the Eastern Beaches and Inner West. It also tells us something about the dynamic of social cohesion in this experience and the impact of modes of policing on social cohesion.

Bondi and Marrickville were suited to the study since both:

- have about the same population;
- have above average, rather than extreme, crime rates (BOCSAR, 2002);

- have councils which appear committed to community safety programmes;
- receive a high level of media coverage of the crime that occurs (particularly Bondi);
- have a high proportion of rental properties;
- have a high migrant population; and
- are about the same distance from the Sydney's central business district (CBD).

Of course there are marked differences: Marrickville was has a generally more stable (less transient) population than does Bondi, which is viewed as a tourist destination and attracts a large number of temporary visitors and holidaymakers, that is, the people present in Marrickville tend to live or work there. Waverley is also generally regarded as a wealthier area than Marrickville, a perception supported by the census data (ABS 2004).

A social profile of Bondi and Marrickville[3]

The following social profile of Marrickville and Bondi provides a brief appreciation of the similarities and differences which existed when comparing the two locations covered by this study and to contextualise the findings.

Population transience and 'the unknown other'

Bondi is an internationally recognised tourist destination while Marrickville is a post-industrial suburb. Marrickville had no takings from tourist accommodation reported during the June quarter of 2003 while Bondi has a significant tourist sector and accounted for nearly 1 per cent of the NSW accommodation total, with takings of $3.3 million from over 23,000 occupied nights (ABS 2004). This is in addition to the considerable numbers of day visitors who pass through the area. Bondi has a number of city-wide festivals and events which attract locals as well as bringing large numbers of visitors to the area.[4] Further, residents from Sydney's western suburbs, including Marrickville, can access Bondi Beach easily by changing trains at Central, Redfern, Sydenham (part of the Marrickville LGA) or Wolli Creek and boarding the bus at Bondi Junction.

Nearly half of the families in Bondi live in flats, apartments or units (48 per cent) compared to just over a quarter for Marrickville (26 per cent) and the state average of 10.5 per cent (ABS 2004). The figures for families living in separate houses are virtually reversed, Bondi 27 per cent and Marrickville 44 per cent, compared to the state average of 80 per cent. Further, the occupancy rates of 93.3 per cent for Marrickville and 90.9 per cent for Bondi are comparable to the state average of 91.1 per cent. The occupation rates for flats, units and apartments of 92.1 per cent (Marrickville), 89.8

per cent (Bondi) and 88.8 per cent (statewide) respectively strengthen the argument that Marrickville's population is slightly more stable than that of Bondi. Contrary to our expectation regarding Marrickville, both areas seem to exhibit more population transience than the statewide average.

Both Marrickville (30.0 per cent) and Bondi (32.2 per cent) have a higher proportion of lone person households than the state average (23.4 per cent). They also have more group households than the state average. Bondi has fewer multiple family households than the state average while Marrickville has more. Population density, that is, the population divided by the LGA area in square kilometres, is significantly higher in Bondi (6,700) than Marrickville (4,600) (DLG 2004: 17–8). Overall, contrary to the state's positive annual population growth rate (1.13 per cent for 1997–2001) the permanent population in both areas is declining (-0.74 per cent for Marrickville and -0.85 per cent for Bondi for the same period).

Cultural diversity

Nearly 50 per cent of the population of both areas was born outside Australia, compared to 30 per cent for the state. Twenty per cent of the population of Bondi migrated from a mainly non-English-speaking country compared to over 30 per cent in Marrickville and 16 per cent for the state. The relatively high number of non-English-speaking background (NESB) people in Marrickville makes it easy for Marrickville's population to be viewed as 'other' by Anglo-Australians. Both communities have below average populations of Indigenous Australians. Bondi's Indigenous population, at 0.4 per cent, is less than 20 per cent of the state average.

Coming from a non-English-speaking background curtails the extent to which some members of the community can develop networks. In the case of Mrs Tan,[5] Marrickville Seniors, she had lived in the area for 10 years but knew very few people. The translator who gave her replies to the interviewer's questions said 'She knows some Vietnamese people in Marrickville but she doesn't go out with them'. Mrs Tuy, Marrickville Seniors, said that she did not know many people either, 'she knows some Vietnamese people, but not Australian'. Yet, she participated in all the events which the Council put on.

Income

Bondi has a higher median income both for families with dependent children and those without dependent children than the state figures. Marrickville is also higher than the state median for families without dependent children and the same for families with dependent children. Consequently, the median weekly income for both areas is higher than the state median. Population estimates by age combined with Centrelink benefit figures reveal that Bondi has a much lower number of households relying on Centrelink (government) benefits than Marrickville.

These figures indicate that Bondi residents are wealthier than Marrickville residents and have more community resources than Marrickville. When these figures are combined with the respective numbers of non-English-speaking people in the populations, there is likely to be less pressure on Bondi's budget to support socio-economically and linguistically disadvantaged residents than on that of Marrickville. However, it is clear from the census data that significant sectors of both communities are relatively wealthy and relatively poor (ABS 2004). The income figures indicate that the gap between the poor and the wealthy is greatest in Bondi (ABS 2004).

Figures provided by the Department of Local Government (DLG 2004: 73) show that Bondi received $712 per capita 'to service the needs of the community' (DLG 2004: 72) compared to $620 per capita for Marrickville Council. This measure of council financial performance provides an indication of the budget available per capita in both areas. The NSW average is $701 (DLG 2004: 72).

Crime

Both Bondi and Marrickville police Local Area Commands (LACs) have similar police staff levels and resources. While this might seem strange, given the difference in populations, one must remember that Bondi receives significant numbers of visitors and tourists compared to Marrickville. These visitors put additional pressure on police resources. The NSW Bureau of Crime Statistics and Research (BOCSAR) (2002) reports that, for the period 1997–2001, crime in Marrickville was stable or declining (except fraud which was increasing), while crime in Bondi was stable or increasing (except motor vehicle theft which was decreasing).

Crime rates in the two areas tend to be above the state average (except sex offences and malicious damage, arson and domestic violence in Bondi) with Marrickville tending to have higher crime rates than Bondi for most offences (exceptions being breaking and entering/burglary and malicious damage). Both areas tend to receive a high level of crime reporting in the media, Marrickville because of its reputation as a violent tough neighbourhood (Sidoti 2001) and Bondi because of its status as an international tourist destination. Crime rates in both communities can be described as high without being extreme (BOCSAR 2002).

Method

The methodology was in two phases. The first phase involved a street administered survey, which identified people who were asked to voluntarily participate in the second phase of focus groups and interviews. Where sufficient representatives from the various target groups did not volunteer, the research assistants approached local organisations for volunteers.[6] In the second phase, focus group discussions and individual interviews were conducted and audio-taped. Our aim was to explore the factors that make people feel safe or unsafe in these LGAs, but the sample obtained is not necessarily representative of the LGAs. Because of the multicultural nature of the communities being surveyed, the survey instrument was translated into 10 languages (Russian, Greek, Hungarian, Italian, Chinese, Spanish, Polish, Portuguese, Vietnamese and Arabic) and arrangements were made for interpreters to attend the focus groups and interviews, as required.

The phase one survey instrument incorporated a series of questions drawn from the earlier CCRR fear of crime study to allow the results to be compared with its findings. The questions included sections on residence/ density, community cohesion – participation in community events and networks, crime victimisation experience, and perception of safety.[7]

As well as these topics, the research assistant was asked to comment on the subject's appearance in terms of apparent gender, age, visible minority status, use of a translated questionnaire, and accent. This was aimed at identifying whether visible minority status contributed to levels of fear of crime or victimisation. Appearance (that is, their 'visibility') was chosen as the indicator rather than directly questioning the subject about their ethnic or racial status. This is important since, for example, many immigrants from non-English-speaking backgrounds living in Bondi do not 'appear' to be different to English-speaking locals with an Anglo-European heritage and *vice versa*. Likewise, some people choose to dress in a manner which identifies them with a particular sub-cultural group, regardless of their heritage.

To allow further comparison of results, the focus group discussions and the interviews of phase two were structured around the same core questions. This provided the researchers with a means of comparing the different data sets to identify any similarities or differences which existed between the findings of the two research projects.[8]

Use of translated surveys

While there were only a small number of translated questionnaires returned (about 2 per cent), the usage rate is not a true reflection of their value. The research assistants reported that many people referred to the translated questionnaire and then completed the English version.

Research results

In phase one of the research, 198 people (consisting of a mixture of residents and non-residents) were surveyed. This included 94 participants in Waverley/

Bondi (62 per cent were residents); and 104 participants in Marrickville (75 per cent were residents).

In phase two, 30 people participated in focus groups and interviews. They were volunteers and the focus groups were organised largely in terms of community demographics: older people, parents, young people and business people.

The majority of non-residents sampled in each local government area came from adjoining suburbs. While in Bondi they sometimes came from more distant suburbs, nearly all claimed to live in Sydney and very few were international or interstate tourists. This indicates that the study was largely successful in surveying residents rather than visitors or tourists.

Community cohesion

Nearly all respondents claimed to know people living in the local community. The proportion that knew many residents was higher in Bondi (49 per cent) than Marrickville (36 per cent). This difference was more marked when only those residing within the immediate area were considered, with the proportion rising to 66 per cent in Bondi but only 39 per cent in Marrickville.

Over 50 per cent of respondents had participated in local public events: fetes, concerts and street carnivals with the participation rate among Bondi locals (66 per cent) somewhat higher than Marrickville locals (54 per cent). Around 40–50 per cent reported being involved in local sporting, religious, educational or cultural organisations, again with the proportion being slightly higher in Bondi than Marrickville.

An index of community cohesion was formed combining three variables: residents known, participation in local events and involvement in community organisations. Bondi residents scored significantly higher (2.8) on this index than Marrickville residents (2.3). Further, figures from the Department of Local Government (2004: 230) show that the expenditure per capita on recreation and leisure activities was significantly higher in Bondi ($72) than Marrickville ($51).[9]

Knowing people in the community did not translate into 'feeling safe' in all circumstances. For example, Kate, parent of Bondi, who worked locally and was a member of several local organisations, said that she felt safe when there were plenty of people, including families, around during the day and early in the evening. She said that 'I think Bondi has a wonderful sense of community' but at night she was afraid of the gangs who came and hung around and deliberately hurt people as a form of entertainment.

Experience of crime

Respondents were asked about their experience of three events: assault, theft and harassment.

Experience of assault (14 per cent) and theft (28 per cent) were the same in both communities. Although the number of respondents who had been assaulted was fairly low, younger males were the group most frequently assaulted. One-third of males under 25 (cf 9 per cent for other respondents) reported having been assaulted. Kate of Bondi exemplifies this when she says that 'my son was bashed up in December, at Centennial Park at the night cinema, by about fifteen blokes'. She goes on to refer to the altruistic fear which parents frequently exhibit when she says 'I'm very careful what I do. I'm not going to be silly and walk alone ... the hard part is getting the kids to think about what they are doing'. Earlier she had recounted two murders in areas of the city frequented by her son. This obviously caused her to feel considerable altruistic fear.

Marrickville respondents reported a much higher experience of harassment, 40 per cent, compared to 18 per cent among Bondi respondents. Experience of harassment increased with age. This was somewhat counter to our expectations as it is young people who tend to be out and about in groups as a available targets for harassment. The types of situations where harassment is experienced require further research.

Over 80 per cent of respondents claimed they would report assault to the police, with the anticipated reporting rate rising to over 90 per cent with theft. However, only 54 per cent claimed they would report harassment to the police; family (30 per cent) or friends (12 per cent) were the preferred source of support for a significant minority. Moreover, only 38 per cent of those who had actually been harassed reported informing the police. This low level of reporting harassment has implications regarding where police focus their high visibility and public order patrols. In the absence of this information from the community, it is likely that police focus on areas identified from crime reports which might not be the same location.

Visible minority status

There was no evidence that being a member of a visible minority (as judged by the research assistants) was related to harassment but these respondents were significantly less likely to anticipate reporting harassment to the police (42 per cent cf 64 per cent).

Risk of crime

Respondents were asked about their perception of the risk of assault, burglary and car theft in the local area. There was a higher perceived risk of crime in Marrickville, with all risks rated at the same level: over 85 per cent of respondents felt at least at some risk of all three events with over 20 per cent often or always worried about them. By contrast, Bondi respondents were nearly twice as likely to nominate some risk of burglary compared to assault. Car theft was seen as somewhere between the other two risks. Only 1 per cent of Bondi respondents claimed to be often or always worried about assault. This is exemplified in statements made by interviewees such as the following:

> *What is the most common crime?*
> It'd have to be theft, for sure ... you always hear about break and enters and car theft ...
>
> Sally of Bondi (young woman)

> I'd say probably ... theft it'd have to be up there I'd say ... and um bashings not quite murder, but definitely bashings and assaults.
>
> Matt of Bondi (young man)

Feelings of safety

Respondents were asked about their feelings of safety in the area both during the day and at night. There were marked differences between the localities and between individuals as the interviews highlight:

> Yes, daytime scared but not really much, night time I don't want to go out because I'm too scared at night, but this lady I know ... she got robbed the other day when she walked somebody took the handbag
>
> Gloria of Marrickville (senior)

> It's dreadful. you have to be suspicious of young kids who probably haven't got a bad bone in their body, but, if they're on skateboards or something you think 'is this mongrel going to [snatch my] bag or something ... of a night, I won't go out.
>
> Enid of Bondi (senior)

Enid of Bondi (senior) also demonstrates that feeling unsafe was not necessarily a result of experience of being victimised:

> Well ... that's the thing, I haven't had a nasty experience but I'm just in fear of it and that hasn't always been ... I mean it's only something that's come in the last perhaps ten years or so or even less. I would think nothing of it even before I had a car, I would walk up to the bus stop to get the bus, go to a movie, come home, kind of thing.

It appears that when people approach their senior years their sense of resilience lessens. If they were to be victimised they feel that they would take longer to get over it. Their ability to re-establish 'normalcy' is reduced as they grow older.

Paul of Bondi (senior) put it this way:

> Everybody says the same thing, [as] an older person they won't go out at night time, and I wonder what the great fear is, apart from being mugged or robbed or anything else, I think that there is the physical damage you suffer if you have been knocked over, 'cause it takes a long time to recover from it.

However, as for himself, he says he has always had plenty of confidence. By contrast, Brian of Bondi (young man) says '... I don't feel I'm safe myself ....'.

Combining the safe and very safe categories, 91 per cent of respondents felt safe in Bondi during the day compared to only 58 per cent in Marrickville. At night, this figure dropped to 49 per cent in Bondi and to a low 30 per cent in Marrickville where 25 per cent of respondents felt very unsafe at night.

In combination, the data suggests that fear of crime is greater in Marrickville than Bondi despite similar reported experiences of assault and theft in the two areas. This supports the CCRR Team's finding (Tulloch *et al.* 1998, see also Hale 1996) that the level of fear of crime (the perceived risk of crime in this case) is independent of the actual crime rate (as reported in crime statistics).

Sense of community and fear of crime

Regarding the level of community cohesion, each area was analysed separately for predictors of feelings of safety. In Bondi, age was the best predictor with older respondents feeling less safe. In particular, the retired Bondi respondents perceived themselves to face a high risk of burglary with 69 per cent perceiving themselves to be often or always at risk (cf only 16 per cent of respondents overall). This finding is consistent with other studies (for example Burnett 2006).

The predictors of feelings of safety in Marrickville differ from Bondi, with experience of harassment a predictor of feeling unsafe at night. The best overall predictor of feelings of safety in Marrickville was the measure of community cohesion. Those who knew more people, participated in community events and were involved in community activities felt safer. The cause of this association cannot be conclusively determined. It maybe that fear prevents participation but it is also possible that participation in community activities and getting to know more people increases a person's feelings of safety.

Among the seniors interviewed this was not necessarily the case. In the Marrickville Seniors group Theresa reported that she had lived there for six years, attended community events but is 'very scared after 6pm'. In contrast to the prediction in the fear of crime literature that people feel safe when there are a lot of people around, Theresa said that she did not like walking around the streets because 'too much people every time walking around in the streets, too much people, I scared too much'. It has to be said that the context in which she expressed her fears was a discussion about bag snatches experienced by elderly women. The obvious question to be explored further is: Who are the 'people' who scare her?

However, the overall survey findings parallel those of Walklate (1997) in Manchester (UK) that in high crime area feelings of 'being known' and 'being a local' are associated with lower fear of crime. Similarly, in the US, Rountree and Land (1996) found neighbourhood cohesion was related to diminished fear of crime in high-risk areas. This is exemplified by Russell, a young Marrickville male, talking about his hometown: 'Yeah, that's where I grew up, I know everybody there and most of them know me so nothing, nothin' bad really happens to me [there]'. It is therefore unfortunate that these results have not resulted in changes to police strategies in NSW, while the British Home Office has adopted a significant community-centred approach to policing (Smith 2007).

Three factors contributed to the variation in Marrickville respondents' perception that they are at risk of assault at night: their level of cohesion with the community, their experience of harassment, and whether they were a member of a visible minority. Those respondents whose level of community cohesion was low, those who had been harassed and those who were not members of a visible minority felt at greater risk of assault. The findings linking harassment and risk perception support other studies that have also linked experience of harassment and fear of crime (for example, Keane 1995).

The finding that those who were not members of a visible minority felt at greater risk of assault may seem counter-intuitive. However, Marrickville has a high proportion of residents from NESB backgrounds and in the current survey, 58 per cent of Marrickville respondents were deemed to belong to a visible minority. What may be termed minority groups in a broad Australian context may therefore form the majority of residents in communities like Marrickville. The higher level of perceived risk by Anglo-Australian respondents accords with US research where whites who perceived themselves as a racial minority in their neighbourhoods had elevated levels of perceived risk of criminal victimisation (Chiricos *et al.* 1997).

There was no evidence of gender differences in perceived risk and feelings of safety, despite the pervasive nature of gender differences in the fear of crime literature (Hale 1996). This was counter to expectations. Two points are worth making about gender and the type of survey data obtained in this study: female respondents saw themselves as equally at risk of assault although their experience of assault was lower than males, and the survey did not distinguish physical and sexual assault, the latter being a particular concern for women (Moore and Shepherd 2007; Tulloch *et al.* 1998; Ferraro

1995). Therefore the item on risk of assault may have meant rather different things to male and female respondents.

Discussion

While providing a starting point, 'sense of community' is a concept that is not easily defined. Therefore, we have adopted the language associated with 'social capital' to more analytically describe the elements of community support central to our research. Putnam has defined 'social capital as those features of social life that enable participants to act together more effectively to pursue shared objectives' (Putnam 1993 as cited in Dollery and Wallis 2003: 87). Portes classifies three types of social capital: *reciprocated exchanges*; *bounded solidarity*; and *enforceable trust* (Portes as cited in Browning *et al.* 2000: 11–12). Browning *et al.* (2000: 12) argue that 'network mediated exchanges encourage the development of bounded solidarity and enforceable trust'. They note that 'social cohesion may emerge as a byproduct of network density and reciprocated exchange' but that this is not 'an inevitable outcome' (Browning *et al.* 2003: 13). The key components of social capital, as defined by Putnam (as cited in Dollery and Wallis 2003: 88), are *networks of civic engagement, norms of generalised reciprocity*, and *relations of social trust*. Our findings suggest that the Marrickville community has less social capital than Bondi. Thus, social capital and social cohesion are the factors we hoped to identify as impacting of people's level of fear of crime.

In the Bondi–Marrickville study we asked people about their community interaction by asking them how many people they knew in the locality, whether they participated in local gatherings, such as fetes, concerts and street carnivals, and whether they were involved in local organisations, such as sporting clubs, educational or religious bodies. Their social capital could then be correlated with their perception of risk and fear of crime. From the results, it could be argued that the impact of community cohesion on fear of crime levels is greater in a community which lacks social capital than on one which has significant social capital, that is, increasing social cohesion activities *as a fear reduction strategy* in communities which already have significant social capital might not be justified.

On the broader scale altogether, however, localised concerns about crime are just one aspect of a number of issues which have the potential to cause anxiety which might find an outlet in crime talk (see Hollway and Jefferson 2000; Girling *et al*, 2000). Concerns about global terrorism, job security, mortgage interest rates, heath care, education, greenhouse gas emissions, possible climate change and the like all have some effect on people's day-to-day lives and can affect their sense of self and security. While we acknowledge these, we are specifically interested in those local conditions which might be influenced through local government policy and policing strategies.

Most crimes can be constructed as, primarily, a policing problem, identifying and arresting the offender, or a council problem, making the environment safer. Crime is a collective (objective) issue while fear of crime is a personal (subjective) issue (Lee 2007: 123; Lupton 1998: 93; Lewis and Salem 1981: 413). The challenge facing those engaged in crime prevention and fear of crime reduction is to recreate fear of crime as a collective issue and then unite individuals to combat it together as a community. This is unlikely to occur unless fear of crime reduction is specifically targeted rather than added as a collateral outcome of crime prevention.

The Cronulla riots of December 2005 indicated a lack of community cohesion in the broader Sydney area but a high level of cohesion among Shire residents (Shire is a term used to describe the St George-Cronulla area of Sydney – since the Lord of the Rings film trilogy residents have become known as 'Hobbits') and Middle-Eastern Australians. Significantly large numbers of people from the same city constructed each other as 'other' with violent results. The Redfern (February 2004) and Macquarie Fields (February 2005) riots together with Cronulla show that, under certain circumstances, a significant number of Sydney residents also identify the police as 'other' under particular circumstances. Arguably, if the police were closer to the communities – viewed as part of the communities – they might have been able to influence those intent on illegal activities and the outcomes could have been different. It is unfortunate that the high visibility strategies employed at present in NSW are possibly hindering police getting close to the community. The paramilitary execution of these strategies also limits opportunities for friendly police-citizen interactions. By aggressively targeting crime hotspots via special operations like 'Vikings' operations', police assist in labeling areas as 'sites of fear', as well as instilling fear in some segments of the community, thus creating impediments to the development of, and access to, social capital for residents (Warr 2005).

'Fear of crime should be considered as important as crime itself and people's responses not seen as irrational or emotional but rather as the result of how they make sense of their daily lives in complex and changing situations' (Blood et al. 2000: 34). There is a danger that fear of crime will be either ignored as a product of sensational media coverage and irrational anxieties or be co-opted by police, politicians and interest groups to create moral panics to justify the reduction of personal freedoms. Basically, it is easy to create heightened fear and difficult to disprove claims once they have been made without appearing soft on crime. While the existence, cause and definition of fear of crime continues to be the subject of debate, there is no doubting that its impact on people's lives extends well beyond their experience or knowledge of victimisation or their consumption of media (Chadee et al. 2007: 149; Tulloch 1999).

Conclusion

We were successful in identifying sense of community as a trait in people with a lower level of fear of crime in Marrickville – the community with the higher level of fear. The situation in Bondi is more complex especially since the higher level of resourcing indicating potentially higher levels of social capital, would allow more support to be given to community projects and activities compared to Marrickville. While Bondi's community cohesion index is higher and levels of fear are lower, there is no evidence of a direct link between the index and lower levels of fear. Further research appears to be warranted, particularly since focus group discussions revealed that people in both areas draw strength from each other in public – the presence of other like minded individuals in public reduced people's fears and made them feel safer. A pre-existing relationship was not necessarily needed, just a demonstration of similar interests. Being alone increased fear.

While it is unwise to generalise, it is fair to say that there are indications that Bondi, and Eastern suburbs, residents fear, or at least resist, visitors from outside their community. Recent years have seen significant local opposition to projects like extending the rail line from Bondi Junction to the beach or constructing a new light rail system from Bondi Junction to the beach. Media reports of anti-social behaviour tend to identify the cause as 'outsiders' rather than residents (Casey 1997: 5). Based on this research, Bondi residents are, generally, fearful of visitors, while in Marrickville, residents are, arguably, fearful of other residents. Interestingly, the CityRail train link means it is possible that, to some extent, both populations are fearful of the same people: residents of Marrickville LGA, who also visit Bondi. Another factor is the argument that cohesion occurs on two axes: horizontally, the cohesion between family and close associates, and vertically, the weaker but more useful links between community members (Warr 2005: 287). It is possible that cohesion in Marrickville and the inner west is more horizontal while in the eastern suburbs it is more vertical. Further research in this area would seem warranted.

As stated earlier, one of the NSWPF's 'key objectives ... [is to] reduce ... the fear of crime' (NSWP 2006: 22). Despite this corporate commitment and claims, its 2006 annual report does not present any evidence that fear of crime has been reduced. There are no specific strategies beyond the crime centred approaches of high visibility policing and sharing information on crime through PACT meetings (NSWP 2006: 29). The expectation seems to be that, despite research results to the contrary, reducing crime reduces fear of crime. Likewise, Council strategies do not appear to specifically set out to reduce fear of crime but include fear of crime reduction as a collateral objective of community safety programmes whose outcomes are easier to measure.

A change to 'purposeful reassurance policing' as described by Burnett (2006) and Crawford (2007) would represent a significant step towards a genuine attempt to reduce fear of crime. High visibility policing, particularly as practiced during operations aimed at reducing public disorder are of questionable value in reducing fear of crime. Likewise, local councils could increase their efforts to develop social capital thus, arguably, increasing community cohesion. Examples of activities which build vertical cohesion are community festivals, cultural festivals and library activities for non-English-speakers (for example, Marrickville Council 2007, 2004; Waverley Council 2006, 2005). While councils do these things to some extent, they are not explicitly presented as an activity which will impact on fear of crime and quality of life within the community. It is not sufficient to put on the event, more should be done to engage with community members pro-actively and encourage their participation, for example, promoting events as safe, and providing appropriate passive security measures with safe shuttle buses to and from events.

A review of the Marrickville and Bondi social plans (Marrickville Council 2004; Waverley Council 2005) shows that their fear of crime reduction strategies are predominantly crime focused. In fact, the term 'fear of crime' does not appear in Marrickville's social plan, although several of the safety strategies appear to address fear of crime related issues (Marrickville Council 2004: 47–59). Both councils engage in community activities as part of their social plans, but, in Bondi, the Council is specifically trying to address fear of crime by maximising the use of public space by people of 'all ages' (Waverley Council 2005: 35; Marrickville Council 2004: 47). Bondi's success in these endeavours is supported by our research. Moreover, local government councils are ideally suited to eschew the traditional top down approach to fear of crime – formal social control – and empower community members – informal social control – thus making use of what Tulloch (1998: 6) refers to as 'lay knowledgability'. This would allow individuals to develop their own strategies for dealing with fear of crime.

Police services should extend their approach to fear of crime beyond the 'get tough on crime' high visibility initiatives by connecting with their communities more. Though in its early stages of development, Burnett (2006) identifies 'befriending' and 'purposeful patrolling' as two projects that can provide results if delivered 'at the right time, in the right place and in the right way' can help reduce fear of crime. In particular 'purposeful patrolling requires that the police officers operate alone, rather than in pairs, and connect with their communities demonstrating a level of concern which people find reassuring. In a sense, police who are too frightened to walk alone in their communities can hardly be expected to convince others that there is nothing to fear.

Befriending and home visit programs, similar to the NSWPF's VIP initiative (NSWP 2006: 30), provide a further opportunity for local government staff to informally visit and reassure older people. In particular, this can help reduce their anxiety about crime and other risk topics. It seems that it is the visit itself – contact with the outside world – and casual conversation that is useful rather than a planned agenda (Burnett 2006).

Renauer (2007), after establishing that social control can 'influence emotional fear of crime' (Renauer 2007: 57), argues persuasively that fear of crime reduction should be addressed by formal and informal social control. The problem is that these approaches are prone to polarisation between formal social control, administered by the police, and informal social controls, administered by community representatives, invariably advised by the police – in effect more of the same. Formal social control by the police inevitably means enforcement operations targeting public order issues and so-called high visibility policing (in NSW, Vikings' operations are an example). This tends to separate the police from their community by minimising opportunities for 'positive [or friendly] encounters' (Renauer 2007: 57) and potentially, allows the police to segregate the community through racial and geographic profiling and other 'intelligence-based' policing strategies.

For community cohesion to be successful, all agencies, the police, community and government representatives, need to work in concert with the broader community to explore the concepts and the community benefits which might be derived from them, especially in the 'most disadvantaged communities' (Renauer 2007: 57). Reassurance policing provides a framework consistent with these principles that could be useful in their implementation. The encouraging results from the Bondi–Marrickville research combined with further encouraging results obtained from reassurance approaches to fear of crime reduction suggest that this approach deserves further support and evaluation. It also offers a policy discourse counter to the 'high visibility' tough on crime approach.

It is the negative impact on quality of life – specifically the impact on individuals – which seems to be the most harmful aspect of high levels of fear of crime. Our research, including the CCRR's project in 1998 (Tulloch *et al.* 1998) showed that in any community there are individuals who are more affected by fear of crime and individuals who are less affected. It seems that high levels of fear and low levels of fear in communities are due to the relative numbers of people who are more or less fearful. The answer, then, is to reduce the negative impact of fear of crime on those individuals most affected.

To some extent, building social capital/cohesion might do this in some communities. It could be argued that, if fear of crime is a problem, the first step is to target the community as a whole and then to help the individuals. In practical terms, it would seem that fear of crime in Marrickville can be reduced to some extent by strategies to improve social capital/cohesion. While in Bondi, reducing fear of crime would require strategies focused on the individuals most affected. Current fear of crime reduction policies and strategies need to take heed of the research and specifically focus on the fear rather than the crime.

One must also remain mindful that fear of crime and, since 11 September 2001, fear of terrorism, are powerful emotional triggers and can be used to justify increased social control and reductions in personal freedom in the name of crime prevention and fear of crime reduction (Lee 2007: 11–4 and 197). There needs to be careful consideration given to what is surrendered, what is promised and what can realistically be achieved in return. Accordingly, there are many issues to be explored and our research will continue in this area.

Notes

1 Unless stated otherwise, the terms 'Bondi' and 'Marrickville', when used in this chapter, refer to the local government areas of Waverley and Marrickville respectively.
2 Vikings operations are an operational strategy of the NSW police that targets 'crime hotspots' with increased police numbers and high visibility low tolerance policing styles.
3 While the ABS report used as a primary reference was published in 2004, the population statistics provided are either from the 2001 census or are estimates based on the 2001 census. Therefore, the figures presented here should be regarded as indicative for comparison purposes rather than conclusive since data collection for this study ended during 2000.
4 For example the *Sun-Herald* City to Surf Fun Run held in August each year and the beach was a venue for the 2000 Olympic Games.
5 All names used are pseudonyms.
6 For example the local Chamber of Commerce and senior citizens groups
7 Questions included the following: What sort of building do you live in? Are you actively involved in any local organisations or committees? If you were to experience, or in the past have experienced one of the following, who would/did you turn to? Responses were multiple choice or 'other' with space for a reply.
8 The research assistants were also required to provide information to the subjects and ensure that their participation was voluntary in accordance with CSU's Ethics in Human Research Committee guidelines.
9 The state average is $59. It should be noted that high numbers of non-residents (tourists), availability of facilities and the population mix, that is, community needs and resources, can impact on this expenditure.

References

Australian Bureau of Statistics (ABS) (2003) *Crime and Safety: New South Wales*, Canberra: Australian Bureau of Statistics.
—— (2004) *NSW Regional Profile*, Canberra: Australian Bureau of Statistics, available at www.abs.gov.au (accessed 5 December 2005).
Bennett, T (1991) 'The effectiveness of a police-initiated fear-reducing strategy', *The British Journal of Criminology*, 31(1): 1–14.
Blood, RW, Tulloch, J and Enders, M (2000) 'Communication and reflexivity: conversations about fear of crime', *Australian Journal of Communication*, 27(3): 15–38.

Bureau of Crime Statistics and Research (BOCSAR) (2002) *Trends in Reported Crime Statistics by LGA and LAC*, Sydney: Bureau of Crime Statistics and Research (NSW).

Browning, C, Dietz, R and Feinberg, SL (2000) *'Negative' Social Capital and Urban Crime: A Negotiated Coexistence Perspective*, URAI Working paper No. 00-07, Columbus, OH: Urban and Regional Analysis Initiative, Ohio State University.

Burnett, A (2006) 'Reassuring older people in relation to fear of crime', in A Wahidin and M Cain (eds), *Ageing Crime and Society*, Cullompton: Willan Publishing, pp 124–38.

Carcach, C and Huntley, C (2002) 'Community participation and regional crime', *Trends and Issues in Crime and Criminal Justice*, 222.

Casey, Marcus (1997) 'Bondi's train off the rails', *Daily Telegraph*, 8 December, p 5.

Chadee, D, Austen, L and Ditton, J (2007) 'The relationship between likelihood and fear of criminal victimization: evaluating risk sensitivity as a mediating concept', *British Journal of Criminology*, 47: 133–53.

Chiricos, T, Hogan, M and Hertz, M (1997) 'Racial composition of neighbourhood and fear of crime', *Criminology*, 35(1): 107–31.

Crawford, A. (2007) 'Reassurance policing: feeling is believing', in A Henry and D Smith (eds), *Transformations of Policing*, Aldershot: Ashgate Publishing, pp 143–68.

Department of Local Government (DLG) (2004) *Comparative Information on New South Wales Local Government Councils 2002-2003*, Sydney: Department of Local Government.

Ditton, J and Farrall, S (eds) (2000) *The Fear of Crime*, Aldershot: Dartmouth Publishing.

Ditton, J, Bannister, J, Gilchrist, E and Farrall, S (1999) 'Afraid or angry? Recalibrating the "fear of crime"', *International Review of Victimology*, 6: 83–99.

Dollery, BE and Wallis, JL (2003) *The Political Economy of the Voluntary Sector: A Reappraisal of the Comparative Institutional Advantage of Voluntary Organizations*, MA: Edward Elgar.

Enders, M (1998a) 'Programs/strategies for reduction of fear of crime', in J Tulloch, D, Lupton, RW, Blood, M, Tulloch, C, Jennett and M Enders (eds), *The Fear of Crime, Vol. 1*, Canberra: National Campaign Against Violence and Crime, pp 213–33.

—— (1998b) 'The transport industry', in J Tulloch, D Lupton, RW Blood, M Tulloch, C Jennett and M Enders (eds), *The Fear of Crime, Vol. 2*, Canberra: National Campaign Against Violence and Crime, pp 203–18.

Enders, M and Jennett, C (2000) 'Fear of crime and sense of community: a comparative study of fear of crime at Bondi and Marrickville, Sydney, Australia', paper presented at the 52nd annual meeting of the American Society of Criminology, 'Crime and Criminology in the Year 2000', 15–18 November 2000, San Francisco, CA.

Ferraro, K (1995) *Fear of Crime: Interpreting Victimisation*, Albany, NY: State University of New York Press.

Girling, E, Loader, I and Sparks, R (2000) *Crime and Social Control in Middle England: Questions of Order in an English Town*, London: Routledge.

Graycar, A, McGregor, K and Makkai, T (2001) 'Drugs and law enforcement', paper presented at the Winter School in the Sun Conference, Brisbane, 3 July.

Hale (1996) 'Fear of Crime: A Review of the Literature', *International Review of Victimology*, 4(2): 79–150.

Hollway, W and Jefferson, T (2000) *Doing Qualitative Research Differently: Free Association, Narrative and the Interview Method*, London: Sage.

Jones, Gemma and Blackwell, Eoin (2007) 'Killed hosing lawn: Violence shatters tranquil suburb', *The Daily Telegraph*, 2 November, p 5.

Keane, C (1995) 'Victimization and fear: assessing the role of offender and offence', *Canadian Journal of Criminology*, 37(3): 431–55.

Lee, M (2007) *Inventing Fear of Crime: Criminology and the Politics of Anxiety*, Cullompton: Willan Publishing.

Lewis, D and Salem, G (1981) 'Community crime prevention: an analysis of a developing strategy', *Crime & Delinquency*, July: 405–21.

Lupton, D (1998) 'The main study', in J Tulloch, D Lupton, RW Blood, M Tulloch, C Jennett and M Enders (eds), *The Fear of Crime, Vol. 2*, Canberra: National Campaign Against Violence and Crime, pp 11–119.

Marrickville Council (2004) *Belonging in Marrickville – A Social Plan for the Marrickville Local Government Area: Supporting Documents*, Marrickville: Marrickville Council.

—— (2007) *Marrickville matters*, 23(4).

Moore, S and Shepherd, J (2007) 'The elements and prevalence of fear', *British Journal of Criminology*, 47: 154–62.

NSW Attorney General's Department (1998) *Crime Prevention Resource Manual*, Sydney: NSW Attorney General's Department.

NSW Police (NSWP) (2006) *NSW Police: Focused on Community Partnership, Annual Report 2005-06*, Sydney: NSW Police.

Pain, R (2003) *The Geographies and Politics of Fear*, available at www.thefreelibrary.com (accessed 23 October 2007).

Renauer, B (2007), 'Reducing fear of crime: citizen, police, or government responsibility?', *Police Quarterly*, 10(1): 41–62.

Rountree, P and Land, K (1996) 'Burglary Victimisation, Perceptions of Crime Risk, and Routine Activities: A Multi-level Analysis Across Seattle Neighborhoods and Census Tracts', *Journal of Research in Crime and Delinquency*, 33(2): 147–80.

Sidoti, C (2001) 'A nation of thugs', paper presented at Refugees, gangs and racial punishment, the Pluto Press Seminar held at the University of Sydney, 27 September 2001.

Smith, J (2007) 'Speech by the Home Secretary, the Rt. Hon. Jacqui Smith, MP, to the Annual Conference of the Police Superintendents' Association of England and Wales', at the Chesford Hotel, Warwickshire, 13 September, 2007.

Sparks, R (1992) *Television and the Drama of Crime: Moral Tales and the Place of Crime in Public Life*, Buckingham: Open University Press.

Tulloch, J (1998) 'Introduction', in Tulloch, J, Lupton, D, Blood, W, Tulloch, M, Jennett, C and Enders, M (eds) *The Fear of Crime, vol. 1*, Canberra: National Campaign Against Violence and Crime.

—— (1999) 'Fear of crime and the media: sociocultural theories of risk', in D Lupton (ed), *Risk and Sociocultural Theory: New Directions and Perspectives*, Cambridge: Cambridge University Press, pp 34–58.

Tulloch, J and Enders, M (1998) 'Strategies and programs', in J Tulloch, D Lupton, RW Blood, M Tulloch, C Jennett and M Enders (eds), *The Fear of Crime, vol. 1*, Canberra: National Campaign Against Violence and Crime, pp 163–90.

Tulloch, J, Lupton, D, Blood, RW, Tulloch, M, Jennett, C and Enders, M (1998) *The Fear of Crime, Vols. 1 and 2*, Canberra: National Campaign Against Violence and Crime.

Walklate, S (1997) 'Crime and community: exploring the interplay', paper presented at the First Australian Institute of Criminology Regional Crime Conference, Wagga Wagga, Charles Sturt University.

Warr, D (2005) 'Social networks in a "discredited" neighbourhood', *Journal of Sociology*, 41(3): 285–308.

Waverley Council (2005) *Waverley Council Social Plan 2005–2010, Volume 2: Social Planning Issues Papers and Action Plans*, Bondi Junction: Waverley Council.

—— (2006) *Waverley Council Annual Report 2005–06*, Bondi Junction: Waverley Council.

Young, J (1988) 'Risk of crime and fear of crime: the politics of victimization studies', in M Maguire and J Ponting (eds), *Victims of Crime: A New Deal*, Milton Keynes: Open University Press.

Chapter 12

Critical voices in an age of anxiety

Ending with the identification of where to begin ...

Murray Lee and Stephen Farrall

You're trying to pretend to love all the people that you think are beneath you
There is no known doubt that they got guns in their hand
See the whole world lives in fear ...
I know it, I know it, I know, I know in my bones ...
                    (The Dears, 'Fear Made The World Go 'Round', 2006)

Fears trace a map of a society's values; we need fear to know who we are and what we do not want to be.
                    (Marina Warner, *No Go the Bogeyman*, Chatto & Windus, 1998)

We began this book by posing ourselves two pertinent questions. The first was 'Where to begin?' and the second was 'Is there anything left to say?'. We suggested that there was, indeed, still something productive to say and we hope the chapters here are testament to this (we skipped the question of where to begin, you will recall). As this book has made clear, critical engagement with, and dialogue about, fear of crime can come from a broad range of (inter) disciplinary fields and theoretical orientations. But perhaps what the chapters in this book best illustrate is that critical engagement with fear of crime is by nature an ongoing and constantly shifting set of discussions. Indeed, if there are two things we have learned from the recent qualitative and critical turns in fear of crime research it is that fear of crime is neither experienced by individuals in a consistent and coherent way (Hollway and Jefferson 2000; Farrall *et al.* 1997; Girling *et al.* 2000) nor is it an unchanging a historical phenomena somehow separable from experience, culture, language, power and knowledge (Sparks 1992; Jackson 2004; Lee 2001, 2007). It is not a stable entity that enlightened researchers will someday know 'the truth' of. With this in mind we now have to address the question of 'Where to end?' (in) secure in the knowledge that our object is, by nature, indeterminate. In short, there is no 'where' at which to locate an 'end'.

We believe this indeterminacy should be seen as a positive thing. If there is one thing this collection of contributions tells us about recent developments in this area of research it is that the field has become more eclectic and varied, reflecting our ability to see fear of crime as multi-faceted. What was once something of a taken-for-granted concept has been deconstructed, reconstructed and deconstructed again. It has been subject to critique from an array of different disciplinary fields and an array of ideological and epistemological positions within these. While it is clear that fear of crime is a problematic construct, many of the essays here have pointed to new and potentially fruitful areas of research which are both innovative and reflexive.

What, then, are the futures for fear of crime research? These chapters illustrate that fear of crime research does not have to be a conceptual and theoretical dead-end dominated by so-called 'administrative style criminology' within government departments. Moreover, they also indicate resistance against reductive and simplistic research is still required and should perhaps be an ongoing project. Indeed, it would be a tragedy if critical scholars simply surrendered the field to bureaucrats and politicians whose uses and abuses of research into fear of crime are well documented. This is a politically sensitive area and it is one that must be approached critically, reflexivity and with a firm knowledge of the likely risks and consequences of engagement. If the history of fear of crime research tells us anything it is that even the most well-intentioned research can have unintended consequences.

We return again here to Figure 1.1 located in Chapter 1 (p. 4). If fear of crime is the consequence of a range sites and institutions and feedback loops the sensitive nature of our interventions can be countenanced. While we are not suggesting Figure 1.1 is the final word on the matter, or that it is all inclusive, it does give us some orientation to the possible uses and abuses of fear of crime – even unintended uses and abuses. Indeed, we regard it as a set of game openings (to use Foucault's terminology) through which one might locate one's own fear of crime research. In mapping and locating a project we might more clearly identify the consequences of intervention. We can ask ourselves are we mapping fear or merely (re)producing it?

It is stated perennially that the field of fear of crime research requires conceptual refinement, clarity of definition, and a clear range of research methodologies. We are uncertain that this alone is enough. It has been precisely this somewhat reductive approach that has resulted in an overly-narrowly focused research methodology (namely the social survey) that unless approached with some theoretical sophistication (both of the subject matter itself and the epistemological biases inherent in survey research) all too often tells us a whole lot about nothing very much at all. Indeed, we would like to turn the debate on its head and suggest that fear of crime research is an area that has suffered as much as it has gained from refinement, narrow and reductive definitions, and a range of methodologies that try too hard to achieve clarity. Do we really need to agree exactly on what fear of crime is, or indeed precisely how it should be measured? Ought we to continue to proceed as if the fear of crime was one thing or reducible to one set of experiences (Farrall *et al.* 2006)? We know the object of study itself is multi-dimensional, subjective and experiential. Research into fear of crime needs to reflect the amorphous nature of the concept and not be tied to a set of methodologies or reduced solely to a stock range of survey questions. Such approaches directly contradict its changing and historically contingent nature not to mention its various localised versions. As Jackson (Chapter 9, in this book) succinctly puts it, drawing from Mary Douglas' work:

> The vocabulary and associations of risk are always semantically denser, more culturally embedded, more episodic in their appearance and more open to politicization than attempts by specialists to numericise and rationalise them can admit.

It follows that if we are to learn something new about fear of crime and its attendant socio-political processes it will come though the application of many and varied approaches which illuminate differing aspects of the phenomenon. And therein lies the challenge for future research.

Many of the chapters here have attempted to expand and challenge narrow definitions of fear of crime (Smith and Pain, Chapter 4; Jackson, Chapter 9; Gadd and Jefferson, Chapter 8; Weber and Lee, Chapter 5); others attempt to challenge methodologies and institute new less reductive programmes of research (Sutton and Farrall, Chapter 7; Chadee, Ditton and Virgil, Chapter 10); while some turn the concept on its head and attempt to situate it terms of sent of power relations (Day, Chapter 6; Loo, Chapter 2; Lee, Chapter 3). Indeed, in a book that announces itself as critical, it is perhaps pertinent to tie this diverse range of chapters together through the variety of ways they address questions of power. The power to define fear of crime in particular ways to particular political ends (Loo, Chapter 2; Lee, Chapter 3; Weber and Lee, Chapter 5); the power of crime fear to operate as a form of social exclusion (Day, Chapter 6; Jackson, Chapter 9); the power of fear of crime discourses to help construct our everyday geographies and subjectivities (Smith and Pain, Chapter 4; Gadd and Jefferson, Chapter 8; Sutton and Farrall, Chapter 7; Chadee, Ditton and Virgil, Chapter 10). It is, as Smith and Pain (Chapter 4) put it:

> ... time to shift the emphasis from authoritative, remote, top-down models of fear to more nuanced and grounded approaches. [T]o highlight the entwined nature of globalised fears and the processes underlying them; to work with the immediate local everyday fears that are already there; and to stimulate further thought about their connections and relationships in the wider world.

We have here both a set of research 'game openings' and a challenge to current and future researchers in the fear of crime field. And so we end with the identification of where to begin.

References

Farrall, S, Bannister, J, Ditton, J and Gilchrist, E (1997) 'Questioning the measurement of the fear of crime', *British Journal of Criminology*, 37: 657–78.

Farrall, S, Jackson, J and Gray, E (2006) *Everyday Emotion and the Fear of Crime: Preliminary Findings from Experience and Expression*, Working Paper No. 1, ESRC Grant RES 000 23 1108.

Girling, E, Loader, I and Sparks, R (2000) *Crime and Social Control in Middle England: Questions of Order in an English Town*, London: Routledge.

Hollway, W and Jefferson, T (2000) *Doing Qualitative Research Differently: Free association, narrative, and the interview method*, London: Sage.

Jackson, J (2004) 'Experience and expression', *British Journal of Criminology*, 44: 946–66.

Lee, M (2001) 'The genesis of "fear of crime"', *Theoretical Criminology*, 5(4): 467–85.

—— (2007), *Inventing Fear of Crime: Criminology and the Politics of Anxiety*, Cullompton: Willan Publishing.

Sparks, R (1992) 'Reason and unreason in left realism: some problems in the constitution of the fear of crime', in Matthews, R and Young, J (eds), *Issues in Realist Criminology*, London: Sage.

Index